International Law and the Reconceptualization of Territorial Boundaries

This book critically analyzes the state-based regime of international law, eliciting its colonial and decolonial origins and proposing a new sub-regional basis for dealing with contemporary global challenges.

Since 1648, public international law has taken many steps to maintain peace and establish a just order. The State is deemed central to each of these efforts. Yet modern challenges, such as environmental mitigation, mass migration, and the need to stimulate economic growth, overwhelm the State. Could a regional approach to these questions, achieved in conjunction with strong sub-national local governance, establish a more effective framework for systemic change? Drawing on a history of colonization and decolonization, while scrutinizing decisions made about the imposition of the State on the basis of colonial boundaries, this multidisciplinary work analyzes why current challenges are unlikely to be adequately addressed through existing governance structures. In response, it advocates for a sub-regional, transnational approach, drawing on analyses of pre-colonial shared histories and contemporary population ethnographies unfettered by hegemonic boundary drawing. The book argues that collaboration across such frontiers in the face of climate and other challenges may offer more feasible approaches to the pursuit of peace than the unquestioned maintenance of state-based structures of inherited privilege.

This book will appeal to scholars and others with interests in international law, international relations, and international politics, as well as in the history and politics of colonialism.

Joshua Castellino is Co-Executive Director of Minority Rights Group International and Professor of International and Comparative Law at the University of Derby, UK.

International Law and the Reconceptualization of Territorial Boundaries

In Pursuit of Perpetual Peace

Joshua Castellino

Routledge
Taylor & Francis Group
a GlassHouse Book

First published 2025
by Routledge
4 Park Square, Milton Park, Abingdon, Oxon OX14 4RN

and by Routledge
605 Third Avenue, New York, NY 10158

Routledge is an imprint of the Taylor & Francis Group, an informa business

A GlassHouse book

British Library Cataloguing-in-Publication Data
A catalogue record for this book is available from the British Library

Library of Congress Cataloging-in-Publication Data
Names: Castellino, Joshua, author.
Title: International law and the reconceptualization of territorial boundaries: in pursuit of perpetual peace / Joshua Castellino.
Description: Abingdon, Oxon [UK]; New York, NY : Routledge, 2025. | Includes bibliographical references and index.
Identifiers: LCCN 2024025879 (print) | LCCN 2024025880 (ebook) | ISBN 9781032821658 (hardback) | ISBN 9781032821665 (paperback) | ISBN 9781003503279 (ebook)
Subjects: LCSH: Boundaries. | Boundary disputes. | Colonization. | Decolonization. | Internaitonal law.
Classification: LCC KZ3684 .C37 2025 (print) | LCC KZ3684 (ebook) | DDC 341.4/2–dc23/eng/20240614
LC record available at https://lccn.loc.gov/2024025879
LC ebook record available at https://lccn.loc.gov/2024025880

ISBN: 978-1-032-82165-8 (hbk)
ISBN: 978-1-032-82166-5 (pbk)
ISBN: 978-1-003-50327-9 (ebk)

DOI: 10.4324/9781003503279

Typeset in Sabon
by Deanta Global Publishing Services, Chennai, India

To Elvira, Radha & Delfín, with the hope of realizing the non-anthropocentric sustainable, peaceful, inclusive and fair societies that so many women and men written out of history, have struggled for, for centuries.

Contents

Table of Treaties

Agreement between Governments of Great Britain & Russia with regard to the sphere of influence of the two countries in the region of the Pamirs (1895) London, 11 March.

Anglo-Russian Agreement (1907) London, 31 August.

Anglo-Russian Treaty (1873) London & St. Petersburg, 21 January.

Brasilia Agreement (1998) Brasilia, 26 October.

Cairo Resolution (1964) OAU Assembly of Heads of State, Cairo, 17–21 July.

Constitución de la República de Colombia 1821, Rosario de Cúcuta, Impresor de Gob. Gral.

Constitution of Mexico (1824), Constitutive Acts of the Mexican Federation 21 January 1824, also *Federal Constitution of the United Mexican States* October 4, 1824.

Convention for Pacific Settlement of International Disputes 1907 (Second Hague Conference, I) Signed on 18 October, Martens Nouveau Recueil (3d) 360, 36 Stat. 2199, T.S. No. 536.

Convention for the Pacific Settlement of International Disputes 1899 (First Hague I), signed on 29 July, 26 Martens Nouveau Recueil (Ser. 2) 720, 32 Stat. 1779, T.S. No. 342.

Dayton Peace Accord (1995), Dayton, 24 November.

Indian Independence Act (1947), 15 August, 10 & 11 Geo. 6. c. 30.

Japan-Korea Treaty (1876), Kokwa, February 26, *1876* (9th Year of Meiji).

Japan-Korea Treaty (1905), Seoul, 17 November 17, *1905* (38th Year of Meiji).

Ley Fundamental de la República de Colombia (1810), Angostrura, 17 December.

Ley Fundamental de Venezuela (1819), Angostrura Constitution, Angostura, August 15.

Lhasa Convention of 7th September 1904 (London: HMSO UK Treaty Series No. 9 (1906). https://treaties.fcdo.gov.uk/data/Library2/pdf/1906 -TS0009. pdf.

Montevideo Convention (1934), *Convention on Rights and Duties of States*, 7th International Conference of American States, Montevideo, 26 December.

Optional Rules for Arbitrating Disputes between Two Parties Only One of Which is a State (The Hague: Permanent Court of Arbitration, 1962).

Optional Rules for Arbitrating Disputes between Two States (The Hague: Permanent Court of Arbitration, 1962).

Peace of Westphalia of 1648, (Westfälischer Friede), signed Osnabrück and Münster, October.

Promise of St Louis to the Maronites (1250).

San Francisco Treaty (1951), San Francisco, 8 September.

Simla Convention (1914), Shimla, 27 April.

The Agreement Between Great Britain, France and Russia, Regarding Syria, Mesopotamia and Eastern Asia Minor, (Sykes-Picot Agreement), May, 1916.

The Lia-tung Peninsula Concession (1898), 27 March 1898.

The Russo-Chinese Anti-Japanese Alliance (1896), secret treaty, Moscow, 3 June.

The Russo-Chinese Declaration (1913), Peking, 5 November.

The Russo-Mongolian Agreement (1912), Urga, 21 October.

The Treaty of Livadia (1879), Livadia, 2 October.

The Treaty of St. Petersburg (1881), St. Petersburg, 24 February.

The Tripartite Kiaktha Conference (1915), Kyakhta, 25 May.

Treaty of Arbitration of 1897, Washington, DC, 2 February.

Treaty of Breda 1667, Breda, 31 July.

Treaty of Bura (1727) Bur River, 20 August, 1727.

Treaty of Confederation of February 1848 Bolivia, Chile, Ecuador, New Granada, Spanish text available www.oas.prg/sap/peacefund/VirtualLibrary/

Treaty of Ezerum (1847) Ottoman Empire – Persia, Second Treaty of Ezerum, for Determination of Boundaries, (101 CTS 85), Ezerum, 31 May.

Treaty of Friendship between Britain & Afghanistan 1855, Peshawar, 30 March.

Treaty of Gandamak (1879), Gandamak, 26 May.

Treaty of Ghulja (1851), also Kulja, Chunguchak, 25 July.

Treaty of Guarantee, 1960, Nicosia, 16 August.

Treaty of Karlowitz (1699), Karlowitz, 26 January.

Treaty of Nerchinsk (1689), Nerchinsk, 6 September.

Treaty of Peace, Friendship, Commerce and Navigation 1832, Santiago, 16 May.

Treaty of Peking (1860), Peking, 2 November.

Treaty of Sèvres (1920), Sèvres, also known as the *Tripartite Agreement*, 10 August.

Treaty of Shimonoseki (1895), also *Treaty of Maguan/ Treaty of Bakan*, Shimonoseki, 17 April.

Treaty of St. Petersburg (1875), St. Petersburg, 7 May.

Treaty of Surrender (1945), USS Missouri, Tokyo Bay, 2 September.

Treaty of Tientsin & Aigun (1858) Tianjin, 16 May.

Treaty of Versailles (1919), Versailles, 28 June.

Union and Defensive Alliance Pact (1865) Lima, 23rd January 1865.

Union, Alliance and Perpetual Confederation (1825), Bogota, 15 March.

United Nations Charter (1945), San Francisco, 26 June.

Vienna Convention on the Law of Treaties (1969), Vienna, 23 May.

Wycliffe Principles, see C. H. Alexandrowicz, 'Paulus Vladimiri & the Development of the Doctrine of Co-Existence of Christian and Non-Christian Countries (1963)' in *The Law of Nations in Global History* [D. Armitage & J. Pitts eds.] ((Oxford: Oxford University Press, 2017).

Table of Cases

Abyei Arbitration (The Government of Sudan / The Sudan People's Liberation Movement/Army) 22 July 2009.

Accordance with International Law of the Unilateral Declaration of Independence in respect of Kosovo (Advisory Opinion) 22 July 2010.

Aegean Sea Continental Shelf (Greece v. Turkey) 19 December 1978.

Alleged Violations of Sovereign Rights and Maritime Spaces in the Caribbean Sea (Nicaragua v. Colombia) 21 April 2022.

Application for Revision and Interpretation of the Judgment of 24 February 1982 in the Case concerning the Continental Shelf (Tunisia/Libyan Arab Jamahiriya) (Tunisia v. Libyan Arab Jamahiriya) 10 December 1985.

Application of the Convention on the Prevention and Punishment of the Crime of Genocide in the Gaza Strip (South Africa v. Israel) Pending.

Arbitral Award Made by the King of Spain on 23 December 1906 (Honduras v. Nicaragua) 18 November 1960.

Arbitral Award of 31 July 1989 (Guinea-Bissau v. Senegal) 12 November 1991.

Arbitral Award of the Special Boundary Panel Determining the Frontier between Guatemala & Honduras Washington, 23 January 1933.

Barbados v. Trinidad and Tobago 11 April 2006.

Bay of Bengal Maritime Boundary Arbitration between Bangladesh and India 7 July 2014.

Beagle Channel Cases 2 May 1977.

Boundaries in the Island of Timor (The Netherlands v. Portugal) 25 June 1914.

Chagos Marine Protected Area Arbitration (Mauritius v. United Kingdom) 18 March 2015.

Continental Shelf (Libyan Arab Jamahiriya/Malta) 3 June 1985.

Continental Shelf (Tunisia/Libyan Arab Jamahiriya) 24 February 1982.

Delimitation of the Border (Eritrea-Ethiopia), April 13, 2002-November 7, 2002 UN Reports of International Arbitral Awards.

Delimitation of the Maritime Boundary in the Gulf of Maine Area (Canada/United States of America) 12 October 1984.

Dispute Concerning Coastal State Rights in the Black Sea, Sea of Azov, and Kerch Strait (Ukraine v. the Russian Federation) Pending.

Dispute over the Status and Use of the Waters of the Silala (Chile v. Bolivia) 1 December 2022.

Dispute regarding Navigational and Related Rights (Costa Rica v. Nicaragua) 13 July 2009.

Eritrea – Yemen Arbitration, Phase I: Territorial Sovereignty and the Scope of Dispute, 1998, (RIAA XXII, 2006) 211–334.

Eritrea/Yemen - Sovereignty and Maritime Delimitation in the Red Sea 17 December 1999.

Eritrea-Ethiopia Boundary Commission 13 April 2002.

Eritrea-Ethiopia Claims Commission 17 August 2009.

Fisheries Jurisdiction (Federal Republic of Germany v. Iceland) 25 July 1974.

Fisheries Jurisdiction (United Kingdom v. Iceland) 25 July 1974.

Free Zones of Upper Savoy and the District of Gex PCIJ Reports (1932) Series A/B, No.46.

Frontier Dispute (Benin/Niger) 12 July 2005.

Frontier Dispute (Burkina Faso/Niger) 16 April 2013.

Frontier Dispute (Burkina Faso/Republic of Mali) 22 December 1986.

Guyana v. Suriname 17 September 2007.

Honduras Borders (Guatemala v. Honduras), *2 R. Int'l Arb. Awards 1309, 1322.*

Indus Waters Kishenganga Arbitration (Pakistan v. India) 20 December 2013.

Island of Palmas (or Miangas) (The Netherlands / The United States of America) 4 April 1928.

Kasikili/Sedudu Island (Botswana/Namibia) 13 December 1999.

Land and Maritime Boundary between Cameroon and Nigeria (Cameroon v. Nigeria: Equatorial Guinea intervening) 10 October 2002.

Land Boundary in the Northern Part of Isla Portillos (Costa Rica v. Nicaragua) 2 February 2017.

Land Reclamation by Singapore in and around the Straits of Johor (Malaysia v. Singapore) 1 September 2005.

Land, Island and Maritime Frontier Dispute (El Salvador/Honduras: Nicaragua intervening) 11 September 1992.

Legal Consequences arising from the Policies and Practices of Israel in the Occupied Palestinian Territory, including East Jerusalem (UN General Assembly request for advisory opinion, pending).

Legal Consequences for States of the Continued Presence of South Africa in Namibia (South West Africa) notwithstanding Security Council Resolution 276, Advisory Opinion, *ICJ Reports* (1971).

Legal Consequences of the Construction of a Wall in the Occupied Palestinian Territory, Advisory Opinion, *ICJ Reports* (2004).

Legal Consequences of the Separation of the Chagos Archipelago from Mauritius in 1965(Advisory Opinion) 25 February 2019.

Legal Status of the South-Eastern Territory of Greenland Case (Nor. v. Den.), 1932 P.C.I.J. (ser. A/B) No. 53

Location of Boundary Markers in Taba between Egypt and Israel, UN Reports of International Arbitral Awards (29 September 1988) Vol. XX, 1–118.

Maritime Delimitation and Territorial Questions between Qatar and Bahrain (Qatar v. Bahrain) 16 March 2001.

Maritime Delimitation in the Area between Greenland and Jan Mayen (Denmark v. Norway) 14 June 1993.

Maritime Delimitation in the Black Sea (Romania v. Ukraine) 3 February 2009.

Maritime Delimitation in the Caribbean Sea and the Pacific Ocean (Costa Rica v. Nicaragua) 2 February 2018.

Maritime Delimitation in the Indian Ocean (Somalia v. Kenya) 12 October 2021.

Maritime Dispute (Peru v. Chile) 27 January 2014.

Minquiers and Ecrehos (France/United Kingdom) 17 November 1953.

North Sea Continental Shelf (Federal Republic of Germany/Denmark) 20 February 1969.

North Sea Continental Shelf (Federal Republic of Germany/Netherlands) 20 February 1969.

Northern Cameroons (Cameroon v. United Kingdom) 2 December 1963.

Obligations concerning Negotiations relating to Cessation of the Nuclear Arms Race and to Nuclear Disarmament (Marshall Islands v. India) ICJ Reports (2016).

Obligations concerning Negotiations relating to Cessation of the Nuclear Arms Race and to Nuclear Disarmament (Marshall Islands v. Pakistan) ICJ Reports (2016).

Pulp Mills on the River Uruguay (Argentina v. Uruguay) 20 April 2010.

Question of the Delimitation of the Continental Shelf between Nicaragua and Colombia beyond 200 Nautical Miles from the Nicaraguan Coast (Nicaragua v. Colombia) 13 July 2023.

Railway Land Arbitration (Malaysia/Singapore) 30 October 2014.

Rann of Kutch Case, UN Reports of International Arbitral Awards (September 29, 1988) Vol. XX, 170.

Reference re Secession of Québec, [1998] 2 S.C.R. 217.

Request for Interpretation of the Judgment of 11 June 1998 in the Case concerning the Land and Maritime Boundary between Cameroon and Nigeria (Cameroon v. Nigeria), Preliminary Objections (Nigeria v. Cameroon) 25 March 1999.

Request for Interpretation of the Judgment of 15 June 1962 in the Case concerning the Temple of Preah Vihear (Cambodia v. Thailand) (Cambodia v. Thailand) 11 November 2013.

Right of Passage over Indian Territory (Portugal v. India) 12 April 1960.

South West Africa (Ethiopia v. South Africa) 18 July 1966.

South West Africa (Liberia v. South Africa) 18 July 1966.

Sovereignty over Certain Frontier Land (Belgium/Netherlands) 20 June 1959.

Sovereignty over Certain Red Sea Islands (Eritrea v Yemen), Award of the Tribunal, October 3, 1996 (including jurisdiction question, adjudicated upon first).

Sovereignty over Pedra Branca/Pulau Batu Puteh, Middle Rocks and South Ledge (Malaysia v, Singapore) 23 May 2008.

Sovereignty over Pulau Ligitan and Pulau Sipadan (Indonesia v. Malaysia) 17 December 2002.

Temple of Preah Vihear (Cambodia v. Thailand) 15 June 1962.

Territorial and Maritime Dispute (Nicaragua v. Colombia) 19 November 2012.

Territorial and Maritime Dispute between Nicaragua and Honduras in the Caribbean Sea (Nicaragua v. Honduras) 8 October 2007.

Territorial Dispute (Libyan Arab Jamahiriya/Chad) 3 February 1994.

The South China Sea Arbitration (The Republic of Philippines v. The People's Republic of China) 12 July 2016.

Western Sahara Case (Advisory Opinion) 16 October 1975.

Yanoamani Indian Case, Case 7615 IACHR 24, OEA/Ser.L/V/11.66, doc. 10 Rev.1 (1985).

Introduction

The *World Baseball Series* is often derided for its audacious claim to being 'global' when it is a US competition in a US sport, played between US teams, with efforts only recently to woo others from amongst its neighbours. The discipline of 'International' law does not evoke such derision despite its claimed origin bias, heavy reliance on doctrine and philosophies from these original jurisdictions, continued dominance by those that claim to have instigated and chronicled it, and its over-representation within the academic discipline, though no longer the practice. Significant reams of writings and textbooks on international law are a bit like reflections of life in Hollywood films where everything of significance seems to transpire in New York, Los Angeles, and Washington, DC, with seemingly little of note elsewhere, not even to diversify settings. In international law, the privileged sites have traditionally been London, New York, and Washington, DC, with the historically important counterpoints against the Anglophone domination being Moscow, Paris, Rome, Madrid, Lisbon, and Berlin. The seat of the discipline was of course determined to be an allegedly neutral location but also in Europe: The Hague. Like in Hollywood films, a lot of this is driven by ignorance of the rest of the world, but also to do with the reach and marketability of the product, rather than its overwhelming qualities or ability to provide global perspectives.

International law is neither sport nor art.

Its practice has been long and varied through multiple pluralistic relationships, in multiple locations between sovereigns who tried, in varying degrees and at various epochs of time, to engage, negotiate, collaborate, persuade, coerce, combat, subjugate, and even annihilate other sovereigns. It is important to understand that the lack of presence of avid chroniclers of the discipline at these moments did not mean that these events did not occur. It just means the chronicles are poorer and less accurate as a consequence.

There has been a slow sometimes grudging awakening within the discipline of international law as various forms of the critique expressed above have led to alternative formulations by Marxist, feminist, and other subaltern

DOI: 10.4324/9781003503279-1

approaches. This is perhaps best encapsulated in the emerging writings of those that describe themselves as coming from the TWAIL tradition, or Third World Approaches to International Law. These writings have improved the 'international' dimension of the discipline, which nonetheless remains heavily tilted towards its origin bias. Yet many of the leading mainstream protagonists over time and at present seem unable or unwilling to meaningfully engage with anything more than a superficial nod to this literature in keeping with political correctness.

This book does not claim to present new theories on how international law ought to be calibrated, measured, discussed, derived, applied, or appropriated. It is rather a study that seeks to reflect on how many modern state boundaries were formed, who they were drawn to serve, and why they are increasingly becoming ineffective in addressing the major crises facing the globe: climate change and its attendant scarcity that is leading to further entrenching inequality while failing to develop an alternative economic model that is not based on resource extraction.

While colonization has been a prominent feature in human existence on the planet, the primary focus in this book lies on the most recent bout of colonization – driven from Europe out towards Asia, Africa, the Pacific, and the Americas. This colonization occurred and was widespread despite the full cognizance of the existence of a legal framework, yet it is difficult to find effective critiques against it from within the discipline at the time at which it occurred. The failure to condemn it was not merely an oversight. It could be reasonably argued that it may have contributed to the emergence of a regional custom whereby European (white) nations determined that they (read each other) were justified in acquiring non-European territory, deriving these principles from their own reading of history and wilfully imposing frameworks on others they unilaterally determined to be 'international'. These frameworks could objectively be determined as being ignorant since they were not based on an engagement and understanding of any other globally or locally existing legal systems, which were simplistically dismissed as 'uncivilized'.

Racial superiority and greed have been acknowledged as the driving forces for the capture of vast territories globally. In this quest while the law as it existed ought to have been a fetter to the acquisition of such territory, it was simply ignored or deemed irrelevant. While new States came into being from the decolonization that took place under UN aegis, these States, configured within pre-existing hegemonic line drawing that suited European powers, were persuaded and supported to accept the system of sovereign States that had been imposed and that was becoming validated through UN membership. While the rhetoric of decolonization drew inspiration from values such as the consent of the governed derived from 'Enlightenment Era' ideas that developed in Europe, two issues were deemed beyond the reach of that process: (a) the physical territorial dimension of the State; (b) the political patronage that maintained the new governments, often through the promise of specific access to economic growth and privileged access to technical cooperation, resources, and development aid from their former colonial powers. The *quid pro quo* bargain involved the new States agreeing to the crystallization and subsequent sanctification of their boundaries, an emerging rule that could then be deemed to be 'international' on the basis of widespread State practice. This State practice did not adequately pay attention to the extent to which the emerging governments had the consent of the governed; nor were other forms of governance, representation, or territorial configurations considered in the transition.

For the most part decolonization was achieved through intense mass mobilization of various tribes, communities, indigenous peoples, nations, and peoples that found themselves within the territorially deemed unit of the colonial State. This mobilization was based on submerging historical antagonisms and alliances on the basis of a shared conviction in the need to rid the territories of colonial influence. In some cases, the transition from colony to new State led to genuine attempts at 'state-building' through the design of composite identities that sought to unite disparate communities under a single national banner. In many cases, such pretences did not exist, and a new dominant hegemon arose, often chosen on the basis of their gender, proximity to power, and majority status. These hegemons, often markedly different in their racial appearance from the colonial masters, came to power in the name of decolonization. The nature of their inheritance was clearly defined: (i) an externally determined territorially based sovereign State; (ii) reliance on an extractivist economic model; (iii) varying degrees of dependence on the former colonial power for immediate and medium-term survival; (iv) predrawn governance structures, including laws and institutions; and (v) newly formed direct access to what had been erected as a 'global economy'. The maintenance of colonial-era land tenure systems was key to such extractivism, with the attempt of the new entities to 'catch-up' on development requiring an escalated pace of that extraction.

The new State's tacit acceptance of the economic architecture – deemed 'international' – was coupled with the element of mutual recognition by each emerging entity of other emerging entities' legitimacy. This provided a veneer that a new global society had emerged on the basis of universal consensus, and this was celebrated through what was an impressively diverse-looking United Nations. Emancipatory language derived from western texts was used to trumpet the success of decolonization with the entire process wrapped up in a solid base narrative effectively encapsulated in the opening paragraph of the United Nations Charter of 1945, i.e. a triumph of the new system's validation of the quest for perpetual peace.

It has been 80 years since the passage of the UN Charter. This period shows that rather than global emancipation and the emergence of perpetual peace, the sanctification of territorial boundaries through international law, upheld by the highest global judicial authority, has baked in systemic injustices. These have not only proved fatal to the quest for perpetual peace, but also set the tone for the escalation of the climate crisis.

While calls for system change reverberate loudly in the face of the polycrises, the remedies being proposed by the sovereign States that are now in charge of the global governance agenda are timid and appear unable to address the nature and scope of the crisis at scale. Instead, the governments of these sovereign States often installed through clientelist politics are often controlled by corporate interests that are hardly dissimilar to those that profited and drove colonial enterprises. These lie at the root cause of the perpetration of the crisis, but their continued profitability despite the crises weakens their ability to lead system change. Instead, beholden to a new climate movement that is beginning to dominate politics they seek to frame compromises: tinkering with systems in the belief that a new compact will emerge, rather than embarking on the ambitious change agenda that climate scientists are urging.

This book is framed to engage those interested in wider system change for sustainability. It argues for the relegation of the importance of the sovereign State, as deeply vested in system preservation, in favour of a regional approach. It suggests instead a framework for the dimensions of what such a regional approach could entail, based on older readings of history than the most recent European colonial adventure which is often presented as the only relevant history of these regions. This approach by contrast is based on the need for a spirit of collaboration rather than competition across existing boundaries to address the three central issues deemed of fundamental importance: (i) a response to the climate crisis; (ii) scarcity-oriented migration that has become a reality due to entrenched economic disparities; and (iii) the need to generate meaningful economic activity that is not reliant on the extractivist model but is more circular in nature.

In order to achieve this the book is divided into two parts, the first part focusing on colonization and international law, while the second part provides the ballast for why a reorganization of territorial boundaries, which was not achieved during decolonization, remains a key pathway forward in generating system change. The first part of the book features the rules governing the title to territory derived from European readings of international law, which it argues were still adequate in creating a bulwark against the mass subjugation and domination of lands by European powers. To demonstrate this the second chapter focuses on a select group of mainly British men who strode across territories, delineating them, drawing lines in the sand, across mountains, and deserts to maintain their hegemony in what they saw as a quest to protect their interests from others – Russian, French, Ottoman, Persian, and others. An insight is offered into three such lines, The Sykes–Picot Agreement, the Durand Line, and the McMahon Line, to illustrate the randomness and deeply vested interests that were behind their delineation and to offer an explanation for how such a formula was unlikely to serve the interests of peace when they subsequently emerged as international boundaries.

The second part of the book is divided into three further chapters. The first examines the extent to which decolonization was truly envisaged as a process by which order rather than justice could emerge. This is followed by an analysis of the state of the world's boundaries from a regional perspective against the framed rules governing territory that have become crystallized in international law post-decolonization, including through the pronouncement of the International Court of Justice. The concluding chapter seeks to contrast these with what are presented as the underlying realities of identity beyond the narrow reading of history as commencing with the colonial and decolonization period. This final chapter seeks to chart the basis for a regional approach, suggesting that any quest for system change needs to heed the wider governance-oriented challenges at stake rather than relying on the hope that governments of sovereign States with their deeply ingrained clientelist orientation are likely to pursue this path.

In concluding, this book emphasizes how the uncontested nature of the most recent bout of systemic colonization in terms of its wrongfulness under international law was compounded through the decolonization process. There is sufficient evidence to suggest that the process was genuinely driven by the purpose of creating the blueprint for a society where international peace and security would be maintained. This work argues that genuine fears of fragmentation that existed at the moment of transition from colonial rule were overplayed in the easy dismissal of governance solutions other than the emergence of the sovereign State. There is a clear indication that the attitudes on display during colonial rule, which are captured in this work through the closer scrutiny of three specific boundaries, were also at play in the process of decolonization. The clearest manifestation of this is the significant wealth that has continued to be extracted from the former colony to benefit the former colonial power, and the extent to which the wealth that remained within the country was siphoned off towards the consolidation of an arms industry which is today among the most significant sectors in international economic life. The constructed extractivist economy was deeply anthropocentric and violent in its inception, but maintaining it has been a source of continued violence that has undermined any notional quest for peace. The book ends by suggesting that the current series of crises present a genuine opportunity for system change, not least because the business-as-usual models are unsustainable. It argues that new tools are necessary, including the regionalist approach, to be able to step up to addressing these, while finally unwinding the colonization and subsequent colonial mindset that has dominated human activity on the planet for three centuries.

Chapter 1

Historical Treatment of Territory and Boundaries in International Law

Introduction

Writing in the *Oxford Handbook of the History of International Law*, Daniel Erasmus-Khan highlights the etymology of the word 'territory' and the importance of boundaries in the following terms:

> The twofold etymological root of the Latin word 'territorium' aptly demonstrates … [an] intrinsic correlation: 'terra' (earth, land), and the suffix '-orium' denoting place … when first appearing in late Medieval Europe, the term 'territory' was to denominate a 'land under the jurisdiction of a city or town'. Alternative theories suggest derivation from the Latin word 'terrere' (to frighten, see also 'terrible'—thus territorium would mean 'a place from which people are warned off'); or consider 'torium' as the root from which derived words such as 'tower', 'tour', and 'torre', which conveyed in Medieval English, Old French, Italian, and Spanish the meaning of both 'a well- rounded building' and 'a position of strength'.[1]

Erasmus-Khan finds these hypotheses complementary rather than contradictory in that the control of a geographical area becomes the basis on which a community could build a socio-economic base, assert this for the benefit of its inhabitants, and maintain vigilance against intruders. Inevitably, the power to assert ownership (or title) against all-comers meant that in its original usage:

> the concept of territory was assigned to smaller political entities alone, such as cities and towns, whereas the position of power of larger kingly or princely entities in Europe, deeply rooted in the Christian-Medieval

1 Daniel Erasmus-Khan, 'Territory and Boundaries' in *Oxford Handbook of the History of International Law* [Bardo Fassbender and Anne Peters eds.] (Oxford: Oxford University Press, 2012) 231.

DOI: 10.4324/9781003503279-2

> theological-political cosmos, was still considered to rest primarily on allegiance of individuals and organizations, not territory.[2]

Despite the significant dominance and impact of European activities in the realm of the determination of contemporary boundaries, and in the extent to which the rules concerning boundary disputes have developed, the annals of history record the earliest 'international' boundary dispute as occurring between ancient kings of Mesopotamia in the Presargonic Period (approximately 2700–2350 BC).[3] The details of the dispute are recorded on a clay cylinder and fragments of vessels. The dispute arose over contested land and a canal along the Tigris River between the city-states of Lagaš and Umma in what is referred to as the Early Dynastic III period. Written from the perspective of Lagaš, the narrative commences by attributing the 'supreme God' of the Sumerian pantheon, Enlil, as determining the border between the entities, with a monument demarcating this erected by King Mesilim of Kiš, whose kingdom lay to the northeast of the two city-states. This contestation is narrated as having commenced as a consequence of a border transgression by King Uš of Umma, who was defeated by the City-God of Lagaš, Ningirsu. Attempts were made to settle the dispute between the city-states through an agreement, however the reparation required to be paid by Umma led to the city-state developing a significantly large debt in agricultural wealth. In later years, King Urlumma, who ascended to the throne, sought to avoid repaying the debt. Instead he diverted water from the canal and commenced an attack on border monuments, which led to a second war and another defeat for Lagaš.[4]

The significance of the dispute lies not only in its being the first recorded but also in its complexity, drawing on questions of possession, agricultural *usufruct*, irrigation rights, the value of delineation, the destruction of property, the first recorded conclusion of a boundary treaty circa 2470 BC, the setting up of a joint boundary demarcation work, and the creation of a buffer zone to prevent future conflict.[5] Over the subsequent four and a half millennia, each of these issues has remained central to boundary disputes, and the likelihood is that with growing scarcity such disputes are likely to escalate. In contemporary terms the pressure of climate change is forcing nomadic

2 *Ibid.*

3 *Ibid.* 228–230.

4 See Frayne, Douglas 'The Umma Lagash Border Conflict' available on CDLI Wiki at http://cdli.ox.ac.uk/wiki/doku.php?id=umma_lagash_border_conflict [last consulted 5 December 2023].

5 Erasmus-Khan (2012) *op.cit.* 1, 230.

communities into areas settled by pastoralists, raising tension in many parts of the world.[6]

In narrating the history of boundaries and territory in international law, Erasmus-Khan highlights the work of the Greek geographer Strabo, who, 2,500 years later in circa 20 BC, advocated for the accurate delimitation and demarcation of boundaries in the interest of peace.[7] By the fifteenth century, the model of juridico-political power that was dominant in matters of governance (mainly in Europe) was complex, vertical, and heterogeneous. Yet that model was gradually superseded as the concept grew that political spaces ought to be ordered along a 'horizontal plane'. This placed territory at the centre stage of political thought in Europe – which it subsequently transposed to the rest of the world through colonization.[8]

Inevitably, as the concept evolved, the nature of seeking to maintain exclusive control of this territory became one of the most distinctive features of exercising political authority, placing fundamental importance on the geographical extent of the territory, and the limit within which established and recognized political power could be exercised. This was fundamental to the evolution and extension of the concept of *dominium* derived from Roman private law and extended to a public law manifestation wherein it signified the territory over which a single, superior, and exclusive power could be exercised: the antecedent to the modern public international law concept of territorial sovereignty.[9] This signalled a departure from prevailing Augustinian doctrine that the ruler existed for the realization of a superior moral purpose, as captured in literature such as *Il Principe* where Machiavelli highlights the quest for political intrigue in seizing and maintaining political power.[10]

The relationship between the modern State and its territory has merited wide discussion in the literature of public international law ever since. Its seminal nature is captured in the evolution of the State and the transmission and dissemination of it as a universal model of governance through European expansion around the world. The document that most clearly asserts the 'State' and 'territory' link is the 'Montevideo Convention of 1933', which identified 'territory' as fundamental to the definition of a State. Nonetheless

6 Paige Jennings, 'Chad: As Deserts Spread South, Pastoralists Face Scarcity & Drought' *Key Trends Report 2019* (London: Minority Rights Group, 2019).

7 Erasmus-Khan (2012) *op.cit.* 1, 230. Also see *Geography* [Loeb Classical Library ed. & H. L. Jones trans.] (London: William Heinemann & Co., 1917) book I, ch. IV, ss 7 and 8. To understand the significance of territory in the ancient Greek world see I. Malkin, 'Land Ownership, Territorial Possession, Hero Cults, and Scholarly Theory' in *Nomodeiktes: Greek Studies in Honor of Martin Oswald* [R. M. Rosen & J. Farrell eds.] (Ann Arbor, MI: University of Michigan Press, 1993) 225–234.

8 Erasmus-Khan (2012) *op.cit.* 1, 231.

9 *Ibid.* 232.

10 Niccolo Machiavelli, *Il Principe* (G. Bull Translation Penguin Classics, original 1532/2003).

while that document was passed and framed in the context of Latin American fear of *reconquista* by European powers, it merely articulated an existing custom that for an entity to exist as a State, dominium over an exclusive territory was core.[11]

The existence or any claim to such existence by two adjacent entities inevitably brought the outer margins of physical territory into direct confrontation. The Latin term *frons*, signifying front, was employed to describe the 'start' of such territory, which developed into the notion of *fronteria*, which in later medieval usage referred to the front line of an army or battle. In European custom the terms 'frontier' and 'boundary' were used as synonyms, though in what had begun to be referred to as The New World, a 'frontier thesis' idea was emerging.[12] Deriving from an authoritative paper delivered by Frederick Jackson Turner at the American Historical Association meeting in Chicago in July 1893, a frontier came to be thought of as a moving line of military and cultural advancement (and on occasion, retreat), which Turner considered the 'outer edge of the wave – the meeting point between savagery and civilization'.[13] Turner's thesis is justifiably criticized as racist and as a *post facto* justification for territorial expansionism in the Americas.[14] However the precedent for such action already existed in European expansion on land and overseas to other continents.[15] Perhaps one of the clearest antecedents is the Roman law conception of *terra nullius* as consisting of all territories that were not occupied by Romans, and thus open to acquisition.[16]

To gain a critical understanding of the role of boundary formation and dispute resolution in the twenty-first century, this chapter is divided into three sections. The first section addresses the question of how territory can be acquired in public international law. The objective of this section is to focus on the notions of occupation and subjugation, highlighting their impact on the capture of vast tracts of territory across the globe. With the overarching purpose of the book as a whole being to argue for a changed approach in settling boundary disputes, the objective of this chapter is limited to drawing attention to how territory was deemed acquired, in order

11 For an influential insight, see Carlos G. Dávila, *The Montevideo Conference: Antecedents & Accomplishments* (Washington, DC: Carnegie Endowment for International Peace, 1934).

12 J. T. Juricek, 'American Usage of the Word "Frontier" from Colonial Times to Frederick Jackson Turner' 110 *Proceedings of the American Philosophical Society* (1966) 10–34.

13 See F. J. Turner, *The Frontier in American History* (New York: Henry Holt, 1921) 3.

14 See generally, Robert Strausz-Hupé, *Geopolitics: The Struggle for Space and Power* (New York: G. P. Putnam's Sons, 1942).

15 See Gregory H. Nobles, 'Breaking into the Backcountry: New Approaches to the Early American Frontier, 1750–1800' 46 *The William and Mary Quarterly* (1989) 641–670.

16 Lauren Benton & Benjamin Straumann, 'Acquiring Empire by Law: From Roman Doctrine to Early Modern European Practice' 28(1) *Law & History Review* (2010) 1–38.

to later comment on the attempts to enable a transfer of sovereignty to peoples that were previously subjugated. With this in mind the second section explores the value of 'historical' title: how it was configured and what salience it continues to have. This section draws on public international law literature written at the time of colonization processes to understand the deemed parameters of 'peoplehood' and how their legitimacy in pursuing title-generating activities was perceived. The third section identifies the role that culture played in framing the blueprint for what subsequently became uncontested as the unit of decolonization that was to follow. While that decolonization could be considered a success in emancipating tracts of African, Asian, and American territories from colonial powers, the vehemence of continued identity-oriented territorial claims and their frenzied articulations require active engagement.

Public International Law and the Acquisition of Territory

While European domination of global history remains small in temporal terms, its influence on generating and labelling norms as universal or international is significant. While China may have the longest documented history in the world, its various dynasties and governors did not deem it necessary to label their actions beyond their frontiers as either norm-creating or as constituting international law or global custom. Thus in understanding how 'public international law' treats the acquisition of territory, the focus inevitably turns to European history and events. The legal framework governing the acquisition of territory has its historical antecedents in the development of *jus gentium*, or the law of nations, itself.[17] Greek and Roman contributions have been fundamental to its transmission into international law, as highlighted by MacIver, writing in 1926:

> The Greeks made very important advances in the science of law, but they never attained to the consistent doctrine or the logical practice which the Romans built up. To begin with, they did not possess ... a term corresponding to the Roman *ius*, the ordered system of which an individual *lex* is merely an example. ... Moreover, the universality of law was far from being recognized. ... The idea that law has a common application to all persons within a political territory was alien to the Greeks. The idea of a universal *ius gentium* was not yet born.

17 For a historical analysis of the development of international law in the context of title to territory, see Georg Schwarzenberger, *International Law*, 3rd ed. (London: Stevens & Sons, 1957) 289–309 AND Georg Schwarzenberger, *The Frontiers of International Law* (London: Steven & Sons, 1962) 43–59.

MacIver's reverence for Rome's contribution is palpable. He writes:

> It was Rome that liberated the universality of law, that transcended the sophistic antithesis between nature and convention, and that first embodied in one comprehensive and unified code the distinctive order of the state.[18]

According to this well-accepted hypothesis the first significant departure point for the emergence of *jus gentium* came from Rome liberating itself from the Twelve Tablets that had created a rigid framework.[19] While this was premised on the need to preserve the special rights of Roman citizens over aliens,[20] the principles under the jurisdiction and judgment of the *Praetor Peregrinus* gradually took on a complexity that considered them superior in many respects to *jus gentium*.[21] Like much of colonial law that subsequently flowed across continents centuries later, *jus gentium* developed in the intellectual circles of the capital and was 'accepted' as universal simply by virtue of its having been so deemed.[22] These origins of *jus gentium* need to be grasped rather than glossed over to critically assess the doctrines that have subsequently become fundamental constraints governing the treatment of territory under international law. The treatment of concepts as 'universal truths' to be handed down as firm doctrine from generation to generation in a rigid manner has overshadowed the distinct cultural contexts in which they were articulated. This has restricted discussions about their content, appropriateness, and applicability in diverse contexts and communities across the globe. As a consequence, a significant part of the sources of public international law deemed to be subsidiary in determining the rules of 'the judicial decisions and the teachings of the most highly qualified publicists of the various nations' suffer from reassurance bias driven from a small segment of nations' participation. That these nations were the first articulators of the

18 Robert M. MacIver, *The Modern State* (Redditch: Read Books Ltd., 1926) 103–105.

19 James Muirhead, *Historical Introduction to the Private Law of Rome* [Henry Goudy & Alexander Grant eds.], 3rd ed. (London: A&C Black, 1916) 89–97. The Twelve Tablets were inscribed in stone as the first form of codified Roman law after a study of the laws of Greece and Greek cities of Italy. *See id.* at 89–90. They became the basis of *jus civile* in Rome and were applicable to all Roman citizens. *See id.* at 82.

20 MacIver (1926) *op.cit.* 18, at 106.

21 Id. at 107.

22 *See id.* at 106; Charles Henry Alexandrowicz, 'The Role of Treaties in the European-African Confrontation in the Nineteenth Century' in *African International Legal History* [Mensah-Brown ed.] (New York: UNITAR, 1975) 35–36, 61–63. Also like the colonial law that was to follow in later centuries, distinctions were made between the rights of citizens and the rights of subjects. Perhaps the most explicit example of these distinctions concerns the system of capitulations that were put in place to safeguard the rights of citizens of the metropolitan states (i.e. the colonizing state) when working abroad.

argument concerning the scope of 'international', that their reference points were their own judicial decisions, and that the standard of their qualifications was determined by their own established institutions of learning, meant that the discipline of public international law derives a very small range of 'highly qualified publicists' with limited experience of global history, often unaware of their own positionality within it.

This work argues that as a consequence of this deep limitation, many existing concepts considered fundamental to determinations of title to territory fail to cater to complexities that are germane to notions of identity and territory.[23] This pertains as much to concepts concerning the acquisition of territory as to determinations of how territorial disputes ought to be settled. Thus *Oppenheim's International Law* highlights, for instance, the lack of unanimity among members of the international community vis-à-vis the modes of territorial acquisition. Yet traditional textbooks present this subject in definitive terms, despite the concept of State territory having changed considerably from the times of Grotius, through the Middle Ages, to contemporary society.[24] Therefore:

> [T]he acquisition of territory by a state normally means the acquisition of *sovereignty* over such territory. In these circumstances the Roman law scheme of 'modes' concerning the acquisition of private property are no longer wholly appropriate.[25]

Irrespective of distinctions between historical acquisition of territory, often based on private modes of acquisition, and contemporary acquisition of territory, usually occurring under greater international scrutiny, the modes of acquisition are described in the annals of public international law as consisting of the following:[26]

23 This is commonly asserted in literature often described as constituting a Third World Approach to International Law; see James Thuo Gathii, 'Promise of International Law: A Third World View (Including a TWAIL Bibliography 1996–2019 as an Appendix)' 114 *Proceedings of the ASIL Annual Meeting* (Cambridge: Cambridge University Press, 2020).

24 *Oppenheim's International Law, Peace* 678–79 ([Robert Jennings & Arthur Watts eds.], 9th ed. (1992).

25 *Id. at* 679.

26 Ian Brownlie, *African Boundaries: A Legal and Diplomatic Encyclopedia* (London: C. Hurst, 1979), sought to provide an authoritative view of the theory and practice behind the acquisition of African territory and boundaries in public international law. Compared to territorial acquisition, territory can be lost through six modes – the corresponding five modes of acquisition and, in addition, the loss of territory through revolt or dereliction. *See also Oppenheim's International Law, Peace, op. cit.* 24, 716–718.

(1) *Cession*: State acquisition of territory through transfer of sovereignty by 'owner state;'[27]
(2) *Occupation*: State appropriation of territory over which another is not sovereign;[28]
(3) *Accretion*: State acquisition of territory through natural or artificial formations, without violating another state's sovereignty;[29]
(4) *Subjugation*: State acquisition of territory through conquest and subsequent annexation, where war-making is a sovereign right and is not illegal;[30]

27 Robert Yewdall Jennings, *The Acquisition of Territory in International Law* (Manchester: Manchester University Press, 1963). Also see J. H. W. VERZIJL, INTERNATIONAL LAW IN HISTORICAL PERSPECTIVE (Heisenberg: Springer, 1970). *See also Oppenheim's International Law, Peace, op. cit. 24*, at 679–682 (explaining that cession may take different forms, including the sale of territory, as occurred in Alaska in 1867 and the Danish West Indies in 1916). One example of a cession is the giving of Bombay by the Portuguese to the British in 1661 as part of the dowry of Catherine of Braganza, who married Charles II. *See* Anthony Farrington, 'Trading Places: The East India Company and Asia' 52 *History Today* (2002) 40.

28 *See generally* Arthur S. Keller, Oliver J. Lissitzyn & Frederick J. Mann, *Creation of Rights of Sovereignty through Symbolic Acts 1400–1800* (New York: Columbia University Press, 1938); NORMAN HILL, CLAIMS TO TERRITORY IN INTERNATIONAL LAW AND RELATIONS (Oxford: Oxford University Press, 1944).

29 *See Oppenheim's International Law, Peace, op.cit.* 24, 696–698. Accretion would include the construction of embankments, breakwaters, and dykes while also covering the augmentation of territory through natural processes such as alluvion, deltas, emerging islands, and abandoned river beds. *Id.*

30 *See* Ian Brownlie, *International Law and the Use of Force by States* (Oxford: Clarendon Press, 1963) 112–122. *See also Application for Revision of the Judgment of 11 September 1992 in the Case Concerning the Land, Island and Maritime Frontier Dispute* (El Salvador/Honduras: Nicaragua intervening) (El. Sal. v. Hond.), *ICJ Reports* (2002) 392 (December 18) (illustrating a modern revision claim based on avulsion). El Salvador's revision claim was based on the avulsion of the river Gaoscorán, in addition to the Carta Esférica and the report of the 1794 *El Activo* expedition. *Id.* at 401. To open revision proceedings, all the conditions contained in Article 61 of the Statute of the ICJ need to be fulfilled. *See* Statute of the International Court of Justice Article 61, 26 June 1945, 59 Stat. 1055, 33 U.N.T.S. 933. The application must be based on 'discovery of some fact of such a nature as to be a decisive factor, which fact was, when the judgment was given, unknown … not due to negligence'. *Id.* art. 61(1). In addition, the application must be made within six months after the new fact is discovered and within ten years after the original judgment. *Id.* Article 61(4)–(5). In the application for revision of the **Land, Island and Maritime Frontier Dispute (El Salvador/Honduras: Nicaragua intervening)*, the Chamber found that El Salvador's request for revision did not satisfy the conditions set down in Article 61 on the basis that the facts alleged were not new facts in the sense intended by Article 61. *Application for Revision of the Judgment of 11 September 1992 in the Case Concerning the Land, Island and Maritime Frontier Dispute* (El Salvador/Honduras: Nicaragua intervening) (El. Sal. v. Hond.), *ICJ Reports 2002*, 409–11.

(5) *Prescription*: State acquisition of territory through continuous and undisturbed exercise of sovereignty over the territory.[31]

Of these modes of acquisition, the two most fundamental to understand contemporary boundary disputes are occupation and subjugation, with the impact of these determining the nexus between self-determination and the post-colonial territorial State.

Occupation as an original mode of acquisition was considered different from one where a State took control of a territory by military force.[32] Rather, occupation was traditionally deemed achieved by the State while serving a State function, which was acknowledged externally upon its performance.[33] Occupation traditionally comprised two elements: possession and administration.[34] First, the territory in question must have been *terra nullius*, or unoccupied by a State, at the moment of possession:[35]

> The only territory which can be the object of occupation is that which does not already belong to any state, whether it is uninhabited, or inhabited by persons whose community is not considered to be a state; for individuals may live on a territory without forming themselves into a state proper exercising sovereignty over such territory. The territory of any

31 *See Oppenheim's International Law, Peace, op.cit.* 24, 705–708 (reflecting the views of leading international jurists in the historical evolution of this concept).

32 See id. at 686–687. Interestingly, the discussion of occupation during times of war is contained in an altogether separate volume of these legal annals. *See Oppenheim's International Law, Disputes, War and Neutrality* [Robert Jennings & Arthur Watts eds.], 9th ed. (London: Longmans, 1992).

33 *Oppenheim's International Law, Peace, op.cit.* 24, at 687.

34 *Id.* at 688. 'Real' occupation is differentiated from 'fictitious' occupation, with the former labelled 'effective' occupation. *Id.*

35 The possession element is reflected in recent Australian case law. See, e.g., *Mabo v. Queensland II* (1992) 175 C.L.R. 1 (Austl.) (discussing the status of Australian territory and its relationship to the aboriginal populations that lived on it at the time of colonization, in the specific context of a case raised by Eddie Mabo). The reasoning in this case was central to the overturning of 200 years of precedent. *See Essays on the Mabo Decision* (1993); Julie Cassidy, 'Observations on Mabo & Ors v. Queensland' 1 *Deakin Law Review* (1994) 37; Michael Legg, 'Indigenous Australians and International Law: Racial Discrimination, Genocide and Reparations' 20 *Berkeley Journal of International Law* (2002) 387, 408–410 (capturing a discussion that began when the UN Committee for the Elimination of Racial Discrimination took objection to Australia's Native Title Act); Gary D. Meyers & John Mugambwa, 'The Mabo Decision: Australian Aboriginal Land Rights in Transition' 23 *Environmental Law* (1993) 1203, 1204–1205 (providing an analysis of the impact of the *Mabo* decision); Gerry Simpson, 'Mabo, *International Law*, Terra Nullius *and the Stories of Settlement: An Unresolved Jurisprudence*' 19 *Melbourne University Law Review* (1993) 195. See also Peter Butt, Robert Eagleson & Patricia Lane, *Wik & Native Title*, 3rd ed. (Canberra: Federation Press, 1998) providing a plain English explanation of the Court's reasoning.

> state however is obviously not a possible object of occupation; and it can only be acquired through cession or, formerly, by subjugation.[36]

This does not mean that the territories needed to be uninhabited: individuals could live on a territory that could still be deemed *terra nullius* if they had not yet organized themselves into governance-oriented entities that laid claim to exercise sovereignty over the territory. Therefore, a clear objective criterion concerning occupation, i.e. *terra nullius*, was deliberately altered by a subjective element that considered the kind of social and political organization that could exist within a territory, as perceived by an outsider to that arrangement. This reading of the doctrine of occupation dominates cases concerning territoriality in international law. For example, in the *Western Sahara Case*, the International Court of Justice determined that the Saharawis were not 'socially and politically organized',[37] and therefore were not occupants of the western part of the Sahara.[38]

The recognized possession by the occupying State was accompanied by a need for it to establish a form of administration over the entirety of the territory.[39] Thus, for an occupation to result in effective title-generation,

> it is necessary that ... [the occupying state] should take the territory under its sway (*corpus*) with the intention of acquiring sovereignty over it (*animus*).[40]

It is assumed that there will be some degree of settlement by non-autochthonous populations, accompanied by a formal act announcing occupation and the intent to extend sovereignty over the territory.[41] A second element flows from this: the occupying State establishing administration to demonstrate its formal exercise of sovereignty in a manner that is externally recognizable, not least to forestall other aspiring sovereign's quest to acquire the same territory. Failures to extend administrative regimes would bring into question the effectiveness of the occupation and, in theory, leave the territory open to acquisition by other sovereigns.[42]

36 *Oppenheim's International Law, Peace, op.cit.* 24, 687 (internal citations omitted).

37 *Western Sahara*, Advisory Opinion, *ICJ Reports* (1975)12, 39 (October 16).

38 *See id.* at 83–102 (separate opinion of Judge Ammoun).

39 *Oppenheim's International Law, Peace, op.cit.* 24, 688–689.

40 *Id.* at 689. This notion itself derives directly from the Roman law governing private property. See generally William W. Buckland & Arnold McNair, *Roman Law and Common Law: A Comparison in Outline*, 2nd ed. (Cambridge: Cambridge University Press, 1952), 70.

41 *Oppenheim's International Law, Peace, op.cit.* 24, 689.

42 *Ibid.*

In many circumstances, colonial flags were raised over newly demarcated territories without effective control over all inhabitants.[43] Robert Jackson advanced this point in the decolonization context, suggesting that many States in Africa could be considered quasi-States on similar grounds.[44] Jackson's work on the nature of the African State was controversial, not least because it set a uniquely European standard against which African States were judged and found wanting.[45] The notion of effective control over *entire* territories nonetheless has deep salience for indigenous peoples who live in isolation, whose subjecthood and subjugation have been predetermined by outsiders without their knowing or acknowledgement of such sovereignty. Indigenous peoples in the Amazon are only notionally subjects of the territorial States that claim jurisdiction over them,[46] with even non-contact tribes deemed subjected to the State on the basis that their territories fall within their boundaries.[47] The colonial acquisition of inhabited territory, based on a subjective determination of the inherent value of the inhabitants' society, was compounded by a deliberate decision not to seek to understand their usage and possession of their ancestral domains. Instead their existence on territories was deemed not to meet the criteria sufficient to generate titular or possessory rights, rendering their ancestral domains *terra nullius* and therefore open to legitimate occupation.

While the colonization of Africa, and to a lesser extent Asia,[48] occurred in the shadow of the dubious rule adopted by the *Berlin West Africa Congress of 1884–85*, which permitted claims to contiguous territories based on possession of the coast, actions in the Americas predate this rule.[49] It would thus be hasty to uncritically accept the State practice that emerged at Berlin as

43 *See* Sharon Korman, *The Right of Conquest: The Acquisition of Territory by Force in International Law and Practice* (Oxford: Oxford University Press, 1996) 135–178, discussing the rights of so-called European states and 'barbarian' political communities.

44 Robert Jackson, 'Juridical Statehood in Sub-Saharan Africa' 46 *Journal of International Affairs* (1992) 17.

45 Siba N'Zatioula Grovogui, *Sovereigns, Quasi-Sovereigns and Africans: Race and Self Determination in International Law* (Minneapolis, MN: University of Minnesota Press, 1996) 182–184.

46 *See* Gavney Moore & Maria Carmen Lemos, 'Indigenous Policy in Brazil: The Development of Decree 1775 & the Proposed Raposa/Serra do Sol Reserve, Roraima, Brazil' 21 *Human Rights Quarterly* (1999) 444; Maria G. M. Rodrigues, 'Indigenous Rights in Democratic Brazil' 24 *Human Rights Quarterly* (2002) 487.

47 Cameron Clark, 'All Quiet on the Waterfront: Uncontacted Tribes in the Modern Era' 40(2) *Harvard International Review* (2019) 10–11.

48 For a treatise on the colonization of Asia, see Harry G. Gelber, *Nations out of Empires: European Nationalism and the Transformation of Asia* (London: Palgrave Macmillan, 2001), linking the events taking place in Europe with their impact on Asian colonization and concluding with succinctly articulated ironies.

49 See *The Scramble for Africa: Documents on the Berlin West African Conference and Related Subjects 1884/1885* [R. J. Gavin & J. A. Betley eds.] (Ibadan: Ibadan University Press, 1973);

established customary international law, since its practice was not consistent among the leading stakeholders and since it treated occupied territories as *terra nullius*.

Subjugation, the other principal means of acquisition, historically occurred through conquest and subsequent acquisition, at a time when war was considered a sovereign right. To acquire a territory through subjugation, (1) the conquering power was required to have established conquest, (2) the state of war was required to have ended, and (3) the conquering power would have needed to have formally annexed the territory.[50] This method of acquisition predominated in Latin America, but was not as frequently employed in later colonization. The spread of the Mongol Empire[51] and the waxing and waning of the Chinese Empire[52] relied heavily on subjugation, though the lack of clear parameters as to what the third condition entails makes these details less certain. The Japanese acquisition of Manchuria in 1934 and its subsequent declaration as Manchukuo[53] fits the parameters more clearly. The country with the largest landmass in the world, Russia, acquired its vast territories through subjugation of smaller indigenous tribes, resulting in eastward expansion by the Rus from their base of settlements in Minsk, Kiev, and Moscow all the way to Vladivostok (literally, conqueror of the East).[54]

Antony Allott, 'Boundaries in Africa: A Legal and Historical Survey' in *African International Legal History* [A. K. Mensah-Brown ed.] (1975) 69.

50 *In Oppenheim's International Law, Peace, op.cit.* 24, 699, subjugation is explained as follows:

> At no period did conquest alone and *ipso facto* make the conquering state the territorial sovereign of the conquered territory, even though such territory came through conquest for the time being under the sway of the conqueror. Conquest was a mode of acquisition only if the conqueror, after having firmly established the conquest, and the state of war having come to an end, then formally annexed the territory. If a belligerent conquered part of the enemy territory and afterwards made the vanquished state cede the conquered territory in the treaty of peace the mode of acquisition was not subjugation but cession. Such a treaty of cession, however, would now be qualified by article 52 of the Vienna Convention on the Law of Treaties(internal citations omitted).

51 Nikolay N. Kradin, 'The Mongol Empire and the Unification of Eurasia' in *The Oxford World History of Empire* [Peter Fibiger Bang, C. A. Bayly & Walter Scheidel eds.] (Oxford: Oxford University Press, 2021) 507–532.

52 Hui Fang, Gary M. Feinman & Linda M. Nicholas 'Imperial Expansion, Public Investment, and the Long Path of History: China's Initial Political Unification and Its Aftermath' 112(30) *Proceedings of the National Academy of Science, USA* (2015) 9224–9229. Also see Franck Billé, Grégory Delaplace & Caroline Humphrey (eds.), *Knowledge & Practice at the Russian, Chinese & Mongolian Border* (Open Book Publishers, 2012).

53 For a perspective on its empire-building potential, see Eri Hotta, *Pan-Asianism & Japan's War 1931–1945* (The Palgrave Macmillan Series in Transnational History) (New York: Palgrave Macmillan, 2007) 107–139.

54 For an early assessment of the spread of the Russian Empire, see this translation listed under Miscellanea [Editors] 'The Territorial Acquisitions of Russia during the Reign of Alexander II' 44(3) *Journal of the Statistical Society of London* (September 1881) 584–588. Also see

The subjugation of indigenous nations was key to the settlement, occupation, and subsequent claim of the Americas by communities of European origin.[55]

By the early part of the twentieth century, the acquisition of title by subjugation became rare because conquering powers typically enforced a treaty of cession and this had become subject to Article 10 of the *League of Nations Covenant*, which outlawed wars waged for territorial acquisition.[56] By the twenty-first century it had seemed implausible that the acquisition of territory through subjugation would still be possible, making the Russian invasion of Ukraine in 2022 and the declaration of Donetsk and Luhansk as independent entities seem to be an anachronism, though similar attempts with Crimea and South Ossetia had not warranted adequate global attention. The Russian acquisition of Crimea fell classically within the parameters of subjugation. The decimation of territories between Iraq and Syria by *Daesh* had already shown how pretending that such activities were beyond the scope of contemporary life was misguided. While not suggesting that wars occurring before the passage of Article 10 of the *League of Nations Covenant* were legal,[57] many jurists appear to assume that such events are beyond blame since they are subject to the intertemporal rule of law.[58] Although the tendency to borrow principles from domestic law has pervaded and impacted the development of international law,[59] respect for property, central to property law regimes in colonial states, was not extended to cover the acquisition of territories beyond the metropolitan State.[60] It has been suggested that the

Frederic Emory, 'Russia in Asia' 15 *Annals of the American Academy of Political & Social Science* (May 1900) 114–120.

55 Howard Zinn, *A People's History of the United States 1492- Present* (New York: Harper Collins, 1980, new edition 2003).

56 League of Nations Covenant art. 10. See also Oona Hathaway & Scott Shapiro, *The Internationalists: How a Radical Plan to Outlaw War Remade the World* (New York: Simon & Schuster, 2017).

57 Christine Gray, *International Law & the Use of Force* (Oxford: Oxford University Press, 2004) 24–50.

58 Literature on international law is surprisingly silent on the aftermath of colonization. While there are considerable sources that comment on the self-determination aspect of this process, few seek to examine the impact of this principle on the domestic polities created. This is perhaps justifiable because it is a greater concern for human rights literature. However, even a glance at the index pages of human rights journals shows that relatively scant attention is paid to the extent to which effective political participation, or true decolonization, has actually occurred within post-colonial states. In sharp contrast, in the 1960s, international society scrutinized decolonization almost as intensely as the current development of modern international criminal law.

59 *See* Gustavo Gozzi, *Rights & Civilizations: A History & Philosophy of International Law* [Filippo Valente trans] (Cambridge: Cambridge University Press, 2010).

60 Joshua Castellino & Stephen Allen, *Title to Territory in International Law: A Temporal Analysis* (Dartmouth: Ashgate, 2003) 29–56. The development of domestic property regimes, along with international law principles as framed here, would have prevented the

signing of treaties ceding subjugated territories would only now be qualified by Article 52 of the *Vienna Convention on the Law of Treaties, 1969*, which would invalidate treaties produced through the threat or use of force in violation of international law.[61] Despite this, questions concerning title to territory and the extent to which they have been legitimately acquired are dismissed by conservative readings of the intertemporal rule of law, which read in this manner buffers actions committed in previous eras from scrutiny of norms and principles deemed modern.[62]

In this way, international lawyers, including the most highly acclaimed jurists and adjudications in courts of law, appear to preclude legal questions that seek self-correction with regard to the well-documented woes of colonialism.[63] While accepting the legitimacy of the intertemporal rule of law, it is nonetheless important to understand the manner in which historical title is treated and the valence that can be attributed to this at a time when there are increasing questions concerning the veracity of the historical narrative and the extent to which it has been constructed and dominated by those close to sites of power.

The Value of Historical Title

In seeking to explore how historical title to territory[64] has been constructed, Kozlowski provides an outstanding overview that is worth engaging with. According to him:

> The concept of sovereignty is often assumed to be coincident with and arise out of the legal title itself. Accordingly, factual restrictions on sovereignty do not automatically infringe on legal title, for example the occupation of territory by rebellion would not change the nature of the legal title possessed by the original sovereign, even though factually it might reduce the size of administered territory. The concept of legal title provides answers to the question: why does a given competence exist and what is its extent? It also provides support to the claims of territorial sovereignty

acquisition of territory through wars. If such wars were nonetheless waged, any unequal or unfair treaties of cession would be invalidated based on domestic contract law, which frames the laws governing treaties.

61 Article 52 *Vienna Convention on the Law of Treaties* (23 May 1969), 1155 U.N.T.S. 331.

62 Castellino & Allen (2003) *op.cit.* 60, 234–235.

63 Edward McWhinney, *Conflict and Compromise: International Law and World Order in a Revolutionary Age* (Leiden: Sijthoff & Noordoff, 1981) 26–27, 65–66. See also Elazar Barkan, *The Guilt of Nations: Restitution and Negotiating Historical Injustices* (Baltimore, MD: Johns Hopkins University Press, 2001) (2000).

64 For a standard narrative on historical title, its construction, and validation, see Y. Z. Blum, *Historic Title in International Law* (The Hague: M. Nijhoff, 1965).

> by one entity (State) versus other entities (States) laying claim to the same territory.[65]

He goes on to distinguish the acquisition of territory by way of 'primary' and 'secondary' acquisitions, leading to important distinctions. Thus:

> if the object of consideration here is historic title, ... analysed as a legal construct, then we may postulate that we are dealing with a principle which must in the end be rooted in international custom, both in term of its construction as well as its legal effects. In order that reliance on such title does not become a camouflage for other recognised rules for determining a State's sovereign rights to a particular territory, it must be considered independently.[66]

Inevitably discussions of the modalities to measure historic title and the value that can be attributed to one narrative of historical title as opposed to another have been the focal point of many cases concerning title to territory. This pertained to the time context in the *Fisheries Case (UK v. Norway)*[67]and *Minquiers & Ecrehos Case (France v. UK)*[68] and the value of such title in the *Rann of Kutch Arbitration* (1968).[69] In *Eritrea-Yemen Arbitration* (1998) [70]and *Sovereignty over Pedra Branca/Pulau Batu Puteh, Middle Rocks and South Ledge* (2008),[71] significant attention was placed on seeking to understand the scope of what constituted historical title.[72] Along the lines argued by Norway in *Anglo-Norwegian Fisheries*, Kozlowski suggests that 'historic title' be interpreted as an equal element in determining the source of sovereignty over territory rather than as a derogation or exception to that norm. Historical title should therefore be treated as a right based on an established, rather than a developing or accumulating, claim. Accordingly,

65 Artur Kozlowski, 'The Legal Construct of Historic Title to Territory in International Law – An Overview' 30 *Polish Yearbook of International Law* (2010) 61–100 at 62.

66 *Ibid.* 63.

67 *ICJ Reports* (1951) 130 discussed in the context of the precept *possessio longi temporis.*

68 *ICJ Reports* (1953) 53.

69 19 February 1968, RIAA XVII, 436, also see the dissenting opinion Bebler p. 482.

70 *Eritrea – Yemen Arbitration, Phase I: Territorial Sovereignty and the Scope of Dispute* 1998 (RIAA XXII, 2006) 211–334.

71 *Sovereignty over Pedra Branca/Pulau Batu Puteh, Middle Rocks and South Ledge (Malaysia v Singapore)* ICJ Reports (2008) 290.

72 The nature of this question means that it pertains equally to discussions concerning the Law of the Seas. In this context see *Juridical Regime of Historic Waters, Including Historic Bays*, Study prepared by the Secretariat, A/CN.4/143, TILC, 1962, Vol. II, pt 54, which has particular salience for the contemporary questions concerning title in the South China Sea.

> Historic title then is not a deviation, but a dimension of the rules that are referred to when defining the scope of territorial rights. It is one of the emanations of a general principle, and hence the determination of a right arising from historic title is dependent only upon the fulfilment of the prerequisite conditions. Their existence should suffice for a determination of a state's right to a disputed territory.[73]

This requires acceptance of two discernible, sometimes overlapping elements of historic title: (a) ancient title, or ancestral domain as referred to in the context of indigenous peoples' claims, that has been established over such a long period of time as to be recognizable by common repute, to the extent that this common knowledge is sufficient; and (b) a consolidated title that has been created or established by a process of prescription or acquiescence, or by continued possession for a time period significant enough to have become accepted by law as being valid. In both cases, but especially in the latter instance, an important measure of the validity of the title derives from the extent to which sovereign authority can be demonstrated to have been exercised throughout the territory. The threshold for discerning such exercise is based on effectiveness, and:

> [O]nly if they are acknowledged as such an exercise can they be deemed to create the sovereignty of a State over territory. It should be noted that an assessment of the sovereign nature of State activities must necessarily take into account the particularities of specific case; the analysis does not presume the achievement of some permanent universal standard of sovereignty without regard to the circumstances in which legal title to territory develops.[74]

Inevitably the demonstration of sovereignty is not the exclusive determinant of historical title, since it requires, in almost equal measure, that such a claim is generally tolerated and accepted by others, that the rights of sovereignty over the territory are exercised in a manner that is relatively unmolested, and that there is clear evidence of third-party acquiescence to the exercise of sovereignty. These are expressed by the International Law Commission as 'toleration of the effective and continued sovereignty of a State over a given territory for a considerable length of time constitutes strong basis for a claim of historic title'.[75]

Using these concepts and measures in a context of geographical landscapes dominated by sovereigns of fairly equal access is relatively unproblematic.

73 Kozlowski (2010) *op. cit.* 65, 67.
74 *Ibid.* 73.
75 *Ibid.* 75.

In other words, understanding the geographical parameters where one European State has hegemony and where that ends in relation to its neighbour is relatively easy. Outside Europe, especially prior to colonization or even after decolonization, such a task takes on significant difficulties, not least since there are questions concerning the lack of consent from the people who would objectively make the territory occupied (i.e. not *terra nullius* and therefore open to acquisition). In general, within European States, identity has played a key role in the formulation and acceptance of sovereignty. Linguistic fault-lines have played a major role in determining physical territorial boundaries, as have geographical considerations. Outside Europe such determinations are often made by external forces (historically European) on the basis of their own interests. This phenomenon needs more careful consideration than has been warranted thus far. A much-repeated reason for its neglect, especially at the time of decolonization, was the fear of the fragmentation of territories at a time of vulnerability, as best captured in the *Cairo Resolution* (1964). Yet the decision to respect colonial boundaries in many cases simply postponed the problem to another era, with scarcities driven by climate change, persistent migration, and competition hastening the arrival of that moment of reckoning. The size of the challenge is well articulated by Fry and Loja:

> Historic title usually originates in ancient normative systems, including tributary, feudal, sultanate, and Islamic systems that predate the Western international legal system. Nevertheless, the rules against which historic title has been tested in international judiciary proceedings generally require that the original titleholder be a state or a central authority that exercised territorial sovereignty over a defined space to the exclusion of other sovereign powers. The rules that apply specifically to these ancient normative systems, where allegiance to authority was personal or religious rather than territorial, have been seen as irrelevant compared to the more contemporary determination of historic title.[76]

The application of the medieval customary norm of *frankalmoign* in *Minquiers & Ecrehos* presents a notable exception to the trend of determining historical title based on factors other than the strict notion of ancient or consolidated title. This work seeks to contribute to developing this further, with acceptance that such a trend is emerging in ICJ jurisprudence, as evidenced by the attribution of value to the importance of the personal allegiance expressed by the *Orang Laut* to the Sultan of Johore in determining

76 James D. Fry and Melissa H. Loja, 'The Roots of Historic Title: Non-Western Pre-Colonial Normative Systems and Legal Resolution of Territorial Disputes' 27 *Leiden Journal of International Law* (2014) 727–754, 727.

the value of historical title in the dispute between Malaysia and Singapore.[77] The ongoing discussions concerning the value of historical titles and how they can be measured also form an important backdrop to the South China Seas disputes,[78] though their expression by a new incumbent global hegemonic power may require closer interrogation if the pitfalls associated with allowing law to serve powerful political interests is to be heeded.[79] The challenge and efficacy of the settlement of boundary disputes in international law in the twenty-first century and beyond will depend on the extent to which a clearer understanding dawns of the differentiated value to be attributed to historical claims generated in non-Western systems that predate colonialism and, in some cases, modern international law.[80] To do this there first needs to be an acknowledgement of the difficulties associated with the acquisition of territory through colonization, and appreciation of subsequent limitations expressed justifiably and sometimes through misunderstanding in the vast decolonization process that proliferated sovereign States through international society.

There was, justifiably, global discomfort at engaging in a disparate normative way with the territorial claims made by *Daesh* as it overran Iraq and Syria. A crucial question that emerged was whether such actions could be recognized as 'title-generating'. The return of the Taliban to governance after subjugation of the previous government installed by foreign occupiers in Afghanistan in 2021 raised questions which return the discussion to what types of governance could be deemed legitimate, and by whom. With conquest and subjugation overruled as legitimate means towards the acquisition of territory the case could be dismissed as the actions of law-breaking private entities rather than a law-generating entity ascending towards being an incoming sovereign, which is challenging and perhaps racist. Even if it were possible to leave aside the barbaric means through which *Daesh* acquired (and subsequently lost) territory, it would be clear that such a significant degree of change to frontiers deemed inviolable could only be achieved through the consent or, at the very minimum, the acquiescence of the existing

77 *Case Concerning Sovereignty over Pedra Branca/Pulau Batu Puteh, Middle Rocks and South Ledge* (Malaysia v. Singapore) *ICJ Reports* (2008) para. 74.

78 See especially Jianming Shen, 'China's Sovereignty over the South China Sea Islands: A Historical Perspective' 1 *Chinese Journal of International Law* (2002) 94ff, and 'International Law Rules and Historical Evidences Supporting China's Title to the South China Sea Islands' 21 *Hastings International and Comparative Law Review* (1997) 1ff.

79 Contrast The-Kuang Chang, 'China's Claim of Sovereignty over Spratly and Paracel Islands: A Historical and Legal Perspective' 23 *Case Western Reserve Journal of International Law* (1991) 23 ff. with Hong Thao Nguyen, 'Vietnam's Position on the Sovereignty over the Paracel and the Spratlys: Its Maritime Claim' 5 *Journal of East Asia International Law* (2012) 174–184.

80 Fry & Loja (2014) *op.cit.* 76, 729.

sovereignty States impacted. The complication however arises from the fact that neither of the existing sovereign States could demonstrate effective control and governance over the existing territories, and significant questions remained concerning the legitimacy of those regimes too. Classical writings in public international law would suggest that original holders, even of titles deemed primitive, would be required to be considered members of the 'family of civilised nations' before any claim could be accepted.[81] This would require holders to have 'international legal personality' to enjoy external recognition of their title.[82] Yet understanding whether recognition as an international legal personality can predate acceptance of a territorial claim presents the classic time-old 'chicken and egg' problem.[83]

If the tribal communities of Syria and Iraq were the original title holders, with either pristine and fully operational or partially submerged title through Ottoman rule, the subjugation and defeat of their rights were achieved through Franco–British collaboration. The subsequent achievement of 'independence' and sovereignty was engineered through the grant of title-generating activities to new hegemons without adequate acknowledgement of the extinguishment of the rights of the holders of the original 'primitive' title. The loss of effective control and the emergence of another title claimant require the existence of a clear set of standards based on law, although none exist. This leaves a spectre of law being forced to wait, to first validate, then bestow legality upon victors of violent contestations. If such activities take hold and serve to call for mutiny it could undermine the edifice of public international law and signal a failure in the general and gentle civilizing mission of international law.

In the context of the ongoing war in Gaza which commenced in 2023, the ICJ Advisory Opinion of 19 July 2024, given in response to a request for such an opinion by the General Assembly touches on many of the themes contained in this book. The General Assembly sought a legal opinion on the following two questions:

(a) What are the legal consequences arising from the ongoing violation by Israel of the right of the Palestinian people to self-determination, from its prolonged occupation, settlement and annexation of the Palestinian territory occupied since 1967, including measures aimed at altering the demographic composition, character and status of the Holy City of Jerusalem, and from its adoption of related discriminatory legislation and measures?(b) How do the

81 Sir Mark Frank Lindley, *The Acquisition and Government of Backward Territory in International Law* (London: Longman Green, 1926) 37–39.

82 Georg Schwarzenberger, 'Title to Territory: Response to a Challenge' 51 *American Journal of International Law* (1957) 313–314.

83 R. Higgins, 'Time and Law: International Perspectives on an Old Problem' 46 *International & Comparative Law Quarterly* (1997) 501 ff.

policies and practices of Israel referred to in paragraph 18 (a) above affect the legal status of the occupation, and what are the legal consequences that arise for all States and the United Nations from this status?"

After a thorough analysis of the issues that underpin the questions posed, key elements of the Court's decision are that: (a) Israel's continued presence in the Occupied Palestinian Territories (OPTs) is unlawful (11 votes to 4); (b) Israel is under an obligation to end its unlawful presence in the OPTs as rapidly as possible (11-4); (c) Israel is under an obligation to immediately cease all new settlements and evacuate all settlers from the OPTs (14-1); (d) Israel has the obligations to make reparations for the damage caused to natural or legal persons in the OPTs (14-1); (e) States are obliged not to recognize as legal the situation arising from Israel's unlawful presence in the OPTs and not to render aid or assistance in maintaining the situation (12-3);(f) International organizations, including the UN, obliged not to recognize the unlawful presence of Israel in the OPTs (12-3). The judgment ends (12-3) with the Court's: ...opinion that the United Nations, and especially the General Assembly, which requested this opinion, and the Security Council, should consider the precise modalities and further action required to bring to an end as rapidly as possible the unlawful presence of the State of Israel in the Occupied Palestinian Territory.[84]

The treatment of issues in this judgement continues a trend by which the ICJ has become increasingly vigilant of the need to broaden its understanding of the kinds of activities that could be considered as generating historical title. Thus, attention was paid to the value of tribal systems in determining sovereignty contours in the Bakassi peninsula,[85] in contrast to a failure to attribute meaningful value to this in Western Sahara.[86] Similarly there were genuine attempts to understand the form of governance in Islamic societies in the *Eritrea v. Yemen* arbitration:[87] a facet that received significantly less attention in Western Sahara where potential title-generating value from religious allegiance to the Sultan as the temporal head of the region merited little reflection.[88] In more recent cases concerning Malaysia, there was engagement with the sultanate system of governance and how it pertained to generating

84 *Legal Consequences Arising from the Policies and Practices of Israel in the Occupied Palestinian Territories, including East Jerusalem* (ICJ, Advisory Opinion,19 July 2024) available at https://www.icj-cij.org/sites/default/files/case-related/186/186-20240719-adv-01-00-en.pdf

85 *Case Concerning the Land and Maritime Boundary Between Cameroon and Nigeria* ICJ Reports (2002) 203.

86 Joshua Castellino, 'A Territorial Interpretation of Identity in International Law: The Case of the Western Sahara' 29(3) *Millennium Journal of International Studies* (1999) 523–559.

87 Territorial Sovereignty and Scope of the Dispute (Eritrea and Yemen) XXII RIAA (1998) 525.

88 Castellino (1999) *op.cit.* 150, 554.

title-bearing activities,[89] while in *Qatar v. Bahrain* attention was paid to the tribute system and the extent to which it could be considered to generate title.[90] This indicates a progressive attitude to settling disputes based on concepts and tenets amenable to the regions and cultures where the disputes arise, rather than to a rigid perception and regurgitation of rules on the simple assertion of the claim they are already 'universal'. Yet this willingness to nuance discussions concerning title to territory, Fry and Loja argue, has had little benefit on the outcome. Instead they found in general that

> the validity of historic title typically depends on whether the original titleholder was capable of exercising territorial sovereignty over the disputed territory. The exercise of other forms of authority, whether religious, personal, tribal, or cultural, is not relevant to the outcome of these cases.[91]

The Role of Culture and Attitude in Determining Boundary Issues

At the core of the problem lies the difficulty that contemporary international institutions such as the ICJ have with cultures different to the normative home of the discipline. While the institutions are no longer dominated by Europeans, the public international legal discourse remains built on European-based ideas, making adherence to such 'knowledge' the most relevant in upholding law. The nature of judiciaries, self and externally portrayed as upholders of existing doctrine, make them less than able to 'advocate' or articulate change. A key perception remains that was articulated in what is still considered a classical international legal text on the subject of the acquisition of territory by M. F. Lindley in 1926.[92] The text of his book, *The Acquisition and Government of Backward Territories in International Law*, is worth reproducing to show the depth of racial superiority that lies behind title to territory questions in international law. Of course in the text Lindley did not see the need to frame a definition of what he perceived to be 'backward'. Rather, he stated:

> At one extreme, it may perhaps be said to be marked by territory which is entirely uninhabited; and it clearly includes territory inhabited by natives as low in the scale of civilization as those of Central Africa. On the other

89 *ICJ Reports* (2008) para. 52–68.

90 *Maritime Delimitation & Territorial Questions between Qatar & Bahrain* (Merits) *ICJ Reports* (2001) 40. Also see Barbara Kwiatkowska, 'The Qatar v. Bahrain Maritime Delimitation and Territorial Questions Case' 33(3–4) *Ocean Development & International Law* (2002) 227–262.

91 Fry & Loja (2014) *op.cit.* 76, 736.

92 Lindley (1926) *op.cit.* 81.

> hand, all that can be said as to its upper limits probably is that it is obviously intended to exclude territory which has reached the level of what is sometimes known as European or Western civilization.[93]

While more generous scholars would insist the text be interpreted in light of the attitudes of the time, its formulation remains remarkable, and its language unduly bold in articulating what is mostly considered received wisdom in terms of the traditionally accepted values of 'civilizations', seized and acted upon by a group of gentlemen (studied further below) who assumed control of literally framing the world in this image. To Lindley's credit his work acknowledged that 'civilization' could be gained as well as imposed, thus rendering a need for a dynamic interpretation of what constituted civilization. Thus, he argued:

> The term [civilization] is a relative one, and as civilisation advances it may cease to apply to territory which would today be said to be included within it; or it may conceivably become applicable to countries which would not, in the circumstances of the present time, be called 'backward'.[94]

Having postulated his view on such territory it became appropriate to articulate a set of rules derived from public international law that could be put in place for the ordered acquisition of such territory. Thus, for Lindley:

> Occupation … can be commenced by a unilateral act of a relatively simple nature and consummated in a comparably short time. It is therefore important to determine what are the conditions that characterize territory that is open to acquisition by Occupation.[95]
>
> Occupation in the broad sense covers not only the process or mode by which sovereignty is extended over a territory that was previously without a Sovereign, but also that by which ownership is acquired in land or goods previously belonging to nobody.[96]

While the rules governing *terra nullius* are derived from Roman law and effectively consist of claiming first ownership over a property, Lindley accepted this could not apply to inhabited property. He wrote:

93 *Ibid.* v.
94 *Ibid.*
95 *Ibid.* 2.
96 *Ibid.* 3.

> when we are dealing with inhabited lands such a rule [acquisition of terra nullius] is of little use, because the point at issue is whether, having regard to the degree of political development and other characteristics of the inhabitants, the territory can be considered to be already under an effective sovereignty, and with this the Roman rules do not deal.[97]

Lindley cites Middle Ages precedents that treated this issue as conquest, where

> the general trend of opinion in the direction of denying sovereign rights to non-Christians, but, even among those who held this view, it was put forward as legitimizing a war of Conquest and not as rendering the lands of non-Christians *territoria nullius* which could be acquired by Occupation.[98]

Any dismissal of such writings and attitudes as being merely synonymous of the time needs to be tempered against other writings by Thomas Acquinas (1227–1274) who argued that 'even' infidels have rights;[99] by condemnation by the Council of Constance (1414–1418) of the so-called *Wycliffe Principles* that denied rights to Poles and Lithuanians on grounds of their being infidels[100] and by writings of Bartolomé de las Casas who argued for recognition of the rights of indigenous peoples, not least in title to territory-generating activities in their native lands.[101] The point here is to emphasize that even among the select group of men with a certain type of education, there were those with less strident domination and exploitation-oriented views of the world, than those who were over-represented among the most highly qualified publicists of public international law.

Aware of some of these discussions of the time Lindley did seek to reflect the contrasting opinions, leading him to classify three distinct opinions on title-generating valences to be attributed to 'native' or those living on 'backward' territories:[102]

97 *Ibid.* 11.

98 *Ibid.*

99 Jean-Pierre Torell, *Saint Thomas Aquinas: The Person and his Work*, Vol.1 (Catholic University of America Press, 2005), 106ff.

100 Charles Henry Alexandrowicz, 'Paulus Vladimiri & the Development of the Doctrine of Coexistence of Christian and Non-Christian Countries (1963)' in *The Law of Nations in Global History* [David Armitage and Jennifer Pitts eds.] (Oxford: Oxford University Press, 2017) 59.

101 Lawrence A. Clayton, *Bartolomé de las Casas* (Cambridge: Cambridge University Press, 2012)

102 Lindley (1926) *op.cit.* 81, 11.

(a) Those who regard backward races as possessing title against all comers;[103]
(b) Those who admit title but are subject to restrictions;[104]
(c) Those who do not consider natives as possessing, making them subject to assumption of sovereignty over them by more highly civilized people.[105]

He concluded that though the publicists in class (a) state their position in different ways they do not materially differ in themselves, with their opinion amounting to 'that wherever a country is inhabited by people who are connected by some political organization, however primitive and crude, such a country is not be to regarded as *territorium nullis* and open to acquisition by Occupation'.[106] By contrast, he concluded that none of the opinions of the people in class (b) provided a satisfactory foundation for the formulation of a rule of international law.[107] For him delving into the discussion of class (c) necessitated additional questions, including what is a State and how to classify those who are not 'full members' of the international family. On the former questions writers in this category take a restrictive view of what is a State. This led Lindley to suggest that

> extending over some three and a half centuries, there had been a persistent preponderance of juristic opinion in favour of the proposition that lands in the possession of any backward peoples who are politically organized ought not to be regarded as if they belonged to no one. But that, and especially in comparatively modern times, a different doctrine has been contended for and has numbered among its exponents some well-known authorities; a doctrine which denies that International Law recognizes any rights in primitive peoples to the territory they inhabit, and, in its most advanced form, demands that such peoples shall have progressed so far in civilisation as to have become recognized as members of the Family of Nations before they can be allowed such rights.[108]

This effectively means that while Lindley located himself as a supporter of the views of those classified as group (a), he allowed for the need for a 'politically defined society'. (He also appears to wear the burden lightly of having to 'progress civilizations' to a point where they could be 'recognized' within

103 Franciscus a Victoria (Salamanca), Dominic Soto, Bartholomew de Las Casas, Ayala, Brunus, Gentilis, Selden, Grotius, Pufendorf, Gunther, Kluber, Blackstone, Heffter, Pasquale Fiore, and others.

104 Vattel, Phillimore, Martens, Pinheiro-Ferreira, Bluntschli, and others.

105 Westlake, Hall, Oppenheim, Lawrence, Dudley Field, Martens-Ferrao, Heimburger, and others.

106 Lindley (1926) *op.cit.* 81, 17.

107 *Ibid.* 17.

108 *Ibid.* 20.

the Family and 'allowed' such rights [sic].) His test for a politically defined society seems to be derived from Austin, who stated that the political character of a society is that 'the bulk of its members must be in a habit of obedience to a common superior'.[109] After exploring these issues and the views of publicists, Lindley concludes:

> in order that an area shall not be *territorium nullius*, it would appear, from general considerations, to be necessary and sufficient that it be inhabited by a political society, that is, by a considerable number of persons who are permanently united by habitual obedience to a certain and common superior, whose conduct in regard to their mutual relations habitually conforms to recognized standards.[110]

It therefore followed that

> if a tract of country were inhabited only by isolated individuals who were not united for political action, so that there was no sovereignty in exercise there, such a tract would be *territorium nullius*.[111]

After an examination of how territory was acquired through European State practice in *every* continent, in a succinct 20 pages he concluded:

> As an induction from all of these instances, extending over four centuries and derived from four continents, it appears that, on the whole, European States, in establishing their dominion over countries inhabited by peoples in a more or less backward state of political development, have adopted, as the method of such extension, Cession or Conquest, and have not based their rights upon the Occupation of *territorium nullius*. As among themselves, the European powers have not disputed the rights acquired by one Power, whatever the method by which those rights were obtained, so long as their own interests were not thereby affected; and, in some cases, it has been recognized that a certain power had the right to acquire territory within a given area in the future.[112]

The difference between consent and non-consent is accounted for:

> If the inhabitants have agreed to place themselves under the sovereignty of the acquiring State, it has been recognized as an act of Cession. If their

109 *Ibid.* 21.
110 *Ibid.* 23.
111 *Ibid.* 23.
112 *Ibid.* 43–44.

> country has been taken possession of by superior force against their will, the mode of acquisition has been regarded as Conquest.[113]

Notwithstanding the failure of rules towards the inhabitants in adjudicating against the wanton subjugation of territory occupied by them, this crucial difference is deemed important for maintaining the integrity of the discipline. But the discussion takes further overtones with regard to even those instances where consent was deemed to have been given. Thus, Lindley states:

> No doubt, in many of the cases of Cession, the native chief did not realize what he was transferring under treaty; but the fact that the form employed was that of Cession shows that the Power concerned did not consider that the territory was one that belonged to nobody. No doubt, also, in many cases the treaties were obtained under compulsion, but forced treaties are not unrecognized in international affairs. The Powers themselves, ... have in a large number of cases accepted sovereign rights from the chiefs, and based their titles upon such cessions, and, unless one is prepared to argue that the maxim *Nemo dat quod habet* has no application to such a case, it must be admitted that the chiefs themselves possessed those rights.[114]

Lindley addresses the question of international law and how it recognizes native sovereignty, concluding that:

> While international law should and does recognize the rights of independent backward races to the extent of distinguishing those territories to which a title may be acquired by the legally and morally legitimate method of Occupation from those which, in the absence of consent on the part of the inhabitants, can be obtained by Conquest – or through Prescription – it does not, at present, go further and say that an acquisition by Conquest is not legitimate. On the contrary, once a Conquest has become *fait accompli*, International Law recognizes its results.[115]

Lindley then sums up his conclusions on what constitutes acquirable territory, the text of which needs to be emphasized, since they have remained central to the rules governing the acquisition of territory:

113 *Ibid*. 44.
114 *Ibid*. 44.
115 *Ibid*. 47.

I Areas which are *territorium nullius* and open to acquisition by Occupation must consist of:

(1) Uninhabited lands; unless they are unsuitable for permanent habitation and are being used for the purposes for which they are suitable, or are islands which are situated within territorial waters, or have been formed by alluvium from occupied territory.
(2) Lands inhabited by individuals who are not permanently united for political action.
(3) Lands which have been abandoned by their former occupants.
(4) Lands which have been forfeited because they have not been occupied effectively.
(5) Seas that are almost entirely surrounded by land which fulfils one of the above conditions.
(6) The belt of the ocean bordering on land which fulfils one of the above conditions to a distance of at least three marine miles from the shore occupied, with possible extensions in the cases of bays and straits.
(7) The soil beneath the bed of the open sea – by starting from beneath the territorial waters.
(8) Portions of the open sea adjoining the territorial belt – by accretions to the neighbouring land.

II Lands inhabited by any permanent political society can be acquired only by Conquest, Cession, or Prescription.

In a third part Lindley also discusses the acquisition of title over open seas, the impact of the Monroe Doctrine (discussed further below), and how acquisition-related matters such as papal grants, discovery, and other forms of acquisition such as conquest, cession, and prescription can be treated. In summarizing what constitutes effective occupation, he finds:

> [that] a valid title to backward territory … depends upon the existence throughout the region, within a reasonable time after the first formal taking of possession or the announcement of a claim to exclusive control, of an administration sufficient for the protection of life and property. What is sufficient will depend upon all the circumstances.[116]

116 *Ibid.* 159.

In discussing native religion, laws, customs, and institutions, Lindley states:

> It is becoming more and more generally recognized that, in conferring upon backward races some of the advantages of modern civilization, it is not necessary, nor as a rule desirable, to force a great change upon them abruptly; and that the process is usually more likely to be hindered than helped by destroying their institutions, imposing upon them institutions which have been evolved to meet the exigencies of an advanced civilization sweeping away the sanctions of their established customs, or hampering them in the exercise of their religion.[117]

Conclusion

The acquisition of territory in international law by colonial powers was achieved against a backdrop of deeply problematic legality, with significant bias of racial superiority. The chance to remedy this through decolonization ought to have presented an opportunity for significant change. Yet the decolonization that eventually did transpire took place along lines drawn on maps by a group of men whose biases and interests became baked into the map of the world. Due to constraints of space and the difficulties of acquiring such knowledge through biased narratives, the next chapter can only explore the actions of a handful of these men. Yet it hopes to show how even these few had an impact on significant contemporary powers, some of whom are likely themselves to shape the next set of contours of human history, based on their own inherited boundaries.

117 *Ibid.* 376.

Chapter 2

A Few European Men and Global Boundaries

Introduction

To emphasize the undue influence that specific men, all drawn from the same education and driven by what appear to be a common set of values, can have on lands and territories far removed from their own, this chapter will seek to trace the lineage of specific lines drawn upon maps. Rather than attempting to attribute blame per se for the actions of these individuals, the purpose of this section of the book lies in seeking to demonstrate the factors considered relevant in drawing boundary lines that have been legitimized in international law, not least through the acquiescence of the sovereign States that are currently sovereign within the lines. The aim of delving into these is to address the impact of the rule concerning the sacrosanct nature of international frontiers in a contemporary setting. Rather than calling for redrawing frontiers or risking further fragmentation and subdivision, this book seeks to do the opposite: emphasize how the lines drawn across human identity that have taken on such salience were unjustified in the first place and ought not to determine in perpetuity how peoples and cultures that exist on the territories today live. The imperative behind this derives from the nature of the collective threats faced within regions, where divided approaches based on artificial States with boundaries configured to suit someone else's specification are unable to address central governance challenges.

To capture the importance of boundaries, Lord Curzon, considered a publicist of high standing within the discipline of public international law and a key authority on boundaries, stated in his much-heralded lecture on Frontiers in 1907:

> Frontiers are the chief anxiety of nearly every Foreign Office in the civilized world, and are the subject of four out of every five political treaties or conventions that are now concluded… Frontier policy is of the first

DOI: 10.4324/9781003503279-3

> practical importance, and has a more profound effect upon the peace or warfare of nations than any other factor, political or economic.[1]

As stated in the introduction the underpinning importance of the boundary is ever more valid today, even if the frontiers are no longer the chief anxieties of the respective foreign offices of the States. This makes an understanding of how the frontiers emerged into history ever more important. To illustrate the role that a group of men with a common purpose had in this process, this chapter will focus on three lines – the Durand Line, McMahon Line, and Sykes–Picot line – while also reflecting on the impact and drivers for these lines against the historical currents of the time. In so doing it will also place these activities against those of competing hegemons: notably Russia and China.

Durand Line

The *Durand Line* that eventually 'established' Afghanistan commenced with the appointment of three boundary commissions by Sir Mortimer Durand when he visited Kabul in 1893.[2] These commissions, consisting of British officers and geographers along with Afghan Commissioners, were charged with demarcating the frontier between British India and Afghanistan, specifically through the *Baluch-Afghan Commission*; the *Asmar Commission*, and the *Waziristan Boundary Commission*.[3] Reflecting on the experience of drawing the boundaries, the special correspondent of the *Englishman* and *Times of India* who accompanied the missions on their entire journey reflected:

> one is thankful to be able to say that the work has finished without loss of life, and that the whole boundary has been gone over excepting some unscalable peaks and a few miles of country which were inaccessible on account of sand. Permanent and visible evidence of the boundary line has been left in the shape of stone pillars, and the inhabitants of the neighbouring tracts – to their expressed great satisfaction be it said – have thus had all doubts and disputes removed.[4]

1 *Curzon on Frontiers*, quoted by Percy Sykes, *Sir Mortimer Durand* (Lahore: Al-Biruni Press, 1977), 205.

2 F. P. Maynard (ed.), *The Baluch-Afghan Boundary Commission of 1896* (Calcutta, India: Baptist Mission Press, 1909).

3 The story of how the Commissions went about their work has been captured in Maynard (1909), which gives the backdrop as well as the hardships encountered in charting through unforgiving territory.

4 *Ibid*. 86.

The achievement is celebrated in terms that show familiar signs of Orientalism, as reflected in the text below:

> All of this, of course, has not been accomplished without great forethought, great tact, and the constant exercise of those qualities of mind and heart in dealing with more or less uncivilized races which seem peculiarly British, and which are possessed by Captain McMahon in an eminent degree. The proof of this is that the demarcation of 800 miles of frontier, almost equal to that between Russia and Europe in length, all of it lying among tribes more noted for their lawlessness and disregard for life than for their manners, and in country which, when not actual desert, has been hitherto regarded as unsafe for British officers to visit, has been settled, much of it rapidly and all of it without incident.[5]

On the 12th of November 1883, (British) India and Afghanistan signed an agreement which validated the demarcation of the boundary between them along what is known as the *Durand Line*. This legitimation is based on what Gul Wazir identifies as reasons that compelled Durand, a Cambridge-trained geographer and international lawyer, to be charged with the task of creating such a frontier.[6]

Principal among these was the threat that Russia was perceived as posing to British India through its growing influence in Persia (1833–1837). Concerned that Afghanistan would fall under Russian influence (it subsequently did) with impact on British control of India, Durand was dispatched to negotiate a *Treaty of Friendship between Britain and Afghanistan* in 1855. Around this time Russia, in full imperial mode, had expanded through Central Asia (discussed further below). Concerned about this expansion so close to frontiers it deemed within its sphere of influence, Britain occupied a mountain pass called Pishin, subsequently validating this occupation through the *Treaty of Gandamak* (26 May 1879), which led to the Second Anglo-Afghan War (1879–1880). As in many other parts of the world, British military interests were protected by the use of collaborators, in this case, Amir Abdur Rahman, who was supported from 1875 onwards, mainly through belief in his abilities to bring tribal territories that were hard to control under British influence. The *Treaty of Gandamak*, which served as a precursor to the *Durand Line*, enabled Britain to assist Rahman Khan to secure the Afghan throne in 1880 in return for his maintaining an exclusive relationship with them. The agreement promised a policy of non-interference in domestic rule, and protection by Britain against external (namely Russian) aggression.

5 *Ibid*. 86–87.

6 For more on the instructions to Durand, see Sykes (1977) *op.cit*. 1.

Gul Wazir argues that the *Durand Line* ought to be invalidated in international law on the basis that it was signed under duress. In explaining this Wazir states:

> The Government [of Rahman Khan] hoped that the delimitation of Afghanistan's North-West Frontier on the 22nd July by [the] Anglo-Russian Commission would satisfy the two rival powers Britain and Russia and allay their countries state of tensions, ... and not lead them moving beyond the boundaries they had already occupied. However that was not to be the case.[7]

Despite superficial promises of non-interference, Britain had adopted what is referred to as a 'Forward Policy'. This was focused on acquisition of influence in South Waziristan (Foreign Department Programme, Sec. E April, 1890 Nos. 15–16) and planned physical encroachments towards Herat Province. The Russians, on the other hand, fresh from Central Asian expansion, were focused on gaining influence among tribes in the territories north of the Pamir plateau, escalating tensions between the two European superpowers far from home. Ostensibly British policy from the mid-1870s onwards aimed to 'protect' India from Russian influence, with Britain as the 'honest arbiter', 'striving only for the best for Afghanistan as well as British India'.[8] As Russia advanced towards Afghanistan, King Abdur Rahman Khan was persuaded about Britain's role as a protector and admitted the *Durand Mission* to Afghanistan, which eventually led to the Agreement of the 12 November 1893.

The 'guidelines' given to Durand are worth reproducing for an insight into the boundary-making:

a. He was authorized to make minor concessions to the King. He was to inform the King of the friendly intentions of the Government of British India in the matter of a tunnel through Khojak and the extension of the railway line to New Chaman. He was to assure the King of the identical interests of the two Governments, British India and Afghanistan, who were threatened by Russia.
b. He was given licence to discuss with Amir Abdur Rahman the whole question of the frontier settlement between India and Afghanistan and authorized to discuss the necessity for the British Government to maintain direct relations with the independent border tribes living along the

7 Babri Gul Wazir, *Durand Line: A Discussion about the Legality of the Signing of the Durand Line Agreement between Afghanistan and British India on the 12th of November 1893* (Kabul: Shah Books, 2007), 28.

8 Percy M. Sykes, *A History of Persia* (London: Andesite Press, 1915) 324–325.

> frontier, especially the Waziris, Afridis and the people of Bajaur, Swat, who the Afghan ruler had persistently tried to bring under his control.[9]

Convinced of the Russian threat by British articulations, King Rahman agreed to define spheres of influence between Afghanistan and British India. He gave up his claim to suzerainty over independent tribes and agreed not to interfere in the affairs of the Waziris, Afridis, Kakars, and other tribes on the frontier of British India. As for the Agreement itself, which delimits the frontier, Articles 6 and 7 are worth examining to understand the spirit of the agreement:

> (6) The above articles of agreement are regarded by the Government of India and His Highness the Amir of Afghanistan as a full and satisfactory settlement of all the principal differences of opinion which have arisen between them in regard to the frontier and both... undertake that any differences of detail such as those which will have to be considered hereafter by the officers appointed to demarcate the boundary line, shall be settled in a friendly spirit, so as to remove for the future as far as possible all causes of doubt and misunderstanding between the two Governments.
>
> (7) Being fully satisfied of His Highness's goodwill to the British Government, and wishing to see Afghanistan independent and strong, the Government of India will raise no objection to the purchase and import by His Highness of munitions of war, and they will themselves grant him some help in this respect. Further, in order to mark their sense of the friendly spirit in which His Highness the Amir has entered into these negotiations, the Government of India undertake to increase by the sum of six Lakhs of rupees a year, the subsidy of twelve Lakhs now granted to His Highness.[10]

Though little known and hardly studied by international lawyers, the Durand agreement laid down a boundary that is 2,400 km long (approximately the distance between Oslo and Rome), stretching from the Pamir Plateau to Koh Malik Siyah. This boundary, not properly delimited on the map accompanying the agreement, mainly sought to define the southern and eastern limits of the Amir's dominion. Commenting at the time of its framing, Fraser Tyler, a political commentator with an inevitable air of superiority, stated:

9 Wazir (2007) *op.cit.* 7, 36.

10 Hamid Wahed Alikuzai, *A Concise History of Afghanistan in 25 Volumes*, Vol. 14 (Bloomington, IN: Trafford Publishing, 2013) 574.

> The Durand line, though perhaps in the circumstances the best line possible, has few advantages and many defects. It is illogical from the point of view of ethnography, of strategy and of geography. It cuts across one of the main basins of the Indus watershed, it splits a nation in two, and even divides tribes. It is surprising that Adbur Rahman accepted such a boundary. It is possible he could not read the map, but was too conceited to admit it. [11]

Even Lord Curzon, who served as Viceroy of India between 1889 and 1903, regarded the *Durand Line* as a ridiculous, injudicious, and not very sensible agreement. It is important to note, however, that his objections were based on what he deemed were apparent 'concessions' made by Durand to the Amir, rather than any concern about tribal populations or unequal contracts. It may be obvious but needs to be stated that no attempt was made, nor was it even considered a factor, to consult the people of the tribal areas and so they did not consent to the Agreement. As Wazir states:

> The Durand agreement cannot be recognized as a valid agreement because it was negotiated without the consent of the people of Afghanistan and the tribal people living in the independent tribal territories.[12]

The relations between Amir Rahman Khan and his counterpart the Amir of Waziristan were traditionally good, with no evidence to suggest that these lines, and the latter's suzerainty over what had traditionally been an independent tribal area, were ever accepted. However, as rumours of the agreement spread, a growing disquiet arose among the tribes about such an agreement being struck without their consent. A *Loya Jirgah* was called, convening the tribes of Waziristan and Zhob, and a joint letter was dispatched to the Governor of Paktia Province to the following effect:

> Dear Governor sahib,
>
> A rumour has spread around here but it is not clear as to who spread this rumour. However, people are saying that in an agreement with the British, Amir Abdur Rahman Khan Sahib has handed over the whole of the Wazirs and Kakr to the British non-believers. We don't know the truth of this rumour. In order to inform ourselves about the reality and truth of the issue, we sent Ghazi Kastorai Khan and a few other men with a

11 Patrick Fraser Tytler, *Afghanistan: A Study of Political Developments in Central and Southern Asia* (Oxford: Oxford University Press, 1967) 188–189.

12 Wazir (2007) *op.cit.* 7, 38.

> letter to Your Excellency. We hope you will inform them about the issue concerned.[13]

The letter received no response, and another *Loya Jirgah* was convened at Wana, where speeches were made about the need for *jihad* to defend the territories and honour of the tribes. One speaker called for restraint until facts could be verified but agreed that if the treaty had been signed without consultation with the tribes, they had a duty to defend their country and honour. Wazir emphasizes a host of other reasons too for the illegality of the treaty, including that it was an ultimatum rather than a treaty of mutual consent; Amir Khan was in the pay of the British and could not be deemed an uninterested party; it was based on the decision of a single man prone to irrational behaviour; it is not clear whether the map was explained to Amir Khan; Amir Khan did not meet the criteria for being an independent Government; the bribes attached to the agreement make it void; it was signed under duress; the map that forms the basis was made in error without due diligence of qualified survey officers.[14]

The physical demarcation was also flawed. In the words of H.H. Dodwell,

> the new boundary line was not based on topographical data, for during the process of demarcation, it was discovered that certain places, marked on the Durand map did not exist on the actual ground.[15]

In the midst of writing his memoirs during the First Afghan War, Durand had been summoned to India much earlier for the Sikh War in 1848. His fragmentary accounts provide adequate insight into his perceptions of the territory and the people.[16] His son, who completed the work and had it published later, did so with the caveat that it was not meant to represent his father's views with regard to British policy in Central Asia. The book unashamedly captures how the establishment viewed Durand. Thus, Lord Mayo in 1870 is attributed with saying:

> Of all men in India, the most likely to exercise influence of a powerful and at the same time persuasive character is Sir Henry Durand. He has great experience of the best mode of dealing with these men; he knows most of them personally; he has a thorough knowledge of the history of modern Indian diplomacy, and a fine appreciation of that mixture of firmness and

13 As reproduced in Wazir (2007) *op.cit.* 7.

14 *Ibid.* 46–61.

15 Horace H. Dodwell, *The Cambridge History of India*, Vol. VI (Cambridge: Cambridge University Press, 1943) 462–463.

16 Henry Marion Durand, *First Afghan War and its Causes* (London: Longmans, Green and Co., 1879).

> kindness which is so essential... I think his great forte is political work, and he possesses the qualities which enable him to govern and direct men by personal influence, which are much more rare than administrative or judicial talent.[17]

Another famous name in boundary-making that we shall shortly turn to, Mark Sykes, also commented on the *Durand line*. He emphasized its positive legacy at a time of Russian expansion into Central Asia during the nineteenth century, which had already enabled them to capture Turkoman. In describing Durand as the 'moving spirit in the India Office', he is full of praise for the legacy of the boundary:

> his profound knowledge of the Central Asian problem and the statesmanlike views he expressed, [were responsible for] a boundary [that] was finally negotiated between two empires that has stood the test of a generation. ...by removing sources of grave misunderstanding and constant irritation, Durand paved the way for the Anglo-Russian Agreement of 1907, which constituted a general settlement of all outstanding questions between the two Powers in Asia.[18]

According to Sykes, his achievements in negotiating peace between two Empires were responsible for Russia working alongside Britain in World War I. This, in addition to what is trumpeted as the durability of the *Durand Line*, leads Sykes to commend Durand as standing out in his generation as the 'great Boundary-Maker and consequently as the great Peace-Maker'.[19]

The importance of Afghanistan in the quest for territory and influence in the late nineteenth century should not be underestimated. Part of the Persian Empire until the assassination of Nadir Shah in 1747, Afghanistan became independent, led by Ahmad Khan, chief of the Abdali tribe and former loyalist to Nadir Shah. Yet Afghan history has been dominated by being seen at various times as 'strategically important' or a 'corridor' or 'buffer' between first Persia and India, then Persia, and aspirations for Russian and British Empires in the region.[20] Persia had already lost influence and territory in the form of Georgia and Armenia to the Russians, but remained keen to maintain influence in Afghanistan through kin communities who traversed the new emerging boundaries.

17 *Ibid.* xxvi.

18 Sykes (1977) *op.cit.* 1, v.

19 *Ibid.*

20 Bernt Glatzer, 'War and Boundaries in Afghanistan: Significance and Relativity of Local and Social Boundaries' 41(3) *Die Welt des Islams* (November 2001) 379–399.

Russian advances through Central Asia were consolidated by the transporting of populations into the newly acquired territories. This was also accompanied by the building of a railway linking Samarkand, Bukhara, and Tashkent to the Russian Empire, all actions viewed as significant threats by the British. Writing in 1884 Durand stated:

> The only statesmanlike course is to endeavour to come to a really frank and friendly understanding with the Power which we have hitherto tried in vain in a half-hearted way to thwart and impede. I would, if possible, embody that understanding in a formal treaty, precisely defining the limits of Afghanistan... recognizing the extension of Russian influence up to those limits.[21]

A rough boundary line had existed between Russia and Britain, alluded to in the 1873 *Anglo-Russian Treaty*. However, the line had not been demarcated due to a lack of geographical knowledge of the terrain. With Russian expansionism on the horizon, the Amir of Afghanistan became keen to delimit the frontier, and as a consequence, a British and Russian boundary commission was constituted in 1884 with Afghan presence. Yet the boundary-making was far from simple: the Russians sought to aggrandize the territory under the Turkomans that formed part of their Empire; the British were keen to consolidate Afghan territory, hoping for a territorial buffer against Russian advances; while Afghan tribes sought to occupy key territories in advance of the arrival of the Commission. The Afghan boundary was eventually delimited by a joint British–Afghan Boundary Commission in 1895.

Sykes quotes Lord Curzon to the following effect:

> It has been a policy of the Protectorates that the Indian Empire has for more than a century pursued and is still pursuing its, as yet, unexhausted advance... The culminating point of this policy on the western side was the signature of the Durand Agreement at Kabul in 1893, by which a line was drawn between the tribes under British and those under Afghan influence for the entire distance from Chitral to Sistan, and the Indian Empire acquired what, so long as Afghanistan retains an independent existence, is likely to remain the Frontier of active responsibility.[22]

The tendency of the interconnection between the men who shaped entire regions is also captured in their writing. For instance, Tate's book, *The Frontiers of Baluchistan*, published in 1909, was born out of his own experience as Survey Officer to the *Baluch–Afghan Boundary Commission*

21 Sykes (1977) *op.cit.* 1, 135.
22 *Ibid.* 222.

(1895–1896) and the *Seistan Arbitration Mission* (1903–1905).[23] He describes a later *Anglo-Russian Convention of 1907*, which recognized the south-eastern corner of Persia as falling within the British sphere of influence. But he also writes about McMahon, who we will turn to next, as leader of the effort to maintain British interest against another empire – the Chinese. Tate highlights his role in Afghanistan:

> To Sir Henry (then Captain A.H.) McMahon was entrusted the task of surveying and demarcating, jointly with an Afghan Commission, the southern section of the frontier, stretching from Domandi, a village on the Gomal River due west of Dera Ismail Khan, westwards to the Malik Siah Kuh, the southern limit of the Perso-Afghan frontier. The length of the boundary to be fixed was something like eight hundred miles, and the work occupied altogether more than a couple of years, from April, 1894, to May, 1896.[24]

McMahon Line

With the longest documented history in the world, there is no lack of sources on China. Archaeological evidence suggests that the earliest Chinese boundaries trace back to the late Neolithic period, achieving clarity by 2000 BCE, as the Bronze Age commenced. As Hay states, 'this leads rapidly to China's first archaeologically identified political state, the Shang (sixteenth century BCE to mid-eleventh century BCE) – a culture distinguished by the centrality of its ritual representations'.[25] The Zhou period (mid-eleventh century to 256 BCE) saw major political, technological, commercial, and intellectual advances, with power becoming increasingly dispersed among multiple centres of authority.[26] In relating this to the formation of states, Hay states:

> From the eighth century BCE onwards, various states expanded, shrank, and sometimes disappeared in the struggle for dominance. Until the formal demise of the Zhou in 256 BCE, all these states acknowledged the otherwise powerless Zhou court as the ritual authority at their nominal centre (although it moved eastward in 771 BCE).[27]

The Great Wall of China is among the most famous boundaries in the world, even though its geographic location today no longer marks the limits of

23 G. P. Tate, *The Frontiers of Baluchistan: Travels on the Borders of Persia and Afghanistan* (London: Witherby & Co., 1909).
24 *Ibid.* 26.
25 John Hay (ed.), *Boundaries in China* (Oxford: Reaktion Books, 1994) 9.
26 *Ibid.* 11.
27 *Ibid.*

a sovereignty State.[28] It was built when China felt threatened by nomadic tribes, in the late sixteenth and early seventeenth centuries under the late Ming dynasty. The relative failure of the wall in protecting the Ming is best captured in the fact that the subsequent dynasty, the Qing, in fact came from north of the wall.

Yet, in examining boundary creation mechanisms in early China, Yates offers an interesting insight into the Chinese perspective on territory:

> Mirroring the mythological organization of space in concrete political and economic policies, by the time of the late Warring States period, each of the contending states had its own land tenure system; one of the most important reforms was instituted by Shang Yang in the state of Qin in the mid-fourth century BCE when, in the course of his radical reconstruction of the laws of that state, he redrew the size of the traditional acre. Shang Yang increased the size of this unit from one hundred to two hundred and forty square paces, and delineated the boundaries of the fields by pathways running north-south and east-west. By this means he is said to have destroyed the feudal (*fengjian*) system of the Zhou and to have created a new system of land tenure in which land could, for the first time in Chinese history, be freely bought and sold.[29]

It is important to note that the internal organization of the State is significantly different from the European conception of the State:

> the Qin organized its entire population into a hierarchy of which the lowest level consisted of five-family units geographically dispersed throughout the countryside in accordance with the strict divisions laid down in Lord Shang's land reform programme… This social organization was coordinated with the land tenure system; above the family was the village, the county, the commandery and eventually the whole state and empire. Thus Qin society resembled an enormous intricately interwoven and interlocking set of mutually responsible cells. This system was based upon contemporary military practice: the Qin army was similarly organized… The disciplinary structure employed by the Qin state may be contrasted with that of early modern European states in that the smallest unit held

28 For more, see Arthur Waldron, *The Great Wall of China: From History to Myth* (Cambridge: Cambridge University Press, 1990).

29 Robin D. S. Yates, 'Body, Space, Time and Bureaucracy: Boundary Creation and Control Mechanisms in Early China' in *Boundaries in China* [J. Hay ed.] (Oxford: Reaktion Books, 1994) 56–80 at 63.

> accountable to government was the family group, rather than the individual. Thereby it created group solidarity *against* the state.[30]

Yates traces this trend through to the modern day, identifying it as a key point of impact in Chinese history:

> In China, the state was never able to 'individualize' members of the population completely: it relied on the family and the lineage to help it control the population, but by so doing it created centres of opposition which prevented it from ever monopolizing entirely the techniques and powers of discipline. Right up to the present time, Chinese people feel as much, if not more, loyalty to their families and lineages as they do to the central government authorities. The tensions between particularistic ties to family and general loyalty to the state and nation has been an enduring feature of Chinese history.[31]

Discussions on boundaries in ancient China also need to pay particular heed to the etymology of the word in Mandarin. Thus, the ancient Chinese word *daxian*, translated to 'great boundary,' refers to death. However, the word has multiple meanings. As Wu Hung narrates:

> as is often the case in Chinese, the word is ambiguous and the concept of 'boundary' has multiple meanings: on the one hand, it means the 'end', 'termination', 'cessation', and 'expiration' of life; on the other, it implies a 'dividing', 'demarcating', 'joining', and 'juxtaposing' of this life and the afterlife.[32]

None of this history or nuance seems to have entered into the kinds of political calculations that McMahon engaged in while preparing the ground for what would become the *McMahon Line*. While his name may be less prominent than some of the others discussed here, his dubious legacy nonetheless remains alive between two of the world's most populous States, neither of which he came from nor attempted to understand, namely India and China, where contestations remain live and may become more lively in the future. In a sterling piece of work that reflects instead on the British Empire's take on boundaries, Noorani provides insights that show further the ignorance and

30 *Ibid.*
31 *Ibid.*
32 Wu Hung, 'Beyond the 'Great Boundary': Funerary Narrative in the Cangshan Tomb' in Hay (1994) *op.cit.* 9, 81–104 at 81.

superiority that led to its framing.[33] This then, in the context of its decolonization through the *Indian Independence Act 1947*, enacted by the British Parliament, became a live frontier. The *Act* did not define the boundaries of India, specifying that these would be the 'territories' that were to form part of the two independent Dominions of India and Pakistan.' Yet British boundary-making on behalf of India traces back to 1846 when Jammu and Kashmir was acquired and became part of British India.[34]

Provisions were subsequently made for boundaries delimiting the two emerging States of India and Pakistan, through 'awards' made by the *Radcliffe Commission* in Bengal and Assam. The transition from the British Empire to Indian independence treated India as the successor State to the British Empire, while Pakistan was considered the seceding State.[35] This had implications for State succession *vis-à-vis the* acceptance of treaties negotiated not only by British-administered India but also by the *East India Company*, tracing back to 1792.[36] Indian writers have long bemoaned the reason for being restricted in defining the State on the basis of British boundary-making between 1846 and 1947. As Sarvepalli Gopal, an influential figure in the Ministry of External Affairs, wrote in his biography of Nehru:

> To assume that nothing mattered in India before the arrival of the British, to revel in the [sic] details of the policy-making during the raj and to recommend compromise alignments, whose sole aim to consideration is that they were indicated by Englishmen, is to exhibit intellectual shallowness. This inclination of some British officials at the end of the nineteenth century to relinquish Indian sovereignty over parts of Aksai China plateau does not provide China with traditional rights to this area.[37]

Besides McMahon, the story on contemporary Indian boundaries also includes Lord Curzon (Viceroy of India), Lord Salisbury (Secretary of State), and Thomas H. Holdich (Surveyor-General of India), all key figures in the boundary-making stakes. Their published attitudes to what they believed they were doing are worth recounting. In the prestigious Romanes Lectures given by Lord Curzon in 1907, he reflected on the importance of such policy:

> frontier policy is of the first importance and has a more profound effect upon the peace and warfare of nations than any other factors, political or

33 A. G. Noorani, *India-China Boundary Problem 1846–1947 History and Diplomacy* (New Delhi, India: Oxford University Press, 2011).

34 *Ibid*. 5.

35 *Ibid*. 2.

36 *Ibid*. 6.

37 Sarvepalli Gopal, *Jawaharlal Nehru: A Biography, Vol. III 1956–1964* (New Delhi, India: Oxford University Press, 1984) 303–306.

> economic… wars of religion, of alliance, of rebellion, of aggrandizement, of dynastic intrigue or ambition… tend to be replaced by Frontier.[38]

In doing so he either appeared ignorant of the impact of the arrival of a colonial power from outside the region into densely populated lands or genuinely believed that the arrival of such a power, laden with a superior culture, would restrict the ambition of local rulers. The statement above appears to have been offered with no sense of irony about the ambition of the power seeking to make the frontier policies in the first place. In a similar vein, Holdich, another name prominent in questions concerning boundaries in international law,[39] explains the nature of the line-drawing as follows:

> A boundary is but an artificial impress on the surface of the land, as much as a road or the railway, it must adapt itself to the topographical conditions of the country it traverses. If it does not, it is likely to be no barrier at all… The first preliminary to a boundary settlement should be, if possible, a reasonably clear topographical illustration of the country concerned.[40]

With this spirit the *McMahon Line* was imagined in ignorance of the traditions in the region. In many parts of the world the failure to pay adequate attention to such issues is condoned due to the lack of a documented history. This rings untrue in the case of the *McMahon Line*, since the history of what can loosely be called the Chinese Empires is well documented, making the decision to exclude its consideration a decision of either pure ignorance about its salience (not least because of the language barrier) or due to a superiority of one culture/race over another.[41] Instead, the *McMahon Line* was drawn to form the eastern sector of the Sino-Indian border in the Himalayas. Formulated in 1914, it commences at the western border of Bhutan, crosses the Indian State of Assam to the Izu Razi Pass, which forms the China–Burma boundary.[42] Burke Inlow's revealing article, written in 1964, explores the genesis of the line and highlights the disagreements between China and India that even led to war in 1962.[43]

The source of the dispute will not be a surprise to scholars of international relations or history: it lies in the attempt by China in 1904 to restore Chinese

38 Lord Curzon, *Frontiers* (Oxford: Clarendon Press, 1907) 4–5.

39 See T. H. Holdich, *The Indian Border Land, 1880–1900* (London: Methuen & Co., 1901).

40 Thomas Holdich, *Political Frontiers and Boundary Making* (London: Macmillan, 1916) 1.

41 Noorani (2011) *op.cit.* 33, 168–209.

42 For more, see the official (British) Indian Government publication, C. U. Aitchison, *A Collection of Treaties, Engagements, and Sanads Relating to India and Neighbouring Countries* (Calcutta, India: Government of India Publications, 1929).

43 See E. Burke Inlow, 'The McMahon Line' 63 *Journal of Geography* (September 1964) 261–272.

rule in Tibet.[44] Britain had maintained an interest in the lower Tibetan plateau, the most fertile part of the region, and was interested in controlling south-east Tibet since it contained what Burlow describes as 'the trunk road' between India and China.[45] British interest in delimiting the boundaries was premised on the belief that its annexation of Assam had brought the entire area under British sovereignty. Britain appeared to believe it exercised some measure of authority over tribes that lived in southern Tibet. Burlow described this claim as tenuous:

> The Bhutans, Abors, Akas, Daflas, Miris and Mishmis, to mention only a few of the tribes in the area, had always resisted authority and moved freely back and forth from Burma to Assam to Tibet and to China, even after Burma was annexed to the Empire in 1885. They had never accepted the Ahom rulers as representing real authority and were not inclined to so recognize the British.[46]

As elsewhere in encounters between colonial powers and independent tribes, the British misread or willingly disregarded the mandate and sway of the Ahoms, as lesser rulers whose claims to authority could be dismissed as over-ambitious. As Burke highlights:

> To [the local tribes in the region] a chief did not hold an office of real political power. British administrators assumed that local chiefs were autocrats and therefore expected them to execute instructions received from the British District Officer or the government native officer. The truth of the matter was that while the tribal chiefs appeared to represent law and order, they were more apt to be mere tax collectors.[47]

The arrival of a Chinese force in 1909 at the Mishmi border prompted a major operation by Britain to explore 50,000 square miles of Assamese territory with a view to incorporating the border tribes into political association with British India to ward off Chinese influence.[48] This did little to stall Chinese control of Tibet and further south, with Chinese influence spreading from the Province of Szechuan towards Nepal and among the tribes of Assam. The Chinese pursuit of territory was slowed by the fall of the Manchu dynasty in 1911, through which Szechuan descended into anarchy, leaving border

44 It is worth noting that the *Lhasa Convention* of 7th September 1904 settled the Sikkim–Tibet frontier.

45 Inlow (1964) *op.cit.* 43, 262.

46 *Ibid.*

47 *Ibid.* Also see E. R. Leach, *Political Systems of Highland Burma* (Cambridge, MA: Harvard University Press, 1954).

48 Inlow (1964) *op.cit.* 43, 262–263.

questions between India, Tibet, Nepal, and China open. In the interim period while China reconsolidated its own governance, British India became more assertive in advocating Tibetan independence and the need to curb Chinese irredentist ambitions further south. One manifestation of this is visible in the statement by the British Minister at Peking, who on 17 August 1912

> informed the Chinese authorities that his government disapproved of China's interference in Tibet's internal affairs; that it opposed the exercise of administrative power by Chinese officials in Tibet and that it refused to recognize China's right to treat Tibet as one of her provinces. The British Minister further insisted that a tripartite convention must be concluded dealing with the various problems involving Tibet, China and British India; that unless China sent delegates to confer on these matters, Great Britain and Tibet would separately make treaties and finally that China was invited to come to such agreement prior to Great Britain's recognition of the Republic.[49]

While this *demarche* warranted no immediate response, the Chinese clarified, in December 1912, that the New Republic had no intention of treating Tibet as a province, though it declined to negotiate any agreement. With Tibet declaring its independence in January 1913, the need for negotiation became stronger, eventually leading to the *Tripartite Conference* held at Simla, India, between 13 October 1913 and 3 July 1914.[50]

The British delegation at the Conference was headed by Henry McMahon, assisted by Archibald Rose of the Chinese Consular Service and Charles Bell, who worked at the Indian Civil Service, was considered by the British to be an expert on Tibet, and was an 'outspoken champion' of Tibetan independence.[51] Ivan Chen represented China, while the Tibetan Prime Minister Longchen Shatra represented Tibet. Of the men at the Conference, Henry McMahon had already built a reputation for boundaries, having been part of the delegation to delimit the Baluchi boundary with Persia (1891) and the Durand delegation to delimit the line between Afghanistan and British India as discussed above.

McMahon's impact on boundaries in Central, East, and South Asia is significant.[52] Besides his Baluchi and Afghan adventures of 1891 and 1893,

49 *Ibid*. 263.

50 The background to the Simla Conference is explored in detail by Alastair Lamb, *The McMahon Line*, 2 vols. (London: Routledge & Kegan Paul, 1966).

51 Inlow (1964) *op.cit.* 43, 263.

52 See W. Kirk, 'The Inner Asian Frontiers of India' 31 *Transactions & Papers* (December 1962) 131–168.

respectively,[53] he was also appointed to arbitrate a dispute between Persia and Afghanistan over water rights in Seistan, a two-year process that seemingly gave him the sense of entitlement – which it may be fair to say from the values attributed to him in his education he probably never lacked[54] – of having significant insight into boundary-making and arbitration.[55]

At the Tripartite Conference, China contested Tibetan claims to independence, non-interference, and boundary delimitation. While admitting no desire to convert Tibet into a Chinese province, it contended that Tibet remained an integral part of China. While there were heated discussions concerning the boundary between Tibet and China, the line between Tibet and British India merited little attention. As Burke narrates:

> What is known is that on 14 March, 1914, as a result of conversations between the Tibetan and British representatives, a line was drawn on a General Staff map (India) of the India-Tibetan border titled 'North East Frontier'. It consisted of two sheets and was in the scale of one inch to eight miles. The map was signed A.H. McMahon and the seal and signature of the Tibetan Plenipotentiary appear immediately below the Englishman's signature. Delhi is given as the place name. Neither the initial nor the signature of the Chinese plenipotentiary appear on this map.[56]

This map was then validated through an exchange of letters between McMahon and Shatra, through which the latter states, 'I now accordingly agree to the boundary as marked in red in the two copies of the maps signed by you'.[57] McMahon's engagement of the Tibetans through this secret declaration was seemingly against the wishes of London and New Delhi,[58] though this was retrospectively ratified.[59] Gupta narrates how McMahon tricked the Chinese through a 'diplomatic sleight of hand' by showing a differentiation on a map at the Conference between Inner Tibet and the Tibet–India border.

53 A. Henry McMahon, 'The Southern Borderlands of Afghanistan' Paper Delivered at the *Royal Geographic Society* (22 February 1897).Subsequently published as A. Henry McMahon, 'The southern borderlands of Afghanistan'. [London: Geographical Journal, no. 4 (April 1897)], 393-415.

54 See especially A. Henry McMahon, 'International Boundaries' 84 *Journal of the Royal Society of Arts* (15 November 1935) 9.

55 Inlow (1964) *op.cit.* 43, 264.

56 *Ibid.* 264.

57 *Ibid.*

58 See Communication from Viceroy Lord Hardinge to London, 23 July 1914 I.O.R.: Pol.464 Pts 5 & 6 L/P & S/10/344 Political and Secret Memo B 206. No 90 of 1914 Government of India Foreign & Political Department.

59 Karunakar Gupta, 'The McMahon Line 1911–1945: The British Legacy' 47 *The China Quarterly* (1971) 521–545, 522.

Since the Chinese repudiated the Convention this effort failed, leading to valid conclusions concerning China's non-acceptance of the *McMahon line*.[60]

The actual line was based on a geographical principle, that of the watershed, which it more or less followed, though there were no explanations for some divergences and errors in understanding its location.[61] China did not ratify the 11 articles that formed the *Simla Convention* (June 1914), though the *McMahon Line* did not appear to be a significant reason for this: other elements of the line between Tibet and China were more of an issue. Despite calls for the resumption of negotiations, no further discussion took place. The *Simla Convention* was finally published in 1929, and the *McMahon Line* began to appear in official maps by 1937. The line was considered by Burke at the time to be more 'political than geographical',[62] though as a frontier between two emerging superpowers, this leaves significant room for tension. It is worth recalling that for McMahon there was a distinct difference between 'frontiers' and 'boundaries' with the former having a wider and more general meaning than the latter. Lord Curzon also appeared to suggest that there was a uniquely Asian practice to understanding boundaries, which 'mark different degrees of planes and responsibilities within a frontier area'.[63] At the time, it appears, that McMahon was persuaded by Lord Curzon's boundaries philosophy as an understanding of three lines: an inner, agreed, and outer strategic line, though the value of that in a modern context is debatable.

In contemporary times China questions the value of the *McMahon Line* on the basis of its validity and historic accuracy. China argues the line is wholly illegal since the *Simla Conference* outcomes were not ratified and the line was not even discussed at Simla.[64] By contrast India as successor State holds that the line is valid since it was on the table at Simla and since no objections had been raised by China in the immediate aftermath. In a report by the *International Commission of Jurists*, it was also held that Tibet was fully entitled to enter into treaties of its own accord.[65] In terms of historical arguments, India argued at that time that history confirmed its boundary as defined by nature, i.e. by the crest of the Himalayan mountain range and the ensuing watershed of its river systems. The Indian government asserted that neither Tibetan nor Chinese influences could be deemed to have gained a

60 *Ibid.* 523.
61 Inlow (1964) *op.cit.* 43, 222, 264.
62 *Ibid.* 267.
63 Inlow (1964) *op.cit.* 43, quoting Curzon (1907) 19.
64 See People's Republic of China, *The Sino-Indian Boundary Question* (Peking: Foreign Language Press, 1962) 51 ff.
65 *Tibet and the Chinese People's Republic* (Geneva: ICJ, 1960) 149–150.

permanent footing on the Indian side of the Himalayas, referencing centuries of Hindu rule in India.[66]

Indian history documents that the entirety of Assam, south of the *McMahon Line*, was ruled by the Ahoms from 1228, who adopted the Hindu religion in the sixteenth century and took Hindu names.[67] By the time the British annexed Assam in 1838, there was effective if loose control of the frontier tracts. In the 1960s, the Chinese contended that the area known as Assam was an extension of the ancestral domain of Tibetans, that the people of the region are of Mongoloid origin and speak a Tibetan Burman dialect. They viewed the local communities as people of the hills as opposed to the plains (as are Indians) and emphasized that even the river names were Tibetan. The Chinese argued that the boundary between China and India should run to the south of the Himalayan foothills, while the *McMahon line* moved the frontier significantly further north, taking in approximately 90,000 square kilometres of Tibetan land. For China, Indian occupation of the area was enforced by troop movements from 1951 onwards in violation of the tribal frontier areas.[68] China argued that official maps drawn by the *Survey of India* (1917) showed the traditional boundary between India and China as significantly south of the *McMahon Line*, that it was only in 1950 that the *Survey of India* map first showed the *McMahon Line* as the boundary between China and India,[69] which was subsequently validated as the political boundary by the official Political Map of India in 1954, based on this line.

While the tension from China's current *One Belt One Road* programme, Chinese relationships with Pakistan, disputes over the Siachen Glacier, and posturing in the Andaman Nicobar Islands over sea routes form numerous sources of anxiety between contemporary China and India, there is evidence of a different relationship over a wider time period. Many texts emphasize a close relationship between India and China, forged over 2,000 years, commencing with the introduction of Buddhism to China in 206 BC under the Han dynasty. History also portrays the relationship as being primarily cultural and religious, though built on the foundation of trade.[70] The power of individuals to override history, a theme well reflected throughout this work, is also at play in this relationship. Thus, Chacko emphasizes how Nehru's

66 Inlow (1964) *op.cit.* 43, 269–270.

67 C. J. Chacko et al., *The India-China Boundary Question: A Legal Study with a Brief Historical Introduction* (New Delhi, India: Indian Society of International Law, 1963).

68 Inlow (1964) *op.cit.* 43, 270.

69 For more on developments in this time period, see Gupta (1971) *op.cit.* 59.

70 See S. Radhakrishnan, *India and China* (Bombay, India: Hind Kitab Labs, 1947) and Probodhachandra Bagchi, *India and China: A Thousand Years of Cultural Relations* (Bombay, India: Hind Kitab, 1950).

reading of history was supported by Prime Minister Chou En-Lai.[71] In fact the latter's statement emphasized the border:

> Since the very ancient days, profound friendship has existed between the peoples of India and China. A border line covering a great distance of nearly three thousand kilometres links together the two nations. Century after century, history has recorded peaceful and cultural and economic inter-change but never war or animosity between our countries.[72]

The independence of India in 1947 and the establishment of the People's Republic of China in 1949 changed this relationship, with the border issue coming into sharper focus. One of the primary reasons for this was the Chinese aspiration to 'liberate Tibet', raising concerns that this would destabilize the border between the countries. In an exchange of letters in 1950, it became clear that the border itself might be disputed, leading Prime Minister Nehru to state in Parliament (20 November 1950) that in the eastern sector of India's northern boundary, 'The MacMahon Line is our boundary'.[73] The crisis became physical in October 1962 when China attacked four points on the border, and then, with China poised to make incursions into the Indian plains, they desisted and called a ceasefire, leading Burke to conclude,

> the action seemed to emphasize further the fact that the Chinese attack was no mere military adventure but rather intended to underscore Chinese demands for a renegotiated boundary between China and India along the McMahon Line.[74]

According to Gupta a primary reason for British interest in convening the *Simla Conference* was to formalize and extend the *de facto* independence Tibet had begun to enjoy since the overthrow of the Manchu dynasty in 1912. An independent Tibet was viewed by the British to be a key buffer zone between the Chinese and British empires.[75] In addition to significant evidence of the non-acceptance of the *McMahon Line*, including by the British, the line was forgotten about until published in Aitchison's Treaties in 1928, though

71 C. J. Chacko et al. (1963) *op.cit.* 67.

72 As quoted in Ramesh Sanghvi, *India's Northern Frontier and China* (Bombay, India: Contemporary Publishers, 1962).

73 K. Krishna Rao, *International Law Aspects of the Sino-Indian Boundary* (New Delhi, India: Indian Society of International Law, 1963) 3. Also see *Trade and Intercourse Agreement (29 April 1954)* and *The Sino-Indian Boundary: Texts of Treaties, Agreements and Certain Exchange of Notes Relating to the Sino-Indian Boundary* (New Delhi, India: Indian Society of International Law, 1962).

74 Inlow (1964) *op.cit.* 43, 271.

75 Gupta (1971) *op.cit.* 59.

with caveats as to its validity.[76] It was, however, in 1935, in connection with the arrest of a British botanist who had illegally entered Tibet that the then Deputy Secretary in the Foreign and Political Department of the Government of India, O.K. Caroe, unearthed the document showing the agreement made 22 years earlier. This breathed new life into the idea that the line was valid among the British and subsequently India.[77]

Mehra's comment, at the end of his introduction, rings true for boundary disputes all over the world:

> In the evolution of boundaries, as of the men who make them and of the people who live on either side, there is a remarkable flux and a variety of developments impinge. In the case of India's north-eastern frontier, this variety is greater, if more complex, for, in the period under review, not only India and Tibet but China, too, is directly, at times even intimately, involved.[78]

Evidence of this complexity in the wider region encompasses mixtures of cultures, religions, histories, and forms of governance besides the significance of geography. Life in the world's highest mountains often leads to different notions of kinship and relationships with territory than on small islands in Northern Europe. Some of these complexities are captured in an edited collection by Crossley, Siu, and Sutton called *Empire at the Margins*.[79] The editors highlight the problematic notion of ethnicity and kinship and the extent to which this equates to Western visions of notions of nationhood. They highlight that the conception in China itself varied significantly, with the Ming (1368–1644) and the Qing (1636–1912) having significantly different perceptions themselves. They assert:

> In the Ming period, a national group within the Empire happened to be very clearly defined – usually by culture, but in some instances by genealogy. The Qing structure was quite different, particularly before the nineteenth century. In that case, a distinct form of rulership bound a group of historically defined populations of northern and eastern Asia into a

76 S. Ghosh, *Truth About McMahon Line* (Calcutta, India: Lalchand Roy & Co., 1962).

77 Gupta (1971) *op.cit.* 59, 528–535.

78 Parshotam Mehra, *The McMahon Line and After: A Study of the Triangular Contest on India's North-eastern Frontier Between Britain, China and Tibet 1904–1947* (New Delhi, India: MacMillan, 1974), xiii.

79 Pamela Kyle Crossley, Helen F. Siu & Donald S. Sutton (eds.), *Empire at the Margins: Culture, Ethnicity and Frontier in Early Modern China* (Berkeley, CA: University of California Press, 2006).

> consolidated conquest elite, and vigorously nurtured a theoretical distinction between them and the objects of the conquest.[80]

They go on to state:

> In the eighteenth century the fading of the conquest was accompanied by many complex changes in the definition and status of the imperially oriented populations, but not with the result that a 'national' population emerged. Rather, the lingering centralities and marginalities of the Ming period remained identifiable, and many regions vigorous, beneath the formal, newly historicized hierarchies of the Qing conquest. The result was a cacophony of cultural dynamics throughout the empire, in some cases producing new clarifications of loyalties, identities, and communities, and in others obscuring patterns that might have been clearer or more meaningful in earlier centuries. All these processes were ancestral to the cultural configurations of modern China and in some cases to the societies of Mongolia, Kazakhstan, Burma, and other neighbors.[81]

This led them to conclude that, '[O]ther than China, no empire of such cultural and ethnic diversity has survived modern statehood and the twentieth century in one piece'.[82] This is also a factor in the attempts by President Xi Jinping to extend Chinese influence across the wider region through the *One Belt One Road* programme.

Russia, China, and Lines on Maps

The regional complexities and the value of boundaries warrant brief commentary on the role of another major European power with stakes in the region, namely Russia. Viewed from the perspective of China's western frontier, the Uyghurs, like the Tibetans also deemed 'splittist' by the current Chinese President,[83] have become an increasing source of concern across the existing boundaries. The waxing and waning of Chinese regional influence along the Silk Route is also a factor here, as are disputes over what constitutes suzerainty and sovereignty. Writing about the Uyghur Nation, sitting on the Russia–China frontier, Brophy emphasizes a 'failure of nation-building'

80 *Ibid.* 2.

81 *Ibid.*

82 *Ibid.* 311.

83 Rowan Callick, 'Xi Jinping Launches New Era for China and the World' 52 *China Before a World in Crisis* (April 2021) available at https://revistaidees.cat/en/xi-jinping-launches-a-new-era-for-china-and-the-world/

among the Uyghur in contrast with the Uzbeks and Kazakhs.[84] Thus while the Uzbeks, Kazakhs, Kyrgyz, and even Turkmen have their own sovereign State, the Uyghur continue to form part of China. Brophy argues that the delimitation of the boundary between Russia and China effectively divided the Uyghur nation, referred to by scholars as 'Soviet Uyghurs' and 'Xinjiang Uyghurs', creating insurmountable pressure on the Uyghurs to inscribe their history within the political boundaries others drew around them.[85]

In narrating the history of the Uyghur, Brophy offers intriguing possibilities of what the map could have looked like in different situations. Writing about the Great Muslim uprising under the Qing dynasty in the 1860s, he states:

> as the violence spread to Xinjiang, the province was partitioned by a string of rebel regimes. The emirate of Yaqub Beg …in Kashgar was the longest lasting and ultimately looked to the Ottoman Empire for confirmation and support. To its north an independent sultan was installed in the Lli Vlley from 1871 to 1882. Meanwhile in Urumchi, today the capital of Xinjiang Uyghur Autonomous Region, Chinese-speaking Muslim (Hui) king emerged, linked by Sufi affiliations to the Muslims of Gansu. In this three-way division of the province we see a set of alternatives to Beijing-centered rule in Xinjiang, which in many ways defined the limits of possibility for the years to follow: Xinjiang as a Kashgar centered, Istanbul-aligned Islamic state; as the next stage in Russia's colonial advance across the steppe; or as a sanctuary for Chinese-speaking Muslim rebels fighting for autonomy in regions further east.[86]

These possibilities faded as the Hunanese army reconquered Xinjiang for the Qing in the 1870s, with it remaining Chinese ever since. The relationship was also impacted by the Russian evacuation of its Muslim populations from Ili and the subsequent signing of the *Treaty of St. Petersburg of 1881*, which facilitated enhanced trade links and the spread of Russian commerce into China's northwest, while extending protection from the Czar to the mercantile networks of Central Asian Muslims in Xinjiang.[87]

While the boundary remained obscure between the two empires for centuries when it was viewed as a tributary-paying frontier zone, the pressure grew towards the end of the Qing period to delineate due to the emergence of Russian Turkistan and British India, both with ambitions to include Xinjiang

84 David Brophy, *Uyghur Nation: Reform and Revolution on the Russia-China Frontier* (Cambridge, MA: Harvard University Press, 2016).

85 Brophy (2016) *op.cit.* 84.

86 *Ibid.* 6–7.

87 *Ibid.* 7.

in their spheres of influence. Both European powers viewed Xinjiang as a buffer between their empires.[88] With the Qing keen on empire-building, they appeared to have adapted Eurasian state-building mechanisms to solidify Xinjiang as a fully-fledged Chinese province.[89] Key to this strategy was commerce:

> In Xinjiang, as much as in the empire's heartland of the Yangtze delta, state-sponsored enterprise and initiatives towards local autonomy saw a new stratum of rich merchants emerge as conspicuous collaborators with the late Qing bureaucracy. Yet these *bays* (an epithet meaning 'wealthy'), as they were known, can be only hazily perceived in the records of Xinjiang's Chinese bureaucracy, and their relations with Chinese officialdom must be studied on the basis of non-Chinese sources.[90]

The governance issues are further confused by both the ease of migration across the Russian–Chinese border and the fact that, due to Russia's treaties with the Qing, Russian Muslims living in Xinjiang enjoyed the same extraterritorial privileges as ethnic Russians. This contributed to the re-creation of Russian forms of native autonomy that were prevalent in Russian Turkistan within Xinjiang.[91] Brophy highlights that this role was best epitomized by the office of the *aqsaqal*, or trading headman, who appeared to mediate the relationship of the trading community with the Russians and the Qing. As the influence of these individuals grew, they became incorporated over time into Qing state-building attempts within the governance system, as the Manchu sought to proactively adopt nationalizing measures to spread Chinese cultural elements among the Muslims from the 1880s onwards.[92] In commenting on the role of the Muslims as frontier communities and how they fit within the Russian and Chinese empires, Brophy states:

> even at its height the Manchu emperors never viewed their Muslim subjects in the same way as did the tsars. Russia was a confessional state sharing a border with the Ottoman Empire and frequently clashed with it in the Caucasus, Black Sea, and the Balkans. In its diplomacy with the Ottomans, Russia positioned itself as a defender of Orthodoxy and champion of Slavic interests and saw its Muslim populations as part of an Islamic world in which its loyalties were potentially divided. The Qing had a very different view of Islam, not influenced by geopolitical strategy or

88 *Ibid.*
89 *Ibid.*
90 *Ibid.* 9.
91 *Ibid.* 10.
92 *Ibid.*

> Orientalist discourse on fanaticism or stagnation of Muslim society. For the Qing, if the empire's Muslims presented a threat, it was because of heterodox customs such as the blind following of charismatic Sufi shaykhs, not any connection to the Ottoman sultan or transimperial hajj networks. In this environment, though Qing officials polices Sufi brotherhoods among the Chinese speaking Hui (Dungans) closely, expressing loyalty in a spiritual sense to the Ottoman sultan as the caliph of all Muslims, even praying for him during communal worship on Fridays, was not treated as a threat.[93]

Despite attempts at integration into China through the identification of Xinjiang as a Chinese province, the dispersal of the Chinese schooling system (the *xuetang*) and other measures, by 1911 the project looked to have failed. From the Chinese side, revolutionary drawings of stars on the flags usually only showed the 18 provinces of China, with the 19th province, Xinjiang, treated more as a colonial dependency. The delicate task of maintaining governance and allegiances fell to the governor Yang Zengxin (1864–1928) who was more circumspect in balancing the interests of non-Chinese elites while also being conservative in listening but resisting calls from warlords and nationalists who urged him to colonize and develop the territory's periphery.[94]

The relatively porous frontier meant that Xinjiang was a thriving trading centre, attracting Muslims from not only Russian Turkistan but also the Ottoman Empire, with the foreign residents forming a positive impression of communal freedom in China in contrast to more restrictive conditions in Russia. The Jadidism movement, a religious movement that avoided questions of sovereignty and focused instead on the implementation of a new method of schooling to advance Muslims, gradually came to be viewed as a threat, leading to the genesis in Chinese scholarship of viewing Xinjiang as posing the dual threat of pan-Turkism and pan-Islam.

Highlighting the challenge of the Uyghur nation, Brophy emphasizes how the Soviet alignment of the regime in Urumchi and the recognition of the Uyghurs as an official nationality of Xinjiang in 1934 were extremely important in developing a national self-conscience. This was in line with the Stalinist notion of the creation of the nation.[95] Stalin had argued that a nation would need to have 'common language, territory, economic life,

93 *Ibid.* 11.

94 *Ibid.*

95 For more, also see Terry Martin, *The Affirmative Action Empire: Nations and Nationalism in the Soviet Union 1923–1939* (Ithaca, NY: Cornell University Press, 2001).

and the psychological make-up manifested in a common culture'.[96] Cultural autonomy contributed, with an important role attributed to Sheng Shicai, a warlord who sought to draw on intellectuals to consolidate this awareness while keeping Muslim opposition in check. However then,

> as now, the initiative was fraught with contradictions. The Uyghur national project was not a product of Soviet or Chinese policy, nor could it be entirely controlled by them. Given the turbulence in Soviet Central Asia in the early 1930s, 'Soviet' notions of nationality were introduced to Xinjiang as much by dissident Uyghurs, runaways from the Soviet Union, as they were through official contacts. This tension meant that Soviet categories of ethnicity were formally implemented in Xinjiang through a highly repressive process, laying the ground for further rounds of violence, and for renegotiation of the relationship between categories of nationality and political authority in Xinjiang. Neither a classic case of state-sanctioned national construction nor of a national liberation struggle in the colonial world, the Uyghurs have had a rocky relationship with both dimensions of the Communist vision for Asia.[97]

In contexts such as the Uyghur claim to nationhood or that of any other similar group, community, minority, or submerged nation that aspires to 'statehood', the immediate question that takes on significant relevance is that of the historical narrative.[98] This often forms the founding legend for the agitation and is often questioned or denigrated by those seeking to deny the legitimacy of such a claim.

In Ben Anderson's parlance, understanding the 'imagined' narrative forms a crucial part of an emerging discourse, but this discourse needs to be qualified against a number of factors. Firstly, the current *de facto* and/or *de jure* sovereign that notionally exercises sovereignty over the 'nation'. As the incumbent power, this State by virtue of its territorial integrity is in the dominant position to question, suppress, and deny any claim. This power is usually backed by the consensus of the community of States, and though there may be some that dissent, they rarely do so solely on the basis of primary arguments of suppressed historical narratives, which have proven to be less than adequate in articulating claims for statehood.

Secondly, there is no forum through which any case of self-determination can be expressed. The most usual manner has been within the State through protests, engagement in an electoral system, or civil disobedience movements.

96 Joseph Stalin, *Marxism and the National Question* (Moscow: Foreign Languages Publishing House, 1947), 15.

97 Brophy (2016) *op.cit.* 84, 20–21.

98 For an undulating narrative of the Uyghur quest, see *Ibid.* 22–52.

While a claim for separate statehood is notionally an expression of a 'right' or at least a claim in international law,[99] the lack of a forum means that its only real expression has to occur within the domestic jurisdiction of a State. This strengthens the hand of the territorial State in two important ways: (a) allowing it a margin of appreciation in how such a claim can be handled; and (b) preventing the claim from being internationalized, especially by recourse to kin and other States who may support the movement but who could technically fall foul of the rule of non-interference in the domestic matters of another State. While States have and may justifiably be condemned for actions suppressing separatist movements, these condemnations rarely add to the prospect of a process that may address the claim. There are far more numerous examples of where suppression of independence claims has been successful in maintaining the territorial sovereignty of the incumbent State than examples such as Timor Leste,[100] South Sudan[101] or Bangladesh,[102] where they led to processes in post-colonial States that eventually yielded a separate State. In each of these cases, the aspiring entities had to use force or resist the use of force by the State for extended periods before the tide on their claim could turn in their favour. As stated by others, more recently, some consensus may be forming that the behaviour of the State in suppressing nationalist claims could strengthen a claim based on 'remedial self-determination'. This, however, needs to be treated with extreme caution, since the consensus has not fully formed, and there are several examples in State practice where the incumbent State's perpetration of gross human rights violations against a population that may be different and may nurture a claim to independence has not succeeded in yielding an independent State. Thus, for every instance of the emergence of a new State such as the three listed above, there are examples of aggressive suppression of claims such as those of the

99 The exception to this would be the 'right of secession' built into the Soviet Constitution, which was triggered by the Baltic States and led to the dismantling of the Soviet Union. See Lauri Mälksoo, *Illegal Annexation and State Continuity* (Leiden: Brill, 2022), 70–139.

100 Douglas Kammen, *Independent Timor-Leste: Between Coercion and Consent* (Cambridge: Cambridge University Press, 2019).

101 Hilde F. Johnson, *South Sudan: The Untold Story from Independence to Civil War* (London: I. B. Taurus, 2016).

102 Jahanara Iman, *Of Blood and Fire: The Untold Story of Bangladesh's War of Independence* (Dhaka: University Press, Ltd., 2019).

Uyghur,[103] Kashmiris,[104] Chechens,[105] Achenese,[106] Kurds,[107] Palestinians,[108] Tibetans,[109] Katangese,[110] and others.

The central problem with these factors is that they take the discourse away from the realm where the force of (legal and other) arguments can be used and relegate the problem to where superior arguments of force win the day. Aside from the fact that settling disputes by force is likely a marker that is counter-civilization due to their significant human cost, the resort to force by an incumbent State in a twenty-first century where access to weapons is profligate, and where methods short of the use of conventional warfare are prevalent, is simply a call that is disruptive of order rather than restorative of it. The brutal genocidal war in Gaza pursued by Israel under cover of a so-called exercise of 'self-defense' against Hamas shows that even when one party has overwhelmingly superior weaponry with a seemingly limitless supply chain of such weaponry, the idea of using force to defend peace is tenuous at best and ineffective in securing such peace. The widescale destruction of life and property in Gaza and the international community's failure to stop it are likely to be a marker of counter-civilization: reductive of the rules-based order and revealing of the hollowness of the alleged pursuit of perpetual peace. Irrespective of the unquestionable legitimacy of Palestinian self-determination, the use of force to achieve this has a history of working against its protagonists, mainly due to the unequal access to weapons between a State and an independence movement. While it is easy to label Hamas a terrorist organisation: the wanton attacks targetting civilians on October 7 reinforce this notion – less contrioversial movements seeking self-determination have also met similar fates. Against this, the war in Gaza is likely to demonstrate that the aggressive suppression of self-determination claims in the manner in

103 Pablo A. Rodríguez-Merino, *Violence, Discourse and Politics in China's Uyghur Region: The Terrorization of Xinjiang* (London: Taylor & Francis, 2022).

104 Shahla Hussain, *Kashmir in the Aftermath of Partition* (Cambridge: Cambridge University Press, 2021).

105 James Hughes, *Chechnya: From Nationalism to Jihad* (Philadelphia, PA: University of Pennsylvania Press, 2013).

106 Elizabeth F. Drexler, *Aceh, Indonesia: Securing the Insecure State* (Philadelphia, PA: University of Pennsylvania Press, 2009).

107 Zeynep Kaya, *Mapping Kurdistan: Territory, Self-Determination and Nationalism* (Cambridge: Cambridge University Press, 2020).

108 Leila H. Farsakh, *Rethinking Statehood in Palestine: Self-Determination and Decolonization Beyond Partition* (Oakland, CA: University of California Press, 2021).

109 Jane Ardley, *The Tibetan Independence Movement* (London: Routledge Curzon, 2002). For a contrast germane to this, also read the Chinese perspective with emphasis on the possession of Tibet in Wang Jiawei & Nyima Gyaincain, *The Historical Status of China's Tibet* (Peking: China Intercontinental Press, 1997).

110 Rene Lemarchand, 'The Limits of Self-Determination: The Case of the Katanga Secession' 56(2) *The American Political Science Review* (June 1962) 404–416.

which Israel has sought to achieve this is unlikely to yield a peaceful long-term result. There are considerably more cross-currents in international society today than in the context for example of Biafra in 1971, where Nigeria's effort to restore its sovereignty when threatened resulted in something of an 'effective' maintenance of State sovereignty. With the monopoly of force no longer as comfortably in the hands of the State, the more brutal the suppression the greater the chance is that it will spur ever more determined desires for independence.

Thirdly, the historical narratives themselves are often contested or difficult to prove. Inevitably the distance of time, the lack of documented evidence, and the fact that power was wielded widely in the creation and agglomeration of States and empires become important factors in understanding or even defeating a claim for separate statehood based on counter-historical narratives that either prove the opposite or, at the very least, cast some doubt on whether the narrative proffered by the claimant to power is the sole and exclusively verifiable narrative. The intermingling of peoples and communities and the writ of powerful capital cities that sought to maintain their hegemony through quasi-sovereign actions such as the collection of taxes, appointment of governors, or the demonstrable adherence to their laws in what were perceived to be the frontiers of their empire often interlay a competing narrative atop the one pressed by the aspirant to power. The fact that these exercises of sovereignty may have been less than universally accepted would not be considered a robust-enough argument against the maintenance of a modicum of effective control by the incumbent sovereign in the region.

A fourth factor that enters the equation is the extent to which the aspirant community's claim to statehood is contested by a third-party neighbour. For instance it is challenging to separate a Uyghur claim for independent statehood from China against the writ of the Kazakh sultans, the rule of the Khans of Kokand, or the emergence of others who may have ascended to power in the Ottoman or the Russian empires that surrounded the Uyghurs.[111] The Xinjiang case and the boundary line between Russia and China are particularly intriguing since it brings territories and communities that were formerly under the influence of another empire, the Ottoman Empire, into a direct competition between two empires who still exercise authority and influence as modern State powers. Brophy refers to this as a 'meeting of the two empires, perched atop a Muslim population'. Then, as with other religious lineages that cross borders elsewhere now, the Muslim population concerned shared much more in common with each other than with the colonial overlords that laid claim to their territory. Notwithstanding, the agreement between the two empires yielded a frontier society. Other commonalities did emerge, for instance, the communities,

111 Brophy (2016) *op.cit.* 84, 53–85.

> had elements in common with China's coastal treaty ports with the dynamic of extraterritoriality shaped by the distinctive environment. While Russian consuls and Andijani merchants collaborated in linking Xinjing to Russia's colonial periphery, their own relationship was also mediated by the structures of Russian colonialism. This led to the emergence of institutions found on the China coast, chief among them the presence of the trading headman, or as *aqsaqal*.[112]

The pragmatism of the Chinese empire was as prevalent then as has been clearly displayed in the free market ideology that modified Chinese communism and transformed the economic fortunes of the State.[113] Many of the traders who sought to trade in the bazaars of Xinjiang often had to do so under false identities provided by or that paid allegiance to the Kazakh sultans. This enabled many Muslims from the Russian empire, including Tartars from the Volga or Siberia, full access. There is significant evidence to suggest that the practice was well known to the Qing for many decades leading up to the middle of the nineteenth century, and the pragmatism of facilitating this despite fears of Russian infiltration into Xinjiang is best manifested in the *Treaty of Ghulja* (1851) that eventually legalized this cross-border trade between the Empires, while providing some restrictions and maintaining the fiction of the disguised identity.[114] Trade continued to be a driver of relationships with the *Treaty of Peking* (1860) easing trade restrictions further. However, notions of identity and interests remained complex. For instance:

> At the outbreak of the Muslim rebellion, Russia's withdrawal of its consuls and the loss of its trading quarters… came as a blow to tsarist commercial interests. The emergence in Kashgar of an Islamic state with ties to Russia's enemies in Kokand was also a source of anxiety, as was the thought that the British might take advantage of Yaqub Beg's weakness to extend their Indian frontier northward. Meanwhile, Kazakh nomads were exploiting the lawless environment to launch raids on Russian caravans from what was formerly Qing territory.[115]

These kinds of moments in history, often not considered as relevant in establishing the 'critical date' at which any given territory's sovereignty could be delineated, nonetheless cast questions on any veracity of singular historical narratives that conclusively 'prove' or 'disprove' claims for separate

112 *Ibid.* 53–54.
113 Ezra F. Vogel, *Deng Xiaoping and the Transformation of China* (Cambridge, MA: Harvard University Press, 2011).
114 Brophy (2016) *op.cit.* 84, 57–58.
115 *Ibid.* 58.

statehood. In the case above, the tensions were resolved by Russian occupation of the Ili, and its announcement that 'it would hold on to Ili for as long as it took the Qing to pacify the rest of Xinjiang'. Brophy adds that '[T]his, of course, was something that many believed the Qing would never achieve'.[116] The Qing attempt to redress the balance involved the mounting of a significant and long campaign throughout the seventh and eighth decades of the nineteenth century, creating refugee flows that added to the complexities of determining a sustainable border between the two empires,[117] until the signing of the *Treaty of St. Petersburg* (1881).[118] By that stage, the Qing had 'successfully' restored their authority over Xinjiang through a variety of measures, including

> reconstruction bureaus (*shanhouju*) modelled on the institutions of the post-Taiping constructions of the 1860s. New city walls and administrative buildings had to be erected, canals dredged and long agricultural land reclaimed. ...much of this work was entrusted to demobilized soldiers... as well as poor Chinese migrants who were enticed to Xinjiang by the farming opportunities that the reconstruction bureaus offered them.[119]

This display of Chinese sovereignty and effective control was different from that of Russia, which built railway lines facilitating trade through the Trans-Caspian Railway to Bukhara and Samarkhand (1888) and Tashkent and Andijan (1889). This created links between the region and the Russian empire, while simultaneously making it more remote from Beijing.[120] As a consequence it could be said that while the Qing had restored the political integration of Xinjiang with China, 'socially and economically its Muslim community continued to face west'.[121]

Sykes–Picot Agreement

In comparison to the *McMahon Line* and the *Durand Line*, the *Sykes–Picot Line* has warranted significantly more attention. It was the product of discussions between Mark Sykes and George M. Picot, set against a wider contestation for territory and influence between European powers against the backdrop of the crumbling Ottoman Empire.

116 *Ibid.* 58.
117 *Ibid.* 66–69.
118 *Ibid.* 74.
119 *Ibid.* 72 quoting Kataoka Kazutada, *Shincho Shinkyo tochi kenkyu* (Tokyo: Yuzanakaku, 1991) at 155.
120 *Ibid.* 84.
121 *Ibid.* 85.

That Sykes described himself as an 'amateur' does not lessen the impact of the work that he undertook. As one biography claims, rather than being an amateur, Sykes was considered 'an interloper in realms where he does not belong, because he is presumed to be neither trained nor as dedicated as professionals'. He is held up instead as a product of class and privilege, 'an example of how far, in what circles, and under what circumstances a young man in his position, and of his nature, could go during the first two decades of [the last] century'.[122] His engagement with the region he was to shape so dramatically commenced in January 1890 when he visited Cairo with his parents, went on holiday to Palestine and Syria, learnt Arabic, and, it is reported, developed some of his later prejudices towards communities from a tour guide who worked for the travel agent Thomas Cook.[123]

He had grown up and lived a privileged lifestyle in luxurious conditions, which included a train of personal tutors and significant global travel with his parents. On these occasions, he was given plenty of opportunities to learn and understand different cultures, with his education including a spell in Monaco due to links between his family and the Princess of Monaco. Like many men referenced in the boundary-making process in this book, Sykes went to Cambridge University where he completed his undergraduate studies between 1897 and 1899. He is reported to have struggled academically while building a reputation for having a uniquely worldly skillset. His formal involvement in the Middle East began in 1905 when he was appointed as honorary attaché to Sir Nicholas O'Connor, the then Ambassador to the Ottoman Empire in Istanbul. This short sojourn made him determined to enter public life and, though unsuccessful twice in winning a seat in Parliament, he eventually succeeded, representing Hull in 1911. With the outbreak of World War I, Sykes was called up for military service and is said to have led his battalion with distinction.

Knowing of his privileged education through travel and reading, Lord Kitchener gave him a commission in 1915 on the general staff of the army and instructed him to undertake a special inquiry that involved travel throughout Asia. On returning to London, Lord Kitchener instructed Sykes to draw up an agreement with M. Georges Picot, on how to 'deal with' Syria, Mesopotamia, and Anatolia. While disapproving of it, Leslie insists that in these negotiations, Mark Sykes was acting as an agent of the Foreign Office, rather than as an individual. As he puts it,

> it could hardly have been otherwise; for in spite of his extensive knowledge (sic!) of Near Eastern affairs, in diplomacy he was a tyro and an

122 Roger Adelson, *Mark Sykes: Portrait of an Amateur* (London: Jonathan Cape Thirty Bedford Square, 1975), 12.

123 *Ibid*. 36, 38.

> amateur; and it is incredible that even the Foreign Office should have given such a one a free hand in negotiations with a trained and exceedingly able diplomatist.[124]

To be able to ground the agreement Sykes was required to gain the cooperation of Imperial Russia, which he is recorded as having achieved with a degree of admiration from the Russian Tsar. As a consequence he was appointed to the Secretariat of the Committee for Imperial Defence upon his return to England in 1916. His role on this Committee was to act as liaison officer between the War Office, the India Office, and the Foreign Office. Among his many duties, he was also required to produce a weekly document known as the *Arabian Report* – which included a commentary and compilation of secret papers, including memos, telegrams, and reports of operations in the 'Near East'. In commenting on the impending division that Mark Sykes was about to sow, one biographer Leslie states:

> He was hampered, and badly hampered, by his recognition of England's duty to her chief ally [France]; but for this the resolution of Arabian affairs would have been simpler by far. Whether an Arab confederation was possible may be doubted; but had France not had claims in Syria the division of the whole area, with the exception of Palestine, into independent Arab States under the political guidance of England, would have been feasible; and the Arabs wanted the help of England and feared France – to them Algiers was an object lesson.[125]

The treatment of Mark Sykes in English history is of someone who fought for Arab emancipation from the yoke of Turkish rule. Leslie narrates the view of Sir Arthur Hirtzel, Deputy Under-Secretary of State for India:

> The idea of the liberation of the Arab peoples from the Turkish yoke originated, as is generally supposed, with Lord Kitchener, but Sir Mark Sykes was the driving power behind the earliest attempts to convert what at first presented itself as a military necessity into a practicable political idea. He threw himself into this task with all his many gifts and all the force of his strong personality, giving expression to it in the proclamation – deliberately Napoleonic in its tone – which was issued to the Arab world on the British occupation of Baghdad, and which strikingly illustrates three of his most marked characteristics – his imagination, his idealism and his sense of the dramatic. He was fully alive to the difficulties that lay ahead

124 Shane Leslie, *Mark Sykes: His Life and Letters* (London: Cassell and Company Ltd., 1923) 21.

125 *Ibid*. 26.

> of Arab nationalism, but he believed that they could be overcome by loyal cooperation between Great Britain and France, and for this too he never ceased to work.[126]

Yet underpinning any sense of capturing power for his paymasters, portrayed as a noble duty, was an impending and racist motivation to keep European powers coming face to face on Asian battlefields, much the same sentiment that led to the articulation of the *Berlin West Africa Conference* and the various other agreements in Africa.[127] Sykes himself acknowledged this in a speech in the Houses of Parliament on 12 August 1913, where he stated:

> The break-up of the Ottoman Empire in Asia must bring the powers of Europe directly confronting one another in a country where there are no frontiers because the mountains are parallel to the littoral, and because there being only three rivers, one moving in a circle and the other running side by side over a level pain it is very difficult for any power to find a frontier. That very awkward geographical situation troubled the mind of Alexander the Great, the mind of Diocletian and the mind of Constantine.[128]

His formation included travel in the region and the writing of what can be described as part travelogue, part ethnography, and part historical account.[129] He describes the wider region in an introduction to one book as follows:

> Here is a land of contrasts, climates, barriers, and diverse physical circumstances. It has been the birthplace of civilization, has given the world the Gospel and Koran, has seen the rise and decline of four great Empires and scores of principalities and dynasties. It has been the battle-ground of all the philosophies and creeds which form the basis of those now occupying western minds, as well as the highway of all conquerors from Xerxes to Napoleon...[130]

126 *Ibid.* 26–27.

127 *The Papers of Sir Mark Sykes, 1979–1919 with special reference to the Sykes-Picot Agreement and the Middle East* from Hull University Archives ISBN-10: 1-85117-079–0; ISBN-13: 987-1-85117-079–1; Publishers' film no. R50041 [8 reels].

128 Leslie (1923) *op.cit.* 125, 202.

129 See, for instance, Mark Sykes, *Dar-ul-Islam: A Record of a Journey Through Ten of the Asiatic Provinces of Turkey* (London: Bickers and Son, 1904). The book is based on a personal account of his journey across the Ottoman Empire. It contains anecdotes of meetings and details of the travel undertaken. While it avoids an *orientalist* tone, it is presented as one of the 'first journeys into the unknown' and is characterized by maps and attempts to chart territory, significant in view of the later work leading to the Sykes–Picot agreement.

130 Mark Sykes, *The Caliphs' Last Heritage: A Short History of the Turkish Empire* (London: Macmillan, 1915) 1.

One of the chief justifications Sykes offers for this book is the need to 'make an impartial and general study of its past history', which he suggests had remained to be written at the time of his book.[131] To Sykes, the Middle East on the eve of his negotiation with Georges Picot could be assessed in his 'intellectual analysis of Islam in transition [as lying] between the influences of the ancient past and of the modern Occident'.[132] As Leslie narrates:

> He divided Moslems into Ancients and Moderns, while pointing out that the Young Turks ideas are in no wise different from those of the Janissaries of the fifteenth century... The Ancient Moslems he divided into: Class I (anti-Christian bigots), Class II (tolerant and scrupulous), Class III (unorthodox mystics), The Moderns he divided into Class I (agnostics), who were Western in culture, but not able to assimilate Nationalism.... Class II consisted of the half educated who apply '...a European Jacobinism to Sunni Mohammedanism.' He recommended Arab rivalry against Turkish dominion and put his greatest hope in Class II of the Ancients. He advised concession, however unpalatable.[133]

The presentation of these 'insights' along with his experience in the region led to Sykes being considered an expert: one of the most knowledgeable voices on the Near East and on Syria in particular. He used this platform to persuade the Foreign Office to respect French interests in the region, even if it meant dismembering the Ottoman Empire territories. This view eventually prevailed despite warnings from the India Office of the impact that this could have on Muslims not only in the region but also in places like India. By December 1915, Mark Sykes was largely determining British policy in Syria, working closely with Lord Robert Cecil in the Foreign Office to make this a reality.

His memoirs, written around that time, are instructive of the nature of this exercise. The dominant narrative around him is of an empathetic individual of deep learning who had an understanding and appreciation of the broader region that had come to be characterized as Asia Minor. The extent to which British military ambitions in the region played a role in his decision-making is somewhat more subdued. Yet his own papers show that Sykes was motivated by the need to gain control of lands in the region, not least to gain influence in Europe.[134] There is clear evidence of close attention being

131 *Ibid*. 2.

132 Leslie (1923) *op.cit*. 125, 243.

133 Leslie (1923) *op.cit*. 125, 243.

134 See Mark Sykes's Letter to Winston Churchill, 'Proposals for Prosecuting the War by Seizing Gallipoli and Constantinople, and Attacking Germany via the Balkans, Austria and Bavaria' DDSY2/4 Foreign Affairs and Travel (1888–1919) 4/81, 27 January 1915 in *Papers of Mark Sykes* (Wakefield: Microform Academic Publishers).

paid to the emerging narrative of Pan-Arabism.[135] In a secret memorandum, Sykes discussed the military objectives of British presence and the threats, stating, '[T]he people, whether nomads, cultivators, or semi-nomads, Sunnis or Shias, are ready to accept our rule, but equally ready to turn against us in event of mishap'.[136] He paid special attention to the prospect of colonization of the Middle East by India and warns that the

> Indian and Arab civilization and mentality are poles asunder, and I am of the opinion that the introduction of Indian methods and Indian personnel should be merely temporary and should form no part of our future scheme.[137]

In a particularly telling paragraph that at once shows his respect for Arabic culture while displaying disturbing levels of sympathy with ideas of racial hierarchy, he states:

> There can be no doubt that the native social standards of Egypt and Syria are far higher than those of India, and owing to language and racial affinity it is from those regions that the civilization of Irak would naturally be drawn. I feel it is my duty to say, therefore, that in my opinion it would be a great mishap if at the outset any action of ours should do anything to impose artificially an alien and lower grade of civilization upon a people who have a natural tendency to a higher and more progressive social state.[138]

Of course, the irony of which lower grade civilization was imposed, the extent to which the great mishap was, and the sheer artificiality of the solution that Sykes would impose is lost in history. Equally less emphasized are the basic lessons on identity in the Middle East given to Parliament and the Prime Minister through 'Evidence of Mark Sykes on the Arab Question'. The following exchange between Lord Kitchener and Mark Sykes is particularly insightful of the general lack of awareness of the region:

Kitchener: Wahabism, does that still exist?
Sykes: I think it is a dying force.[139]

135 'Report on Pan-Arab Party in Syria' 5 September 1915 4/90 DDSY2/4 Foreign Affairs and Travel (1888–1919) in *Papers of Mark Sykes* (Wakefield: Microform Academic Publishers).
136 *Ibid.* 2.
137 *Ibid.* 3.
138 *Ibid.* 3.
139 'Evidence of Lieutenant-Colonel Sir Mark Sykes, BART MP, on the Arab Question' Meeting held at 10 Downing Street, Thursday December 16, 1915 at 11.30 am, 4/95

In a particularly telling part of the testimony, Sykes reveals the blueprint for what would become the agreement with Georges Picot:

Balfour: What sort of arrangement would you like to have with the French? What would you say to them?

Sykes: I should like to retain for ourselves such country south of Haifa as was not in the Jerusalem enclave, which I gather the French themselves admit. I think it is important that we should have a belt of English-controlled country between the Sherif of Mecca and the French.

Prime Minister: You mean the whole way from the Egyptian frontier to Haifa, except the enclave?

Sykes: I think it could be argued to the French that they were not giving up very much, assuming the enclave is large enough to contain the head of the Dead Sea and enough of the Jordan for the pilgrims to go to.

Balfour: What do you leave the French in Syria?

Sykes: That leaves the French from the 'e' in Acre up to as far as they like to go round the Gulf of Alexandretta.

Kitchener: They want to go right round?

Sykes: If they include all that is Syria they might exclude a part elsewhere. They are only giving up what lies between Acre and the beginning of the Jerusalem enclave, which will be about 20 miles.

Balfour: We have always regarded this 90 or 100 miles of desert upon her eastern side as a stronghold of Egypt; now you propose still further east of that to give us a bit of inhabited and cultivated country for which we should be responsible. At first sight it looks as if that would weaken and not strengthen our position in Egypt.

Kitchener: I think what Sir Mark Sykes means is that the line will commence at the sea-coast at Haifa. These Arabs will then come under our control, whereas if we are off the line we lose control over the south.

Balfour: What do you mean to give exactly?

Sykes: I should like to draw a line from the 'e' in Acre to the last 'k' in Kerkuk.

Lloyd George: Do you propose that this should be the first step before you take any military action?

Sykes: I think it is essential that we know where we are.

DDSY2/4 Foreign Affairs and Travel (1888–1919) in *Papers of Mark Sykes* (Wakefield: Microform Academic Publishers).

Lloyd George: Before you begin?
Sykes: I think we should begin to prepare for military action.[140]

Towards the end of 1915, with an Allied victory looking more imminent, Sykes was drafting proposals on what the future of the Ottoman Empire should be.[141] His reasoning, far from any belief in the emancipation of the Arabs from the Turks, is outlined as threefold: (i) the command of the Persian Gulf; (ii) the overland route to India; and (iii) the effect of the development of the arable wealth of Mesopotamia (both north and south) on Indian economics problems.[142] Sykes foresaw two ways in which the 'change of administration is imposed on Turkey':

(1) In the event of the Ottoman Government concluding a separate peace with the Triple Entente, it may be convenient to maintain the supremacy of the Sultan over the Asiatic territories intact in name, but allotted in spheres of commercial and administrative influence to the powers of the Entente and certain neutral states.
(2) In the event of the Ottoman Government continuing the war to the end, the division of the Empire into territorial possession of the various powers can hardly be avoided.[143]

In his note, he considers the advantages and disadvantages of each proposition against the backdrop of a variety of disaggregated British interests. In preparation of the documents that eventually formed part of the agreement, Sykes even examined maps for accuracy. Thus, in a memorandum of 6 May 1915, he clarified spellings and gave general approval for his map of Türkiye.[144] He also paid attention to the links between the territory and trading partners, as witnessed in the discussion of the lines to be drawn around

140 *Ibid.* 4–5.
141 'Notes by Mark Sykes' Document 4/96 of 1915 DDSY2/4 Foreign Affairs and Travel (1888–1919) 6 May 1915 in *Papers of Mark Sykes* (Wakefield: Microform Academic Publishers).
142 *Ibid.* 1.
143 *Ibid.*
144 See 'Letter: Emery Walker Ltd.', London to Walter Wilson, sending a map for "*Turkey*" by Mark Sykes for approval and asking for spellings to be settled' Document 4/83 DDSY2/4 Foreign Affairs and travel (1888–1919) 6 May 1915 in *Papers of Mark Sykes* (Microform Academic Publishers). For earlier, undated maps in Mark Sykes papers, see 'Outline Map of Turkey in Asia', form Document Nos. 69/4 to 78/4 taken from DDSY(2)/4/78, (3) Foreign Affairs and travel (1888–1919) in *Papers of Mark Sykes* (Wakefield: Microform Academic Publishers).

Mosul, where significant justification is given based on practicalities and logistics.[145]

The *Sykes–Picot Treaty* itself was based on the findings of the *Sir Maurice de Bunsen Commission*, which had been charged to find a solution to the dismemberment of the Ottoman Empire and its potential impacts on the 'recognized interests' of the European powers.[146] From a British perspective, the treaty was an attempt to create a French buffer between Britain and Russian territory. This is reflected in the full title of the agreement: *The Agreement Between Great Britain, France and Russia, Regarding Syria, Mesopotamia and Eastern Asia Minor, Commonly Known as the Sykes–Picot Agreement of May, 1916*.

Sykes' first official engagement with determining what would happen post-Ottoman rule came in the form of his being made Lord Kitchener's personal representative on an inter-departmental committee set up in London to 'consider the future of Asiatic Turkey'.[147] Known as the *De Bunsen Commission*, after its chairman Maurice de Bunsen, this consisted of a range of representatives of Whitehall offices (Foreign Office, War Office, Admiralty, Board of Trade, and India Office) tasked with understanding how British long-term interests could be secured. The Commission was formed at a time when European Powers' interests were clear, so it was required to work in a context of

> what should be done with Asiatic Turkey after Turkey and the Turks had been defeated and what the Allies would claim there: Russia had demanded Constantinople and the Dardanelles; France would expect Syria; and potential allies such as Italy and Greece would have their ambitions too.[148]

Yet British interests themselves were less clear, with significant involvement of the Government of British India, and the *De Bunsen Commission* had to not only articulate what those interests were but also how they could be secured, especially since Britain had already agreed to Russian demands over Constantinople and the Dardanelles in return for Russian acquiescence over British claims to Persia. Through the Commission's deliberations, it became apparent that the claim to be made by Britain was for the Persian Gulf and Mesopotamia, in an attempt to counter Russian influence through Istanbul

145 See 'Memorandum on Ports and Railways of Syria and Mesopotamia', by Major S F Newcombe, DDSY2/4 Foreign Affairs and Travel (1888–1919) 4/87 17 July 1915 in *Papers of Mark Sykes* (Wakefield: Microform Academic Publishers).

146 The physical dimensions and map of Türkiye at the time were particularly intriguing, though largely ignored in seeking to understand European interests. See Isaiah Bowman, 'A Note on the Political Map of Turkey' 1(2) *Foreign Affairs* (December 1922) 158–161.

147 Adelson (1975) *op.cit.* 123, 180.

148 *Ibid.* 181.

(Constantinople), French domination in Syria and through loans made to Russia to enable its involvement in the region, and the growing links between Türkiye and Germany.[149] In any case, a determination was emerging among members:

> To leave the Ottoman Empire as it was before the war would not only endanger British interests, but would lose an opportunity of settling the problem of its Asian provinces 'once and for all'.[150]

In pursuit of this objective Sykes proposed two potential solutions:

> The first called for the Allies to partition all but Turkish Anatolia among themselves, with Russia to receive a northern, France a middle, and Great Britain a southern part of the Asian provinces. Sykes's second 'solution' involved keeping the area 'nominally independent, but under effective European control' in Allied 'zones of political and commercial interests'. Both the partition solution and the spheres-of-interest solution stipulated the need for a British Mediterranean port and railway link with British Mesopotamia.[151]

The railway line proved a key prerogative to achieve the aims set out, and Sykes sought to convince his members by highlighting the economic advantages that such a venture would bring, in terms that involved 'development for southern Mesopotamia' but which also presented trade links with India through the ports. A key element in convincing members, reluctant to agree to the significant costs of building what would effectively become a thousand-mile railway line between Rowandiz and Haifa was to stress that it would allow the British to be self-contained, and not reliant on 'the dead weight of intrigues and incompetent pettiness which is characteristic of [French] methods'.[152]

Later in May 1915, having engaged with the French, Sykes proposed another approach to determining the fate of the 'Asiatic provinces of Turkey'. This involved dividing the Ottoman Empire into five historical and ethnographical provinces, consisting of Anatolia, Armenia, Syria, Palestine, and Iraq-Jazirah. This idea of devolved government, Sykes suggested, would free the provinces from the central hold, enabling them a chance to engage

149 *Ibid.* 182.
150 *Ibid.*
151 *Ibid.*
152 See Mark Sykes, 'The Question of a Railway Connecting Haifa with the Euphrates', 19 April 1915, Cab/27/1.

in their own development.[153] As the outbreak of war became imminent, Sykes was sent on a mission to the region to test reactions to the *De Bunsen Commission* report and to observe the military and political situation in the region. This enabled him to engage with a number of different actors, all keen to influence British actions in the conflict. Among these were some moderate Syrian nationalists who believed that Syria would be better served by staying within the realm of British interests, though they would likely have been outnumbered by others keen to stay within the French realm. In any case, their support, led Sykes to another 'solution' to be included in the *De Bunsen Commission* report, namely Mesopotamia, Palestine, and Syria be controlled by Britain as a single unit, 'united by language...under the nominal role of the Sultan of Egypt and the spiritual dominion of the Sherif of Mecca'.[154]

Sykes also undertook a mission to India, where he engaged with the Government of British India to gauge their interests and to ensure that their own interests in the region were catered for. He returned to London in December 1915, with what Adelson described as 'an ambitious scenario in mind for the Arab world', some of which was based on his personal aspiration to 'run the Arab show' as a new chief from Cairo.[155] The goal required British commitment to orchestrate an Egyptian offensive against the Turks. This was a calculated bid to win over the Arabs, playing to Arab nationalists' desires for the overthrow of Turkish rule, achieved strictly under British influence to maintain its hegemony. While this was not agreed to by the War Committee, a concession was made to enable Sykes to engage with the French to glean their appetite for such an offensive.[156] The initiative eventually led to secret negotiations that brought about the *Inter-Allied Agreement of 1916*, subsequently known as the *Sykes–Picot Agreement*. Throughout the latter half of 1915, while Sykes was on his trip to India, the French sought to consolidate their position and mobilized to articulate their own interests through their representative François Georges-Picot, a professional diplomat and First Secretary at the French Embassy in London. The French position was clear: 'France would take nothing less than all of Syria and Palestine except for the Holy Places'.[157]

This opening gambit was gradually tempered as France, in light of some military defeats in the East, became more willing to engage in diplomatic initiatives to 'win over' the Arabs. This involved some reneging on claims to Palestine, in return for agreement on a French sphere of influence which

153 Mark Sykes, 'The Proposed Maintenance of a Turkish Empire in Asia without Spheres of Influence', 3 May 1915, Cab 27/1.

154 Mark Sykes' letter to General C Calwell, 16 July 1915, FO/882/13.

155 Adelson (1975) *op.cit.* 123, 196.

156 *Ibid.* 197.

157 *Ibid.* 199.

included control of the Syrian coast and the city of Mosul. From this position, expressed in the meetings at the (British) Foreign Office, Lord Nicolson charged Sykes to negotiate an agreement with Georges-Picot, emphasizing the need for the emergence of a confederation of Arab States under an Arabian prince.[158] Using maps Sykes had drawn up in previous memos, Sykes and Picot commenced the process, and over three days in January 1916, they divided the region into a northern area under French protection and a southern area under British protection. The negotiations went into greater detail:

> Bordering on the proposed Arab 'confederation' would be a French 'Blue' area along the Syrian coast and Great Britain's 'Red' area at the head of the Persian Gulf. In these areas, the French and British were free to 'establish such indirect administration or control as their desire'. Since Alexandretta fell within the French 'Blue' area, the British took the Palestine ports of Haifa and Acre, thus giving them the land link between the Mediterranean and Mesopotamia that made possible the thousand-mile-long desert-railway scheme from Haifa to Rowanduz, that Sykes had proposed in the De Bunsen Committee meetings. In exchange for such a concession on Palestine, Picot made sure that Mosul fell within the French area... of the Arab 'confederation'.[159]

Making this agreement a political reality required not only the concurrence of the political establishments of France and Britain but also the tacit agreement of Russia, based on the *Declaration of London* of December 1914, according to which France, Britain, and Russia had agreed to consult each other on the peace terms arrived at in the aftermath of the fall of the Ottoman Empire. Thus, both Sykes and Georges-Picot sought an audience with Russia, with the French in a considerably more difficult position since their territory overlapped with Russian interests in the region. However, having gained such an agreement, the *Sykes–Picot Agreement* began to become a realistic prospect.

While the agreement was meant to be secret, Lenin's ascension to power in the Soviet Union provided an opportunity to reveal the secrets behind Imperial Russia's earlier negotiations, and the agreement was made public and received strong criticism for avarice among the Imperial powers, where their indifference to the rights of native populations was emphasized.

The complexities that the agreement sought to negotiate are addressed in its text:

> It was necessary to harmonize the territorial ambitions of France and Russia, the vital and traditional interests of Great Britain in the Ottoman

158 *Ibid.* 200.
159 *Ibid.*

> hinterland of the Persian Gulf and the Imperial British waterway of the Suez Canal and the Red Sea.[160]
>
> It was necessary to do everything possible to maintain concord and unity, not only between European Allies, but between European Allies and Arab Allies. It was necessary to fulfil previous British undertakings to King Hussein of the Hejax and the Arabs. It was necessary to make some provision for the treatment of Palestine, or at least of Jerusalem, on some other basis than that of unfettered Arab rule. And it should be borne in mind that at the time the clash of interests between France and the Arabs, and therefore between Great Britain and France, threatened to become acute.[161]

The document and the dismembering of the Ottoman Empire into two spheres of influence are often justified in British writing about the agreement as necessary due to French interests in the region. Thus the argument is that this was a respectful way in which Britain, who assumed the mantle of being the 'protector of Arabs', through individuals such as Sykes and others, was forced to pay heed to long-nourished French interests in the region, which dated back at least to the *Promise of St Louis* to the Maronites in 1250. This had spawned a legacy that made the Syrian territories important in Napoleonic times and had been cemented through the adoption of French language schools across the region.[162]

As the text states:

> In brief the Arrangement so reached provided for the recognition and upholding of an independent Arab State or a Confederation of Arab States in the regions of Syria and Mesopotamia; but part of this Arab State or Confederation of States was placed under indirect French control and part under similar British control. That in the western party of Syria and in the south-eastern Asia Minor, including Cilica and an area extending to Sivas, France should be allowed to establish such direct or indirect administration as she thought fit. That in the southern part of Mesopotamia Great Britain should have the same privilege; and that Jerusalem and the surrounding district should be placed under an international administration.
>
> This Arrangement, with certain modifications, chiefly with regard to Palestine, formed the basis of the territorial provisions of the Treaty of Sevres.[163]

160 Leslie (1923) *op.cit.* 125, 253.
161 *Ibid*
162 *Ibid.* 257.
163 *Ibid.* 257–258.

Duggan highlights the importance of Syria as a lynchpin that potentially held Mesopotamia, Arabia, and Egypt together. This was in line with the thinking of Abdul Hamid, who articulated a vision that brought together autochthonous communities that had long enjoyed a form of independence during the decentralized Ottoman rule since the fifteenth century.[164] He did this by investing heavily in rail links from Damascus to Constantinople and Baghdad, which enhanced Syrian trade. Yet the growth of foreign influence towards the end of the nineteenth century was palpable, in the form of French missionary influence, the incursion of American schools, and the increasing quest for the creation of Jewish colonies within Syria and Palestine. The rise of the Young Turks came in the face of a growing movement towards Arab independence and reunification, and the attempt to impose one language (Turkish) and culture on the region led to serious repression and flight among Syrian intellectuals.

In seeking to supplement its position as being in favour of protecting the Arabs, Sir Henry McMahon, Governor General of Egypt, transmitted a document to the Cherif in Cairo on 25 October 1915

> in which Great Britain undertook, conditional upon an Arab revolt, to recognize the independence of the Arabs of the Ottoman Empire 'south of latitude 37 degrees' except in the provinces of Bagdad and Basra where British interests require special measures of administrative control and also except where Great Britain 'is not free to act without detriment to the interests of France.[165]

Unknown to the Arabs at that time the last sentence was necessitated by the secret *Sykes–Picot agreement* of 5 March 1915, which simply assumed French predominance in Syria. Duggan attributes the McMahon document as renewing the push towards Arab nationalism, with greater impetus for the emergence of an Arab Empire that included Arabia, Syria, and Mesopotamia.[166]

Drawing on documents declassified in 2007, Barr highlights the French role in the Middle East, including through the funding of terrorist movements.[167] Commenting on the *Sykes–Picot Agreement*, he states:

164 Stephen P. Duggan, 'The Syrian Question' 11(4) *Journal of International Relations* (April 1921) 571–572.

165 *Ibid.* 576.

166 *Ibid.*

167 James Barr, *A Line in the Sand: Britain, France and the Struggle for the Mastery of the Middle East* (London: Simon & Schuster, 2011) 1.

> In 1915 Britain and France, wartime allies then too, tried to resolve the tensions that their rival ambitions in the region were causing. In the secret Sykes-Picot agreement they split the Ottomans' Middle Eastern empire between them by a diagonal line in the sand that ran from the Mediterranean Sea coast to the mountains of the Persian frontier. Territory north of this arbitrary line would go to France; most of the land south of it would go to Britain, for the two powers could not agree over the future of Palestine. The compromise, which neither power likes, was that the Holy Land should have an international administration.[168]

It is important to note the temporal dimension to this kind of empire carving. It had been a central feature of the centuries to date and had already been responsible for the decimation of indigenous tribes in North America and South America in the face of European expansionism. In that specific temporal context, the *Scramble for Africa*, that commenced in 1885 had already yielded the *Berlin West Africa Treaty*, establishing European spheres of influence in Africa. In stark contrast, by 1910 Latin American States had already sought to throw off European influence in a bid to establish themselves as legitimate independent entities from that point onwards. There was also a strong anti-imperialistic critique emerging from the United States, with its then President Woodrow Wilson who genuinely believed in notions of democratic governance and abhorred the idea of the extension of European rule. There were plenty of supporting statements made to this effect in advance of the eventual articulation of such a sentiment in the Atlantic Charter at the end of World War. There was also support for an anti-imperialistic agenda emerging from Russia, where Lenin rose to power on the back of the overthrow of such forces to forge a new Soviet Union. Thus, as Barr put it, while, '[C]rude empire-building of this type had been common in the nineteenth century, ...it was already unpopular by the time the Sykes-Picot agreement was signed'.[169]

Interestingly in providing insight into the background of George Picot, Barr highlights his formation against the 'Fashoda' debacle, which led many to lose faith in France's ability to defend its national interests abroad. This had led Georges-Picot and a group who sought influence at the Quai d'Orsay to deal with Britain directly and more forcefully in the future without surrendering French interests.[170] In serving as French consul in Beirut, Georges-Picot was also well aware of Arab nationalist aspirations, having been petitioned

168 *Ibid.*
169 *Ibid.* 2.
170 *Ibid.* 21.

for French support in this cause, a petition that was difficult to support in view of significant French financial interests in the Ottoman Empire.[171]

The two parties gained the assent of Russia through an exchange of letters in May 1916, though the agreement was kept secret, 'a reflection of the fact that, even by standards of the time, it was a shamelessly self-interested pact, reached well after the point when a growing number of people had started to blame empire-building for the present war'.[172]

As Kedourie highlights in the opening paragraphs of *In the Anglo-Arab Labyrinth*, the

> genesis and subsequent official interpretations, of the McMahon-Husayn correspondence are essential to the understanding of a great deal of Middle-Eastern diplomatic history during and after the first world war, as well as the Palestine dispute in the 1920s and 1930s.[173]

McMahon served as British High Commissioner in Egypt between July 1915 and March 1916, during which time the *Sykes–Picot Agreement* was imagined, negotiated, and drafted. As indicated in the narrative concerning British interests in the region, there was a determination to work through the Sharif of Mecca, Husayn, in a bid to underpin British actions through a form of agreement with the Arabs. With Husayn unquestionably accepted as the spiritual leader of Mecca, he became the focal point for many of the elements that fed into British policy. Thus, there were concerted efforts to bring the Sharif onto the British side, in a bid to convince him to lead the Arab quest for the independence they lost to the Turks.[174] This was part of a wider plan, as articulated in the correspondence below from Sir Reginald Wingate, Governor-General of Sudan, to Sir Edward Grey, the then Foreign Secretary:

> I am well aware that it may be considered futile to talk of the formation of a new state without territory, without capital and without a ruler but however Utopian it may be there can be no doubt that when the psychological moment comes all Moslem eyes will be turned upon Great Britain to whom they look for support in this – perhaps the supreme crisis – in their religious and national existence, and if I may venture to say so, I think it is for us to take the lead and to consolidate on our side – as far as

171 *Ibid.*

172 *Ibid.* 32.

173 Elie Kedourie, *In the Anglo-Arab Labyrinth: The McMahon-Husayn Correspondence and Its Interpretations 1914–1939* (Cambridge: Cambridge University Press, 1976) xi.

174 See *Correspondence between Sir Henry McMahon (His Majesty's High Commissioner at Cairo) and The Sherif Hussein of Mecca, July 1915-March 1916* (London: HMSO Cmd 5957, 1939).

> we possibly may – the divergent views of the various Moslem nationalities and Communities.[175]

The shared vision emerging in the British Foreign Office was to view the emergence of an Arab Caliphate or confederation in 'the Asiatic provinces of Turkey', with the Sharif of Mecca as Caliph, headquartered in Mecca due to its sacred status. These imperialistic actions at a time of a new awareness about the need to foster the aspirations of smaller nationalities brought about by Woodrow Wilson's conviction to this end, coupled with the perceived strength of the Jewish diaspora and their articulation for an independent homeland amidst the Caliphate, played perhaps the most significant role in the geographical and political future of the Middle East.[176]

In a letter dated 14 July 1915, addressed to Sir Henry McMahon, the Sherif Hussein of Mecca states:

> the whole of the Arab nation without any exception have decided in these last years to live, and to accomplish their freedom, and grasp the reins of their administration both in theory and practice; ...and ...found and felt that it is to the interest of the Government of Great Britain to support them and aid them to the attainment of their firm and lawful intentions (which are based upon the maintenance of the honour and dignity of their life) without any ulterior motives whatsoever unconnected with this object.[177]

In view of this the letter asked for five specific aspects concerning its relationship with Britain. First, it called upon Britain to support the call for an Islamic Caliphate from the Red Sea up to the border of Persia, bordered on the north by Mersina and Adana up to 37 degrees latitude and on the south by the Indian Ocean. Second, it pledged support from the Sherif to accept economic preference for England in all agreements pertaining to enterprise within this region. Third, to agree to mutual military help and support in light of any third-party aggression. Fourth, a guarantee of neutrality should one party enter into an aggressive conflict with a third party, and/or a discussion about the prospect of joining forces. And fifth, for Britain to acknowledge the abolition of foreign privileges in Arab countries.[178]

175 Wingate Papers FO371/2486, 77713/34982, private letter from Wingate to Grey, Khartoum 15 May 1915.

176 Kedourie (1976) *op.cit.* 174, 45–50.

177 *Correspondence between Sir Henry McMahon (His Majesty's High Commissioner at Cairo) and The Sherif Hussein of Mecca, July 1915-March 1916* (1939) 3. For a list of other documents towards the formation of a Jewish homeland, see *Documents Relating to the McMahon Letters* (London: Jewish Agency for Palestine, 1939).

178 *Correspondence between Sir Henry McMahon (His Majesty's High Commissioner at Cairo) and The Sherif Hussein of Mecca, July 1915-March 1916* (1939) 4.

The focus on the boundary makers and their aspirations ignores the movements and discussions within Arab society that were ongoing at that time. As Farah states, one key aim of Arab nationalism had been to unite Arabs under one banner:

> As nationalism gathered force in the Arab World during several decades, its only discernible aims had been political freedom and unification for Arab peoples who existing political divisions separating them.[179]

Farah shows the extent to which promises to respect Arab nationalism were raised and dashed by Britain and France in the lead up to and aftermath of World War I. He states:

> Arab nationalists joined the Allies in World War I with the understanding that they would have full independence and unity at the end of the war. When the time of fulfilment came in 1919–20, Fertile Crescent Arabs gained no independence and, worse yet, lost whatever regional unity they had enjoyed under the administration supplied by the Ottomans. Their lands were parceled out by decree of the League of Nations as mandates of the French and British according to a prior arrangement worked out by their representatives in the Sykes-Picot agreement of 1916. In the arbitrary dismemberment that ensued to conform with the policy interests of France and Britain political entities emerged respecting neither geographical, nor ethnic, nor historical boundaries. Localism, ethnic and sectarian separatism were emphasized through what may be regarded as a deliberate policy on the part of the mandate authorities to weaken the nationalist cause. What semblance of unity the nationalist movement had enjoyed to date was now dissipated in the intensified struggle to combat the new separatism.[180]

Writing in 1963, the points made by Farah have significant pertinence half a century later, as the Middle East continues to face grave uncertainties and strife. Farah stated:

> The French and British mandates in the inter-war period contributed to the crystallization of political thinking among Arab leaders. Democratic institutions and new concepts of political organization for the expression of political views were grafted by the mandatory powers onto unreceptive societies: tribal and feudal in structure, theocratic in spirit, and lacking in

179 Caesar E. Farah, 'The Dilemma of Arab Nationalism' 8(3) *Die Welt des Islams* (1963) 140–164 at 140.

180 *Ibid.* 143.

> the political sophistication required to make democracy workable. As the strains of the impact mounted, they produced general maladjustment and led to distortion and abuse not only of the means but also of the declared ends of democratic government. Europe contributed to the confusion firstly by introducing parliamentary institutions before there existed a strong predisposition for them and secondly by tampering with the democratic process when it tended to work against the imperial interests of the mandatory powers; witness British attitudes in Iraq and the French in Syria.[181]

The idea of looking beyond the sovereign State as the only form of legitimate governance in contemporary times, in the region and beyond, would draw on thinking within the Pan-Arab movement at the time of independence. The region had its own governance system of emirates which are still maintained in some States, notably the United Arab Emirates. Realization of this prospect requires an abdication of power by the male regimes that have gained ascendancy in the name of decolonization, driven by strong unification sentiments among States over seven decades old. This requires the articulation of an overarching narrative that has to be inclusive and forward-looking, fully accepting the extent to which outside actions have divided the *ulemma* and *dhimmi* but honest about the extent to which the greed of indigenous ruling families and clans were contributing factors. Any such attempt would need to invoke the idea of Arab unity, which flourished before floundering against the twin objectives of external hegemons and ambitious proxy rulers. As Farah asserted in 1963,

> the dilemma of Arab nationalism can be solved if present trends favoring greater collaboration of Arab states through the agencies of the League of Arab States should persist. The League is the only surviving product of efforts hitherto expended by Arab nationalists to bring about unity. Overlooking its misgivings in the area of political action, the League has demonstrated its capacity for constructive accomplishment in areas where the obstacles to the realization of Arab nationalist aspirations are noticeable: the economic, social and educational. If the League should be permitted and encouraged to pursue its efforts in these areas unencumbered by the political rivalries of its members the political ends of Arab nationalism will be served.[182]

The prospect of such an eventuality is paved with significant difficulties. It requires, first, the articulation of a medium and long-term vision for the Arab

181 *Ibid*. 146.
182 *Ibid*. 163–164.

world in 2050 and beyond, where the human capabilities of its population are not made subservient to continued fragility caused by war and deprivation. It is equally clear that any attempt to forge unity based on the negatives of the past, such as the anti-colonial revolt or opposition to Israel, is unlikely to knit a narrative that is progressive. Farah's statement in 1963 is equally valid half a century later:

> Lasting unity can be achieved only through a gradual process of awakening of the average Arab to an appreciation of what nationalism means for himself and for his society. Arab nationalism has prospects of accomplishing its mission, partly because of powerful forces at play and partly because in world moving towards greater unity it is in tune with the trends the modern age.[183]

Other Men, Other Places, More Lines on Maps

This chapter has touched on a small subsection of men put in positions where they could determine the fate of entire territories. Others could be added with many other boundaries warranting deeper research. The rules on title to territory, examined later in this book, had already emerged from European adventurism in the Americas through people such as Christopher Columbus who is still revered.[184] In fact Portugal's drawing of a map showing its dominance by 1501 was regarded as a major leap forward in charting global geography.[185] Tracking each other to gain influence in the new world, the rivalry between Spain and Portugal was significant, though no documentary evidence has yet been collected and analyzed about the direction of the discussions between the monarchs on the great boundary questions between them.[186]

The Church and the Papal Bulls play a significant role in that mission, with that history also needing to be aired, understood, and imbibed. Vander Linden highlights the fact that the controversy over the Papal Bulls of Alexander VI, which led to the colonial expansion of Spain and Portugal, was also caused by its timing:

183 *Ibid.* 164.

184 While there are many sources available in Spanish, Portuguese, and even Italian, see, in English, John Boyd Thatcher, *Christopher Columbus: His Life, His Work, his Remains, as Revealed by Original Printed and Manuscript Records, Together with an Essay on Peter Martyr of Anghera and Bartolome de las Casas, the First Historians of America*, 3 vols. (New York & London: G. P. Putnam's Sons, 1903–1904) x, 670; vi, 699; vii, 775.

185 P. J. J. Valentini, 'The Portuguese in the Track of Columbus' 21 *Journal of the American Geographical Society of New York* (1889) 167–196 at 167.

186 *Ibid.* 174.

> Promulgated at a critical moment in the evolution of Europe, a moment marked by the rise of the modern states and the decline of the papacy, they belong to a period of political and religious transition. If they have obtained so extraordinary a prominence, it is because of the mass of various and important events with which they were associated: the rapid enlargement of the geographical horizon, colonial expansion, religious propaganda, the foundation of international law, the transformation of the relations between Church and State.[187]

There remain many valid questions about the efficacy of the promulgation and the reasons behind it. In Hugo Grotius's public international law writing, the impression of Alexander VI was that of a mediator, seeking to find a solution between two competing colonial powers.[188] However, Vander Linden is not convinced:

> no one of these different bulls has the appearance of an arbitral decision. They are acts of papal sovereignty, in favor of a single power. They are essentially grants, as one sees by running through the series of designations given to these acts by the documents themselves.[189]

His conclusion on assessing the motivation for the Papal Bulls and the extent to which the boundary drawn was influenced by Columbus is definitive:

> To sum up, then, the bull of demarcation, like the other bulls delivered to Spain in 1493, constituted at first a grant exclusively Spanish; it was in large part, if not wholly, shaped by the chancery of Ferdinand and Isabella; the line of demarcation itself, which played so important a part in subsequent transactions, had been suggested and probably first devised by Christopher Columbus. Moreover, the different bulls of that year were but successive increments of the favors granted to the Spanish sovereigns, Alexander VI being at that time but an instrument in their hands. Friction with Portugal was increased rather than diminished by the granting of these bulls. Far from recognizing the prior rights of that country in the Atlantic, the Holy See restricted them more and more, in the interest of Spain. The difficulties between the two powers were smoothed away by

187 H. Vander Linden, 'Alexander VI and the Demarcation of the Maritime and Colonial Domains of Spain and Portugal, 1493-1494' 22(1) *The American Historical Review* (October 1916) 1–20.

188 See Hugo Grotius, *De Mare Libero*, cap. III. [Alexander VI.] (Leiden: Brill, 2009) 'lectus inter illos [Lusitanos et Castellanos] arbiter'.

189 Vander Linden (1916) *op.cit.* 188, 11.

> their own diplomatic means and Portugal distinctly repudiated the incidental arbitration of the pope or of any other authority.[190]

History will also have its share of those who, within the parameters of the power structure, sought to question, challenge, and speak reason to power. One such person was Las Casas, who could be deemed:

> Arguably the most important person of the age after Christopher Columbus (1451–1506), Las Cases was involved at almost every stage, major event, or controversy of the Conquest in one fashion or another. Las Casas, who became a priest and later a Dominican friar, was formed by the powerful forces of the epoch. But he was also a principal actor and eyewitness to the Conquest, and his writings and hot rhetoric helped fashion how Europeans and Amerindians clashed and adapted to each other in the unique environment following Columbus's first voyage 1492–1493. ...unlike Columbus, who only became celebrated centuries after his death, Las Casas achieved notoriety among his fellow countrymen in his lifetime because of his radical stands in defense of the Indians.[191]

In another era from the later adventures of Sykes and others, Las Casas first travelled to the Americas in 1502 with his father to visit Santa Domingo, the capital of the Spanish colony Espanola. The Las Casas family were merchants whose fortunes depended on the higher volumes of trade that were opening up with the New World. This quest also came in the aftermath of the intolerant Christianity of Spain in 1492, which was characterized by brutal warfare between Christians and Moors. The new settlers and colonizers landing in the Americas carried their warlike traditions with them, forcing the Amerindians into absolute submission, sometimes justifying this as necessary to spread Christianity and 'civilization'.[192]

In documenting the uniquely cruel and insensitive behaviour of the Spanish in their encounter with the Amerindians, Las Casas attracted consternation from those who viewed him as a traitor. His narrative, termed the Black Legend, was countered by the White Legend constructed by Spanish patriots, to show that Spain was no different from other European powers in their overseas adventures and that in the carriage and dissemination of Christianity to the Americas, Spain had played an important civilizing role.[193]

190 *Ibid*. 20.

191 Lawrence A. Clayton, *Bartolome de las Casas and the Conquest of the Americas* (Chichester: John Wiley and Sons, 2011) 4.

192 *Ibid*. 6.

193 *Ibid*. 7.

Conclusion

The documentation and adulation of European men who negatively impacted the world's boundaries far from their own territories remain and is even celebrated in history without any hint of discomfort. Here are the words of Winston Churchill, describing Sykes:

> of the young men who made their way to the fore after service in the Boer War, none set out with a more determined and original programme than Mark Sykes. Though surrounded by every luxury and every temptation to lead an idle, pleasant country life, his fancy turned to the desert rather than the moors... to some piece of Imperial service single-handed in the unknown East rather than to the enjoyment of the home duties of a country gentleman.[194]

He even comments on his motivations as being

> [F]illed with an adventurous spirit which was abroad after the Victorian Jubilee and led so many into African or American adventures, Mark Sykes betook himself to travel in the Near East without any hope of finding treasure or any desire to change the religious views or territorial ownership of those amongst whom he wandered. He acquainted himself with the Levantines and the Palestinians, and even more with the Arabs and Turks. He went where few if any had ever been before, and mapped out roads and countries which neither the War Office nor the Royal Geographical Society with their combined knowledge could cover or compass.[195]
>
> He was clearly marked out for service in the East. He became an invaluable factor in all that intricate and remarkable policy which split the Arab from the Turk, divided the Moslem world at a most critical juncture, and eventually furnished important forces on the desert flank of Allenby's armies.[196]

Sykes is perhaps more accurate in describing himself:

> I am not an Anglo-Saxon, but a Woldsman, consequently a pirate; we came from the North Sea, we did, and we have always been the same. We massacred and destroyed all the wretched flint-making people and drove them off the Wolds, and now they live between York and Selby. We call everyone a *giaour* and a foreigner who lives beyond a twenty-two mile radius of this house. Our men are tall and have dark hair and fair

194 Winston Churchill, 'Introduction', in Leslie (1923) *op.cit.* 125, v.
195 *Ibid.* vii.
196 *Ibid.*

> moustaches, and we are all pirates. Come and buy a horse or sink our fishing boats, and the price or indemnity we shall get out of you will astonish you! ... We are not money-makers, like the Yalmeli, but seizers and snatchers, like our foregathers who came here.[197]

Among this group of men many emerged from Cambridge University with a sense of entitlement and a belief of their right to conduct international affairs, manufacturing a singular narrative of doing good. Thus as Lovat, in his address to the *Central Asian Society* at Cambridge, sought to 'recite afresh... in the briefest possible form, the successive steps by which the special position of Great Britain in the Persian Gulf has been created'.[198] His argument drew three unilateral pronouncements, all made around 1905, by British men who reiterated the importance of the area to British interests (Lord Curzon, Under-Secretary of State for India, Lord Landsdowne, Foreign Secretary, and Sir Edward Grey). These statements do not reiterate a special position for Britain in the Gulf: they express a determination on the part of the British to play such a role. In his text, formulated in 1908, Lovat explored British engagements in the area since the first visit of Ralph Fitch in 1583 to the Middle East to paint a picture of a trading nation keen to foster ties and wield influence to the exclusion of others who may seek to do so. The 'protection' of native populations from these outside influences and the negotiations to keep others who may have similar aims outside the privileged circle occupy significant intrigue and paint a picture of British interests that would perhaps be less feted in contemporary writings.

But perhaps the motivation was simply a sense of racial superiority. In his last will and testament, Cecil Rhodes stated:

> I contend that we are the finest race in the world and that the more of the world we inhabit the better it is for the human race. Just fancy those parts that are at present inhabited by the most despicable specimens of human beings what an alteration there would be if they were brought under Anglo-Saxon influence, look again at the extra employment a new country added to our dominions gives.

Rhodes' own deviousness, like the men who shared his belief system, literally drew lines on maps over 150 years ago that are the cause of significant bloodshed, strife, and destitution. That this was done out of superiority is unquestionable. The travesty lies in how little these decisions are interrogated, understood, and how old forms of tyranny, which allow the nature

197 Leslie (1923) *op.cit.* 125, 3.

198 Lovat Fraser, *Some Problems of the Persian Gulf – Proceedings of the Central Asian Society* (London: Central Asian Society, 1908), 4.

of the territory to govern the fate of the people, drive modern international society. This chapter covered a small list of such individuals, excluding many obscured by history, some still heralded as visionaries. Public international law as a discipline has never taken ownership of how such decisions were made or their legitimacy. Worse, decisions are still made in a modern context that draw on the rules developed during this period despite the limited intellectual and human history of their formulators.

The double-speak of history does not simply require a revisionist view of the motivations for colonization. Indeed, writing in 1921, Gibbons already highlighted the extent to which the mandate system developed by Woodrow Wilson to pay heed to the aspirations of smaller nations was in fact not much more than a 'scheme to disguise under the cloak of virtuous self-abnegation the intention of the conquerors of Germany to divide among themselves Germany's overseas possessions'.[199]

While there has often been *post-facto* rationalization under law for colonial activities and boundary-making, Gibbons finds little evidence of this. He states:

> Concealment of mandatory intentions, and denial of the authority of the League of Nations have been the consistent policy of the Allied Premiers. Since April, 1919, the allotment of the mandates, the drawing of boundaries and the rules for governing mandated territories have been matters of direct negotiation between the powers in actual possession of German and Ottoman territories at the time of the Armistice. These powers did not wait until the Council of the League was formed. The residuary trustee idea is a farce, since the Entente Powers are interested in the League of Nations only as a convenient instrument to use in furthering their own foreign policies.[200]

The historical veracity of this statement can be proved easily through an understanding of the sequencing of events. In the words of Gibbons:

> The mandates for the former German colonies and Ottoman Empire were decided upon before the Covenant of the League of Nations was adopted. The ownership of these territories had been a matter of secret negotiations among the Entente Powers during the war.[201]

199 Herbert Adam Gibbons, 'The Defects of the System of Mandates' 96 *Annals of the American Academy of Political and Social Science* (July 1921) 84–90 at 84.
200 *Ibid.* 85.
201 *Ibid.*

This raises questions about the authenticity of the rhetoric emanating from the League of Nations, subsequently reified by the United Nations, concerning the principle of self-determination and the need for territories to be held 'on trust' until a successful transition could be achieved. It was clear that the acquisition of territories, until their eventual decolonization was seen as no more than a European gain for influence, fought against each other's interests, and only mildly impacted by actors from the region. The template for the secret arrangements with regard to addressing the Ottoman lands, addressed in this chapter, was already developed in agreements between Britain and Belgium concerning the disposal of German possessions in East Africa, and between Britain and Japan in connection with former German colonies in the Pacific.[202]

Precise accusations can be levelled against the Allies' avarice in land-grabbing territories in the aftermath of the Great War, which were disguised as altruistic motivations. While partisan in his critique due to a sense that the Americans ought to have engaged in this game more, Gibbon's points are telling:

> There is much to wax indignant about and to denounce in the way of self-appointed mandatory powers allotting to themselves the mandates, and in the way they have exercised them during the first two years of League of Nations experiment. We can find a true bill against the Entente Powers on the following counts: (1) conspiring with each other to thwart the spirit of the mandate plan by violating the agreement and solemn undertaking of the first paragraph of Article XX of the Covenant; (2) ignoring the Covenant stipulations concerning Class 'A' mandates; (3) refusing to recognize the distinction they themselves made in Article XXII between Class 'B' and Class 'C' mandates; (4) anticipating by secret agreement the provision of Article XXII that the 'degree of authority, control or administration to be exercised by the mandatory shall be explicitly defined in each case by the Council'.[203]

While the *Sykes–Picot Agreement* took place prior to the *Treaty of Versailles*, the subsequent treaties that built on the Agreement clearly were in violation of the spirit of Article XX, as indicated by Gibbons. This would particularly apply to the *Treaty of Lausanne* and *Treaty of Sèvres*, and the *Tripartite Agreement of 1920*, which reinforced the *Sykes–Picot Agreement*.[204] Additionally, there was tacit acceptance in discussions concerning the dis-

202 *Ibid.*

203 *Ibid.* 85–86.

204 For more on this, including the actual maps and the reasoning behind their drawing, see Bowman (1922) *op.cit.* 147, 158–161.

integration of the Ottoman Empire that there were communities deemed to have reached a level of development whereby their standing as independent nations ought to have been provisionally recognized. Despite this explicit provision (Article XXII) and understanding, no attempts were made to gauge the wishes of the population or to make it play a significant role in how the mandates were governed. In the words of Gibbons:

> The British and French Governments have negotiated between themselves boundaries of the territories they coveted and intended to hold and exploit, with no consideration for ethnographic frontiers. The existence of former Ottoman communities 'as independent nations' has not been 'provisionally recognized'. Syria has been artificially divided between France and Great Britain, and the Palestinians have seen an alien regime, which threatens their existence, foisted upon them by force.[205]

As better documented in Africa and Latin America, this chapter has sought to show how a sense of racial superiority enabled men to draw lines upon maps where no white foot had ever trod in South Asia, East Asia, Central Asia, or the Middle East. They permitted themselves the right to give away mountains, rivers, and lakes to each other, often justifying this as being in the interests of peace and prosperity. The blueprint they left behind is one of divided communities, with a legacy of centralized power in the form of a sovereign State, usually controlled by an ethnic group closest to the outgoing power, who could step into the units created, take charge, and ensure the continued resonance and hegemony of the system. The role of public international law in this process was simply to serve as a servant to power, unable to question it or hold it to truth. As we shall see in the next chapter, rules were formulated instead, deemed to be part of customary international law, that uphold the territorial sovereignty of such units, thereby cementing power structures and putting them beyond reach of communities.

205 Gibbons (1921) *op.cit.* 200, 88–89.

Chapter 3

The Rules Governing Title to Territory and Their Adjudication in International Law

Introduction

Judge Dillard famously said that it was for the people to determine the fate of the territory and not the territory the fate of the people.[1] Yet it is the determination of the territorial unit on grounds that were often unconnected with the inhabitants that enabled the formation of the colonial territorial unit. This was then transformed into the modern State during decolonization using a set of rules that were ascribed to being sacrosanct in public international law. The consequence of this is the emergence, seemingly for posterity, of entities that neither have historical coherence nor are they based on geographical features that may have contributed to their distinctiveness. The right to exercise exclusive sovereignty was bestowed on these entities as they emerged from decolonization, with the caveat that this exercise of sovereignty be restricted to the physical dimension of the territories allotted to them. The appearance of the post-colonial State into the firmament of States was validated by a process of recognition within the claimed territorial dimensions, dismissing other possibilities for territorial modification. This left kin communities, sometimes even nations, divided across frontiers, sometimes created artificial minorities to ensure effective control of assets, and sowed seeds of enmity that have contributed to significant states of war in many parts of the world.

The principle of self-determination – as a process by which oppression and subjugation could be overcome – was seized by many movements whose aspirations for freedom were not realized by decolonization. The international legal framework that protected occupied territories proved unable to safeguard territories in the Americas, Africa, and Asia from avarice, resulting in mass European colonization from the fifteenth century to the twentieth century. This chapter aims to show how, in the quest to unravel that colonization, 'international law' was equally culpable: this time in the articulation

1 *ICJ Reports* (1975). Also see G. Distefano, 'The Conceptualization (Construction) of Territorial Title in the Light of the International Court of Justice Case Law' 19(4) *Leiden Journal of International Law* (2006) 1041–1075.

DOI: 10.4324/9781003503279-4

of the rules framing decolonization that may have appeared to maintain short-term peace but which in reality, proved ineffective in the longer term. To achieve this the chapter will outline the rules governing title to territory, highlighting their rationale. In articulating these and emphasizing the underlying motivations for them, this chapter hopes to provide insights into why they need serious reconsideration if the quest for perpetual peace is to remain a live project.

Judge Dillard's statement, contained in an appending judgment, arose in the context of an advisory opinion from the *International Court of Justice*,[2] where Morocco sought, *inter alia*, a legal determination of whether the territory of the Western Sahara was *terra nullius* at the time of Spanish colonization commencing in 1884.[3] The principle of *terra nullius*, articulated in the context of *jus gentium* (the law of nations), was extrapolated from basic property rights.[4] As established in the opening chapter, the only territory open to legal or legitimate acquisition was territory that was uninhabited.[5] The *post-facto* determination of such inhabitation, without accurate historical documentation, would be difficult at the best of times. Innate racism accorded subject-hood to some but not other parts of humanity, and as a consequence, the occupation of territories was justified on the basis that its inhabitants had not acquired property rights to their territory.[6] Indigenous communities living on their ancestral domains, claimed or not, were most significantly impacted by this.

Beyond the racism that deemed them underdeveloped and 'in need of emancipation' from their alleged lack of history, various legal tools derived from European perspectives differentiated use (*usus*) from ownership (*possessio*) of land, rendering them akin to flora and fauna – as objects on a territory, rather than subjects whose consent was needed in any engagement. Sins of omission and commission defeated the principle of *terra nullius*, enabling vast portions of the globe to fall under (mainly) European influence.[7] The

2 Advisory Opinion on the Western Sahara, *ICJ Reports* (1975).

3 See generally T. Hodges, *Western Sahara: The Roots of a Desert War* (Westport, CT: Lawrence Hill, 1983) 210–211 (outlining the political factors underlying the reference of the case for the advisory opinion). Also see M. N. Shaw, 'The Western Sahara Case' 44 *British Yearbook of International Law* (1978) 118; T. M. Franck, 'The Stealing of the Sahara' 70 *American Journal of International Law* (1978) 694.

4 J. Castellino & S. Allen, *Title to Territory in International Law: An Intertemporal Analysis* (Dartmouth: Ashgate, 2003).

5 H. F. Jolowicz & B. Nicolas, *Historical Introduction to the Study of Roman Law*, 3rd ed. (Cambridge: Cambridge University Press, 1972) 259–263.

6 R. L. Barsh, 'Indigenous Peoples in the 1990s: From Object to Subject in International Law?' 7 *Harvard Human Rights Journal* (1994) 33–86.

7 See especially, *Partitioned Africans: Relations Across Africa's International Boundaries 1884–1984* [AI Awisaju ed.] (London: Palgrave Macmillan, 1985). See generally *Colonialism in Africa 1870–1960* [L. H. Gann & P. Duignan eds.] (Cambridge: Cambridge University

successor post-colonial territorial State, now in more autochthonous hands, has prolonged this arrangement into posterity in many of these places. So, even after colonization, the consideration of the inhabitants as not really belonging to their territory under different disguises has continued to facilitate the pursuit of colonizers' objectives at whatever price that may come for the indigenous population. For instance well-documented memos discussed before UK tribunals reveal that the British knew that Chagos islanders were settled in the islands for two, perhaps even three generations. However, they simply decided to evacuate these communities when their perceived defence interests were to be served. This was achieved by categorizing these communities as transient labourers:

> cynically likening the Chagossians to migratory birds and congratulating themselves on how their ruse had worked and that the UK had avoided UN scrutiny over its planned breach of Article 73 of the Charter.[8]

The legitimacy and injustice of these situations are beyond the remit of this book,[9] although those engaged in this debate accept the practical constraints of attempting to roll back the clock to dispense *post-facto* justice.[10] While not dismissing these efforts, this chapter is more focused on the rules that continue to perpetrate injustice.

The single premise that underpins this book can be stated succinctly: there is likely to be increasing contestation of the State's national boundaries in the next two decades.[11] Understanding how these disputes can be tackled within

Press, 1969) (discussing the principles and actions during the period in question); J. Flint, 'Chartered Companies and the Transition from Informal Sway to Colonial Rule in Africa' in *Bismarck, Europe, and Africa* [S. Förster, W. J. Mommsen & R. Robinson eds.] (Oxford: Oxford University Press, 1988) 69 (pointing to the commercial aspect under which such appropriation occurred).

8 G. Robertson, 'Who Owns Diego Garcia – Decolonisation and Indigenous Rights in the Indian Ocean' 36(1) *University of Western Australian Law Review* (2012) 1–32, 15.

9 For more on reparations for colonialism and slavery, see J. Torpey, *Making Whole What Has Been Smashed: On Reparations Politics* (Boston, MA: Harvard University Press, 2006); R. M. Spitzer, 'African Holocaust: Should Europe Pay Reparations to Africa for Colonialism and Slavery' 35 *Vanderbilt Journal of Transnational Law* (2002) 1313; E. Barkan, *The Guilt of Nations: Restitution and Negotiating Historical Injustice* (Baltimore, MD: Johns Hopkins University Press, 2001); E. Posner & A. Vermeule, 'Reparations for Slavery and Other Historical Injustices' 103(3) *Columbia Law Review* (2003) 689; R. L. Brooks, 'Getting Reparations for Slavery Right – A Response to Posner and Vermeule' 80 *Notre Dame Law Review* (2004–2005) 251.

10 See generally C. Evans, *The Right of Reparations in International Law for Victims of Armed Conflict* (Cambridge: Cambridge University Press, 2012). Also see J. Castellino, *Calibrating Colonial Crime* (Bristol: Bristol University Press, 2024).

11 This is supported by empirical work undertaken by Dzurek. See D. J. Dzurek, 'What Makes Some Boundary Issues Important?' *IBRU Boundary and Security Bulletin* (Winter

pacific fora is crucial, but framing effective rules beyond short-term maintenance of peace is equally imperative since the nature of the contestations could otherwise become violent.[12] This trend is already visible in two distinct actions since the start of the twenty-first century: the attempt that succeeded for a significant period by '*Islamic State*' to erase the *Sykes Picot* Line on grounds of its illegitimacy;[13] and the deeper invasion by Russia of Ukraine on the grounds that the country itself did not exist but was part of a wider Russian sovereign State. Both cases highlight how little attention is paid to the establishment of an effective forum for the pacific settlement of disputes. The so-called rules-based international order has also been completely shredded by Israel's inhumane and disproportionate attack on Gaza, allegedly in response to the Hamas attack of 7 October 2023. Highly organized male violence is instigating ever-greater hate in societies, generating anger and dimming prospects for peace. These scenarios rely on violent contestations of the territorial dimension of units with problematic presentations of 'facts' distilled and disseminated for political purposes. The impact on global peace and security has been significant, accompanied by a wide-scale loss of lives. The conflicts will also leave a legacy of significant damage, not least to the environment, while also disrupting the urgent efforts needed to address that existential crisis. Despite attention through the ages for the establishment of a dispute resolution forum at the international level, drawing on the responsibilities of the international community of States in resolving and upholding cross-border dispute resolution, the possibility of such a forum existing seems remote, with the current proxy for that mission – the UN Security Council – having outlived its utility in maintaining international peace and security, most visibly in failing to restore international peace and security in the face of the genocide perpetrated by Israel in Gaza.

1999–2000) 83–95 available at https://www.durham.ac.uk/media/durham-university/research-/research-centres/ibru-centre-for-borders-research/maps-and-databases/publications-database/boundary-amp-security-bulletins/bsb7-4_dzurek.pdf, and 'What Makes Territory Important: Tangible and Intangible Dimensions' 64 *GeoJournal* (2005) 263–274.

12 The empirical support for this can be gleaned in the work of P. R. Hensel, 'Territory: Theory and Evidence on Geography and Conflict' in *What Do We Know About War?* [J. A. Vasquez ed.] (Boulder, CO: Rowman & Littlefield, 2000) 57–84. The author claims that a quarter of military conflicts explicitly involve territorial issues. Violence in territorial disputes is also more likely to be met with a military response than other disputes.

13 This title is in inverted commas, since the claim to a religion, namely Islam, is questionable. The international community had no option but to accept the reality of the entity behind these actions, but it is appropriate that the claim to a religion be problematized by the use of italics, since the actions bear no relation to the message preached by that religion, instead constituting an affront to the multitudes within that faith-based community who do not subscribe to the values professed in their names.

Against the backdrop of the rise in territorial conflicts, this chapter reiterates the rules governing contestations of international boundaries. Internal contestations not involving an international frontier for changed governance within States (intra-state conflict) remain within the considerable margin of appreciation afforded to States in exercising their territorial sovereignty. This must be acknowledged as a potential threat to peace and security but will only marginally be touched upon in this work. Thus questions about sub-state entities seeking secession will merit brief consideration only if they touch on an international frontier.[14]

This chapter is divided into four sections to tackle this agenda. The first section justifies the principal assumption that territorial disputes are likely to increase in the next two decades. The second section explores and critiques the role of international law, first in failing to codify appropriate rules to uphold the rule of law in colonial struggles and, second, for unproblematically applying rules derived from a limited European frame to the settlement of territorial disputes in a rigid manner. This section ends with an articulation of what ought to be priorities for the international community in tackling the increased pressure on international frontiers, among them, support for the international adjudication of disputes. The third section develops the argument by briefly exploring fora that could serve the pacific settlement of disputes, suggesting that the ICJ, the least imperfect of these based on its track record, ought to warrant greater support. This section rebuts arguments about the decline of the Court, suggesting that these cyclical pronouncements are not a fair assessment of the Court's contribution, especially from the lens of territorial disputes. The final section ends with a practical discussion about overcoming weaknesses and perceived weaknesses in the system.

The Blurring of Lines

Over 85% of the world's current States could be considered post-colonial, spreading across the Americas, Africa (with the notable exception of Ethiopia, formerly Abyssinia), every part of Asia (except China and Japan), all of the Pacific, and a significant number of European States, including former Soviet

14 For more on secession, its position in international law, and its current manifestations, see C. Walter, A. von Ungern-Sternberg & K. Abushov (eds.), *Self-Determination and Secession in International Law* (Oxford: Oxford University Press, 2014); R. D. Sloane, 'The Policies of State Succession: Harmonizing Self-Determination and Global Order in the Twenty-First Century' 30 *Fordham International Law Journal* (2007) 1288; A. Pavkovic & P. Radan, *Creating New States: Theory and Practice of Secession* (Aldershot: Ashgate 2007); R. Trisotto, 'Seceding in the Twenty-First Century: A Paradigm for the Ages' 35 (2) *Brooklyn Journal of International Law* (2010) 419: G. Anderson, 'Secession in International Law and Relations: What are We Talking About?' 35(3) *Loyola of Los Angeles International & Comparative Law Review* (2013) 343.

countries, Scandinavia, and others like Cyprus, Ireland, and Malta. The vast majority of these gained independence in the last seven decades, with a considerable portion of the non-island States inheriting boundaries from the colonial era. While most of this experience concerned European colonization, Europe also experienced its share of colonization and empire, though its borders, in general, have evolved over a considerably longer period.

In most parts of Africa and Latin America, the inherited boundaries bear little resemblance to the human geography of the territory, with frontier disputes foreclosed by the rule concerning the *inviolability of frontiers*[15] adopted by regional leadership[16] and endorsed by the international community.[17] This rule undermined separatist forces which may have dismembered fledgling States that were emerging, creating ethnolinguistic and religious tensions with prospects of immense bloodshed. The emphatic statement of the inviolability of frontiers failed to stop *all* violent conflicts, as communities attempted to carve out States that ensured their own hegemony rather than accepting subjugation from a rival community, tribe, clan, or nation.[18]

The rule concerning the inviolability of frontiers spans various decades of the nineteenth and twentieth centuries as discussed below.[19] The following three statements present a sampling of these.

(1) In reporting on the discussions of the *Pan-American Congress* held in Lima in 1864, leading to the framing of Article 9 of the *Union and Defensive Alliance Pact of 23rd January 1865*, Alvarez writes:

> The parties promise...not to grant or recognize any protectorate or superior rights which affect their sovereignty and independence, and ...not to alienate another nation or government any part of their territory. This stipulation, however, does not prevent those parties possessing contiguous

15 S. Lalonde, *Determining Boundaries in a Conflicted World: The Role of Uti Possidetis* (Montreal: McGill-Queen's University Press, 2002).

16 For the context of the Cairo Conference, see C. J. Lee (ed.), *Making a World After Empire: The Bandung Movement and its Political Afterlives* (Athens, OH: Ohio University Press, 2010).

17 Most recently by the Badinter Arbitration Committee, established to arbitrate between the different Yugoslav Republics, but which deliberated on the eventual dissolution of the state. See generally S. Terett, *The Dissolution of Yugoslavia and the Badinter Arbitration Commission* (Dartmouth: Ashgate 2000); P. Radan, 'Secession and Self-Determination: The Case of Slovenia and Croatia' 48 *Australian Journal of International Law* (1994) 183; P. Radan, 'Post-Succession International Orders: A Critical Analysis of the Workings of the Badinter Commission' 24 *Melbourne University Law Review* (2000) 50.

18 T. M. Franck, 'Clan and Super Clan: Loyalty, Identity and Community in Law and Practice' 90(3) *American Journal of International Law* 359 (1996).

19 See the section on the *inviolability of frontiers* II(i).

territory from making cessions which may be intended to fix better their limits or frontiers.[20]

(2) One hundred years later, meeting in July 1964 against the context of wider discussions concerning African decolonization and its future, the newly formed *Organisation of African Unity*, at its First Ordinary Session, passed a resolution that stated, among other elements:

> *Considering* that border problems constitute a grave and permanent factor of dissention;
>
> *Conscious* of the existence of extra-African manoeuvres aimed at dividing African States;
>
> *Considering* further that the borders of African States, on the day of their independence, constitute a tangible reality;
>
> ...
>
> 1. SOLEMNLY REAFFIRMS the strict respect by all Member States of the Organization for the principles laid down in paragraph 3 of Article III of the Charter of the Organization of African Unity;
>
> 2. SOLEMNLY DECLARES that all Member States pledge themselves to respect the borders existing on their achievement of national independence.[21]

(3) Dispatched by the *European Commission* to Yugoslavia with the threat of dissolution and session of that State, the *Badinter Commission*, set out Opinion No. 2 in 1992 that reaffirmed:

> The Committee considers that, whatever the circumstances, the right to self-determination must not involve changes to existing frontiers at the time of independence (*uti possidetis juris*) except where the states concerned agree otherwise.[22]

20 As narrated by Alvarez in discussing Article 9 of the *Union and Defensive Alliance Pact of 23rd January 1865*, which was drafted at the Pan-American Conference in Lima on 15 November 1864. See A. Alvarez, 'Latin American and International Law' 3 *American Journal of International Law* (1909) 286.

21 *Organization of the Heads of African States*, AHG/Res.17(I) passed Cairo, July 1964. Full text at: http://www.au.int/en/sites/default/files/ASSEMBLY_EN_17_21_JULY_1964_ASSEMBLY_HEADS_STATE_GOVERNMENT_FIRST_ORDINARY_SESSION.pdf. Also see S. Touval, *The Boundary Politics of Independent Africa* (Cambridge, MA: Harvard University Press, 1972) 88–89.

22 Opinion No. 2, Badinter Commission, see Allain Pellet, 'The Opinions of the Badinter Arbitration Committee: A Second Breath for the Self-Determination of Peoples' 3(1) *European Journal of International Law* (1992) 178–185 at 184.

Irrespective of the injustice with how frontiers were constructed, the legitimacy of these inherited boundaries was guaranteed by statements such as the three discussed above. Yet in many circumstances, the proof of whether they would stabilize boundaries depended on the depth of historical feelings of shared nationhood and the behaviour of the post-colonial State in formulating its national identity and then guaranteeing meaningful equality to the communities or nations that became constituents of the territorial State. The eight decades of post-colonial experience reveal evidence of schisms as well as accommodation. It is worth focusing briefly on a few regions to demonstrate.

In Latin America, where decolonization occurred between 1810 and 1825 along lines drawn under Spanish ecclesiastical law, the inherited boundaries made little sense, not least because there was no attempt to gauge the subjecthood, consent, or ethnographic conception of indigenous nations.[23] Instead, use of the doctrine of *uti possidetis* legitimized *de facto* boundaries as *de jure* parcelling out possession of territories and ignoring ancestral domains – problems that remain central today. States emerged from colonization using the concept of self-determination without irony. They reiterated that the principle of *terra nullius* no longer applied to the entirety of the Americas, making strong statements to this effect at the early *Pan American Congresses* at the dawn of the twentieth century.[24] While this aimed to safeguard against European *Reconquista*, it re-emphasized the lack of legal personality for indigenous peoples, especially non-contact tribes, who were deemed not to engage in 'title generating activities' according to legal canons of others. The emerging States maintained claims against each other, many that dominate the docket of the *International Court of Justice* throughout its existence.

The other equally problematic region for the lack of coherence of boundaries is in West Africa. In a famous statement in 1890, Lord Salisbury stated in the British House of Lords:

> We [the white man] have been engaged in drawing lines upon maps where no white man's foot has ever trod; we have been giving away mountains and rivers and lakes to each other, only hindered by the small impediment that we never knew exactly where the mountains and rivers and lakes were.[25]

The impact of boundaries in West Africa is startling. They divide nations while forcing antagonistic communities together. The doctrine of *uti possidetis* was

23 C. Doyle, *Indigenous Peoples Title to Territory and Resources: The Transformative Role of Free Prior & Informed Consent* (New York & Oxon: Routledge, 2015) 11–70.

24 Alvarez (1909) *op.cit.* 403, 19.

25 Lord Salisbury, 1890, quoted by Judge Ajibola, in *Territorial Dispute (Libya v Chad)* ICJ Reports (1994) 6, 53.

applied here too, to ensure transition. As with the *Pan American Congress* statements, continent-wide support for *uti possidetis* can be evidenced, as captured in the *Cairo Resolution* quoted above. The States nonetheless maintained claims against each other and in West Africa, nearly every State has raised boundary issues for legal adjudication before the ICJ. Eight of 15 states that form the Economic Community of West African States (ECOWAS) have submitted territorial disputes for international adjudication in the last three decades: Benin, Burkina Faso, Guinea, Guinea-Bissau, Mali, Niger, Nigeria, and Senegal. This also spreads to the Maghreb. If the Western Sahara disputes, those between Chad and Libya and between Libya and Tunisia, are added, it leaves Algeria, with major territorial claims against its Moroccan border, as the only State in the wider region that has not been involved in a territorial dispute submitted to international adjudication, though it maintains such claims.[26]

The next two most contentious areas for land boundaries are the Middle East and the Caucasus. Middle Eastern boundary issues are dominated by the previously discussed *Sykes–Picot Agreement,* which divided Ottoman Empire lands between Britain and France.[27] The value of commercial interests peaked with the discovery of oil in the region and meant that rather than decolonization, the governance of the region was carefully handed over to proxy rulers who maintained Western hegemonic interests, most visibly in the Gulf States, and only recently challenged in the Levant. Unlike in Africa, where Pan-Africanism was mooted as an idea but failed, in the Middle East, the idea of an Arab consciousness subsumed the transition debate,[28] and while a form of independence arrived, it was restricted to pre-drawn boundaries ruled by regimes favourable to the *status quo*.[29] The lack of debate concerning boundaries in the national and international space allowed tensions to fester, and wider socio-economic failures and growth in inequality as captured in the famous *Arab Spring* saw this expressed in the most despicable manner through the activities of *Daesh*. It could be argued that the growth of this force and its ability to mobilize transnational support through messaging about injustices – real and perceived – directed mainly at frustrated men within the Muslim community may be a consequence of not creating adequate fora where injustice could be tackled fairly through the force of argument rather than the argument of force. This type of mobilization has

26 F. E. Trout, 'Morocco's Boundary in the Guir-Zousfana River Basin' 3(1) *African Historical Studies* (1970) 37–56.

27 See W. Laquer & B. Rubin, *The Israel-Arab Reader: A Documentary History of the Middle East Conflict*, 4TH ED. (New York: Facts on File, 1984) 12–14.

28 See G. Antonious, *The Arab Awakening* (London: Simon Publications, 1938).

29 O. Bengio & G. Ben-Dor, *Minorities and the State in the Arab World* (London: Lynne Rienner, 1999). Also see G. Biger, *The Boundaries of Modern Palestine 1840–1947* (London: Routledge, 2004).

become a blueprint and is currently fragmenting societies through the targeting of frustrated Christian men by far-right movements in OECD countries and Hindu men in India and among the Indian diaspora. It emphasizes the role gender rather than religion plays as a driver of violence perpetrated in the misdirected name of combating injustice. Rather than listening, the world's foreign policies in the Middle East and elsewhere remain motivated by demonstrably futile attempts in using overwhelming force to maintain order.[30]

Questions concerning identity are also alive in the Caucasus, where the Soviet regime drew boundaries calculated to maintain Russian prominence in the nations that constituted the USSR from Stalin's reign in 1930 onwards.[31] While the break-up of the Soviet Union was met with fanfare, the fate of Russian-speaking populations was abandoned to the exigencies of each State within which they found themselves. In the immediate aftermath of the transition, Russia was beset by structural and financial problems that persist under authoritarian leadership. The spread of EU influence and the extension of NATO membership eastward were mobilized as a new threat, which was reimagined through messaging directed at Russian-speaking populations within many of the new States. Russian invasions of South Ossetia and Crimea did not warrant significant attention, nor did Russia's effective control over Donetsk and Luhansk. Yet many were then horrified by the wholesale invasion of Ukraine by Russia. As in Latin America and West Africa, the boundary disputes that exist on the fringes of the former Soviet empire are acute but seem further away from resolution through an international forum.

The last region to merit focus is the question of maritime boundaries in the South China Sea. While land disputes in Southeast Asia are less likely than in other parts of the world, partly due to geography and the existence of many littoral States, the dispute over maritime boundaries has been heating up as China first stridently asserted its sovereignty,[32] and then commenced to spread its influence in gaining preferential access to trade routes through the Belt element of the *One Belt One Road* policy. This global region is perhaps the least likely to engage in international adjudication, yet two cases emerged for international adjudication seeking resolution to contestations over islands and maritime boundaries between Indonesia, Malaysia, and

30 J. Castellino & K. A. Cavanaugh, 'Transformations in the Middle East: The Importance of the Minority Question' in *Multiculturalism and Minority Rights in the Arab World* [Will Kymlicka and Eva Pfostl eds.] (Oxford: Oxford University Press, 2014) 53–73.

31 See V. Cheterian, *War and Peace in the Caucasus: Russia's Troubled Frontier* (London: Hurst, 2008).

32 E. Franckx, 'Dots and Lines in the South China Sea: Insights from the Lap of Map Evidence' 2 *Asian Journal of International Law* 89–118 (2012); S. Yee, 'The South China Sea Arbitration (Philippines v China): Potential Jurisdictional Obstacles and Objections' 13(4) *Chinese Journal of International Law* (2014) 663–739.

Singapore.[33] The looming questions concerning China's claim over the South China Sea will likely emerge with greater force or will be submerged by vastly differential power imbalances between the contestants.[34] It remains early to predict whether these disputes would seek full international adjudication, but it could be argued that the use of the International Court of Justice or the Permanent Court of Arbitration ought to be welcomed over other solutions.

The Adjudication of Disputes: The Rules of the Game Thus Far

The current international boundary regime consists of rules, principles, and norms that international politics and courts of law have relied upon in negotiating and adjudicating territorial disputes. This section briefly discusses these, explaining their rationale while highlighting where such rules may need reframing. This section ends by highlighting the need for greater support for non-legal considerations under the principle of *equity infra legem*.[35] The central argument advanced is that the default position in the settlement of territorial disputes has adhered to rules reified by the Court, but the quest for perpetual peace instead requires greater engagement with parties in advance of the development of the dispute, to enable specific consideration of solutions *ex aequo et bono*. This would improve the quality and longevity of settlements on the basis of equity.

The rules governing the settlement of international disputes are discussed extensively in the annals of public international law. This section intends to summarize the most pertinent ones germane to the title to territory.

Inviolability and Intangibility of Frontiers with Consent Required for Change

This rule is the bedrock on which the international society of States rests. It ignores questions concerning the 'quality' or 'legitimacy' of frontiers, opting for a blanket approach of preventing frontier change without State party consent. While the rule has been broken regularly and comes under persistent pressure in border regions, these threats are considered rule violations rather than challenges to the rule or indicators of the emergence of a new rule. The inviolability of frontiers remains fundamental to maintaining peace

33 *Sovereignty over Pulau Ligitan and Pulau Sipadan* (Indonesia v. Malaysia), *ICJ Reports*, 2001, 575, 682 (October 23).

34 International Relations scholars in particular will note the similarity of this situation to the famous *Melian Dialogue* captured in Thucydides.

35 For a relatively detailed judicial opinion, see Judge C. G. Weeramantry in *Case Concerning Maritime Delimitation in the Area between Greenland and Jan Mayen* (Denmark v Norway) Judgment of 14 June 1983, *ICJ Reports* (1983).

and security since it is the basis of State sovereignty and exclusive jurisdiction within a defined territory. When followed strictly, it channels all frontier disputes to interstate discussions.

One fundamental difficulty that remains is the extent of the globe's undelimited political frontiers. In many cases, frontier demarcations are based on erroneous, misleading, or even fraudulent cartographic information.[36] Even in such cases, the application of the principle requires parties to engage in direct dialogue or other pacific settlements, including through more accurate delimitation. The requirement for State consent for change remains a fundamental general principle of public international law.

Uti possidetis juris *and* Terra Nullius

To identify territory as falling within the boundaries of a (usually post-colonial) State, international law uses the 'sword and shield' doctrinal tools of *uti possidetis juris* and its older companion principle, *terra nullius*.[37] Despite its Roman law origins,[38] restatements of *uti possidetis juris* perpetuate its salience, underpinning its legitimacy in the international laws governing territory.[39] The doctrine guarantees the territorial rights of existing stakeholders[40] and posits 'that new States will come to independence with the same boundaries that they had when they were administrative units within the territory or territories of one colonial power'.[41] The need for order is its central aim, especially during transitions where the fear of chaos and insurgence was uppermost in new sovereigns' minds.[42] Derived from the Roman law norm of *uti possidetis ita possidetis*,[43] the doctrine translates, 'as you possess, so you

36 *Case Concerning the Temple of Prear Vihear* (Cambodia v Thailand) *ICJ Reports* (1962).

37 Joshua Castellino, 'Territorial Integrity and the Right to Self-Determination: An Examination of the Conceptual Tools' 33(2) *Brooklyn Journal of International Law* (2008) 503.

38 See generally Jolowicz & Nicolas (1972) *op.cit.* 5, 259–263.

39 Pellet (1998) *op.cit.* 22; Radan (2000) *op.cit.* 17; M. C. R. Craven, 'The European Community Arbitration Commission on Yugoslavia' 66 *British Yearbook of International Law* (1995) 333; M. Weller, 'The International Response to the Dissolution of the Socialist Federal Republic of Yugoslavia' 86 *American Journal of International Law* (1992) 569. For a range of cases in which the ICJ has considered the doctrine of *utipossidetisjuris* see Castellino (2008) *op.cit.* 37 at n.34

40 See generally K. H. Kaikobad, 'Some Observations on the Doctrine of Continuity and Finality of Boundaries' 49 *British Yearbook of International Law* (1983) 126–127; S. R. Ratner, 'Drawing a Better Line: Uti Possidetis and the Borders of New States' 90 *American Journal of International Law* (1996) 590.

41 M. N. Shaw, 'The Heritage of States: The Principle of Uti Possidetis Juris Today' 67 *British Yearbook of International Law* (1996) 97–101 (1996).

42 See generally *Order & Justice in International Relations* [R. Foot, J. L. Gaddis & A .Hurrell eds.] (Oxford: Oxford University Press, 2003).

43 See Muirhead (1916), *op.cit.* 89–212.

possess'.[44] This possessory interdict enabled a Roman *praetor* to prevent the 'disturbance of the existing state of possession of immovables, between two individuals',[45] by awarding possession to the incumbent unless the claimant could establish better grounds,[46] thereby maintaining order.[47] Unlike in international law, the original possessory interdict required the possession to have been acquired *nec vi, nec clam, necprecario*, i.e. without force, secrecy, or permission.[48] In its use to deflect conflict at a time of transition, the repurposing of the doctrine in international law ignored the requirement over the original conditions of how possession was acquired. In its contemporary interpretation, the need to determine how the territory was acquired continues to be ignored; instead, the doctrine is simply used to justify the permanent *status quo*. It also establishes a test for 'possession' that is not used in equal measure to apply to indigenous peoples' relationship with their ancestral domains.

'Snapshot' or 'Critical Date'

Critical date has become a central feature in territorial disputes between States,[49] with its interpretation following the reasoning articulated by Judge Huber in the *Island of Palmas (or Miangas) (United States v. Netherlands)*:[50]

> If a dispute arises as to the sovereignty over a portion of territory, it is customary to examine which of the States claiming sovereignty possesses a title—cession, conquest, occupation, etc.—superior to that which the other State might possibly bring forward against it. However, if the contestation is based on the fact that the other Party has actually displayed sovereignty, it cannot be sufficient to establish the title by which territorial sovereignty was validly acquired at a certain moment; it must also be shown that the territorial sovereignty has continued to exist and did exist

44 J. Castellino & S. Allen, 'The Doctrine of *UtiPossidetis:* Crystallisation of Modern Post-Colonial Identity' 43 *German Yearbook of International Law* (2000) 205.

45 J. B. Moore, 'Memorandum on *UtiPossidetis*: Costa Rica-Panama Arbitration 1913' in *The Collected Works of John Bassett Moore* (Oxford: Oxford University Press, 1944) 328.

46 *Ibid.*

47 In the late Republic, the *Praetor Urbanus* was responsible for the administration of *jus civile*, and the *Praetor Peregrinus* held the same position with regard to *jus gentium*. See Muirhead (1916), *op.cit.* 43, 219.

48 Jolowicz (1972), *op.cit.* 5 at 259 n.2.

49 For an early articulation of this principle, see L. F. E. Goldie, 'The Critical Date' 12 *International & Comparative Law Quarterly* (1963) 1251. For a recent articulation by the ICJ, see *Frontier Dispute* (Burkina Faso v. Mali), *ICJ Reports* (1996) 554, 586–587.

50 *Island of Palmas* (or Miangas) (U.S. v. Neth.), 2 R. Int'l Arb. Awards 829 (Perm. Ct. Arb. 1928).

> at the moment which for the decision of the dispute must be considered as critical.[51]

Read in conjunction with the critical date – usually the departure of the colonial ruler – the *de jure* title to territory was simply handed over to new incumbents based on administrative lines drawn by departing colonial regimes. The new ruler was deemed, from this point on, as exercising sovereignty over the territory as a successor State, with aspirant's claims to sovereignty dismissed as disruptive of the peace.[52] Thus, the critical date, usually an arbitrary moment of colonial departure, is the determining factor in determining the territorial dimension of the modern State[53] even though the emerging State's territory may have been unified by a colonial power through belligerent use of force for a limited period of time.[54] No flexibility is extended to readings of the critical date: if challenged, there would be disagreements as to the importance of particular events, dates, and ultimately the fate of the territory.[55] Permitting challenges to the critical date is considered dangerous to the peace, risking opening a continuously available process, defeating the quest for order. As a result, the most significant ramification for the future of a territory is the snapshot[56] of that territory on the critical date. The doctrine of the critical date determines the fate of a territory on the basis of a singular moment that becomes all-encompassing in terms of its future.

51 *Id.* at 839. See also *Legal Status of the South-Eastern Territory of Greenland Case* (Nor. v. Den.), 1932 P.C.I.J. (ser. A/B) No. 53 (Aug. 3) (an early interpretation illustrating the ICJ's subsequent articulation of the idea).

52 Castellino & Allen (2003), *op.cit.* 4, at 10.

53 N. S. Marques Antunes, 'The *Eritrea-Yemen* Arbitration: First Stage – The Law of Title to Territory Re-Averred' 48 *International & Comparative Law Quarterly* (1999) 362, 363–365.

54 Western Sahara, Advisory Opinion, *ICJ Reports* 1975, 45 (October 16). Also see J. Castellino, 'National Identity & the International Law of Self-Determination: The Stratification of the Western Saharan 'Self'' in *Accommodating National Identity: New Approaches in International and Domestic Law* [S. Tierney ed.] (The Hague: Kluwer, 2000) 257, 270–281.

55 KA Cavanaugh, 'Rewriting Law: The Case of Israel and the Occupied Territories' in *New Laws, New Wars? Applying the Laws of War in 21st Century Conflicts* [D. Wippman & M. Evangelista eds.] (Leiden: Brill, 2005) 227.

56 *Frontier Dispute* (Burk. Faso v. Mali), *ICJ Reports* (1986) 554, 658. The judgment explains: *[U]tipossidetis* applies to the new State (as a State) not with retroactive effect, but immediately and from that moment onwards. It applies to the State as it is; i.e. to the 'photograph' of the territorial situation then existing. The principle of *utipossidetis* freezes the territorial title; it stops the clock, but does not put back the hands.

Applicable Evidence, Including Reliance on Maps Drawn by Colonial Treaty Law

The ICJ has been reluctant to accept the strength of maps as evidence of territorial claims. In *Territorial & Maritime Dispute between Nicaragua and Honduras in the Caribbean Sea*,[57] the ICJ cited prior arbitration cases, namely *Island of Palmas (or Miangas) (United States v. Netherlands)*[58] and *Arbitral Award of the Special Boundary Panel Determining the Frontier between Guatemala and Honduras*.[59] In the former, the Permanent Court of Arbitration stressed that '[a]ny maps which do not precisely indicate the political distribution of territories ... clearly marked as such, must be rejected forthwith'.[60] In the latter, the PCIJ found that maps presented by the parties provided only 'slight value', since they did not show the extent to which administrative control was actually exercised.[61] The value of maps was also addressed by the ICJ in *Frontier Dispute (Burkina Faso v. Mali)*.[62] In *Nicaragua v. Honduras* cited above, the presentation of maps was merely seen as

> [E]ssentially serv[ing] the purpose of buttressing their respective claims and of confirming their arguments. The Court finds that it can derive little of legal significance from the official maps submitted and the maps of geographical institutions cited; these maps will be treated with a certain reserve.[63]

The problematic nature of cartography as a mainly colonial enterprise does not feature significantly in arguments used in international law. Yet relief maps, as an imprint of a territorial footprint, could only be indicative of the

57 *Territorial and Maritime Dispute between Nicaragua and Honduras in the Caribbean Sea* (Nicaragua v. Honduras), *ICJ Reports* (2007).

58 *Island of Palmas (or Miangas)* (USA v. Netherlands), 2 R. Int'l Arb. Awards 829 (Perm. Ct. Arb. 1928).

59 *Honduras Borders* (Guatemala v. Honduras), 2 R. Int'l Arb. Awards 1309, 1322 (Special Boundary Tribunal constituted by the Treaty of Arbitration between Guatemala and Honduras 1933).

60 *Island of Palmas (or Miangas)* (USA v. Netherlands), 2 R. Int'l Arb. Awards at 852.

61 *Honduras Borders*, 2 R. Int'l Arb. Awards at 1325 ('[A]uthenticated maps...are also to be considered, although such descriptive material is of slight value when it relates to territory of which little or nothing was known and in which it does not appear that any administrative control was actually exercised'.)

62 See *Frontier Dispute* (Burkina Faso v. Mali) *ICJ Reports* (1986) 554, 582 (December 22). Maps were considered in and of themselves indeterminate in constituting territorial title, or 'document[s] endowed by international law with intrinsic legal force for the purpose of establishing territorial rights'.

63 *Territorial and Maritime Dispute between Nicaragua and Honduras in the Caribbean Sea* (Nicaragua v. Honduras) *ICJ Reports* (2007) para. 217.

ebbs and flows of population. This theme is further developed in the last part of this book.

Importance of Effective Control, Ccolonial Effectivitiés (droit d'outre-mer) *and Applicable Law*

The issue of effective control within territorial boundaries receives scant attention with a tendency towards the simple assumption that the colonial power *must have* exercised effective control through a regime of colonial law. In *Nicaragua & Honduras* a distinction is attempted to determine what behaviour of a colonial power could give rise to *colonial effectivités*. The judgment states:

> [A]cts performed *à titre de souverain* which are in principle relevant for the purpose of assessing and validating *effectivités*, and those acts occurring after such critical date, which are in general meaningless for that purpose, having been carried out by a State which, already having claims to assert in a legal dispute, could have taken those actions strictly with the aim of buttressing those claims.[64]

It suggests that the new sovereign's acts post-critical date are not relevant in assessing the value of *effectivités*, which reveals the overarching value attributed to colonial rule over other demonstrations of sovereignty.[65] In *Territorial & Maritime Dispute between Nicaragua and Honduras in the Caribbean Sea*, the disputants contested two legal issues concerning *uti possidetis juris*: (1) the extent to which the judicially -determined line extended to the maritime areas and the disputed islands;[66] and (2) the extent to which documentary evidence established the extent of the local authorities' control.[67] Nicaragua argued that the Spanish authorities had exclusive jurisdiction over the territorial sea, and therefore the sea could not be included in the local authorities' justifiable claims under the doctrine of *uti possidetis juris*.[68] While the ICJ regarded the *uti possidetis juris* line as germane to territorial title and boundary delimitation at the moment of decolonization,[69] regardless

64 *See Territorial and Maritime Dispute between Nicaragua and Honduras in the Caribbean Sea* (Nicaragua v. Honduras), *ICJ Reports* (2007) para. 117.

65 *See also* Sovereignty over Pulau Ligitan and Pulau Sipadan (*Indonesia v. Malaysia*), *ICJ Reports* (2001) 575, 682.

66 See *Arbitral Award Made by the King of Spain on 23 December 1906* (*Honduras v. Nicaragua*), *ICJ Reports* (1960) 192, 199–200.

67 Territorial and Maritime Dispute between Nicaragua and Honduras in the Caribbean Sea (*Nicaragua v. Honduras*) *ICJ Reports* (2007) 150.

68 *Ibid.*

69 *Ibid.* para. 151.

of whether the boundaries were on land or sea,[70] the Court found it difficult to see how *uti possidetis juris* could be used to determine sovereignty over the islands.[71] Articulating an important linkage between *terra nullius*, *uti possidetis juris*, and effective control, the Court stated:

> It is well established that 'a key aspect of the principle [of *utipossidetis-juris*] is the denial of the possibility of terra nullius'. However, that dictum cannot bring within the territory of successor States islands not shown to be subject to Spanish colonial rule, nor *ipso facto* render as 'attributed', islands which have no connection with the mainland coast concerned. Even if both Parties in this case agree that there is no question of the islands concerned being *res nullius*, necessary legal questions remain to be answered.[72]

The ruling echoed the judgment in the *Land, Island, and Maritime Frontier Dispute (El Salvador/ Honduras: Nicaragua intervening)* case, where similar difficulties were faced in attributing non-allocated islands to competing administrations.[73] The Court stressed:

> [W]hen the principle of *uti possidetis juris* is involved, the *jus* referred to is not international law but the constitutional or administrative law of the pre-independence sovereign, in this case Spanish colonial law; and it is perfectly possible that that law itself gave no clear and definitive answers to the appurtenance of marginal areas, or sparsely populated areas of minimal economic significance.[74]

The *uti possidetis juris* line has limited value in such circumstances, raising fundamental questions about the nature of *colonial effectivités* and the extent to which it generated title-claiming activities. At face value, *colonial effectivités* consist of 'the conduct of the administrative authorities as proof of the effective exercise of territorial jurisdiction in the region during the colonial period'.[75]

Pleadings in cases concerning title to territory devote significant attention to establishing evidence of effective control over a particular territory, claiming that this control justifies the claimed territory as part of a unified whole

70 *Ibid.* para. 156.
71 *Ibid.* para. 158.
72 *See Territorial and Maritime Dispute between Nicaragua and Honduras in the Caribbean Sea* (Nicaragua v. Honduras), *ICJ Reports* (2007) 157.
73 *Land, Island and Maritime Frontier Dispute* (El Salvador v. Honduras: Nicaragua intervening) *ICJ Reports* (1992) 351, 558–559.
74 *Ibid.* at 559.
75 *Frontier Dispute* (Burk. Faso v. Mali), *ICJ Reports* (1986) 554, 586.

with the rest of the State's territory.[76] In its determination the Court is forced to scrutinize evidence indicating the right or practice that generates territorial title,[77] often relying on the quality of the presentation of evidence to determine its historical veracity.[78] In *Western Sahara*,[79] Morocco and Mauritania produced evidence supporting their effective control:[80] Morocco as successor to the Sherifian State;[81] Mauritania via a network of allegiances identified as part of the *Bilad Shinguitti*, precursor to modern Mauritania.[82] The appointment of representative *sheikhs* by Sherifian Imperial cities was deemed evidence of effective control, while Mauritania countered with the articulation of a system of customary laws that governed the use of watering holes and transitory passages through the desert as equally compelling evidence of such control.

In *Frontier Dispute (Burkina Faso v. Mali)*, the Court identified *colonial effectivités* as 'the conduct of the administrative authorities as proof of the effective exercise of territorial jurisdiction in the region during the colonial period'.[83] Such *colonial effectivités* fulfils limited conditions of effective administration over a territory, which is extrapolated to emphasize title to territory under colonial law. In *Kasikili/Sedudu Island (Botswana v. Namibia)*, the parties relied on a document showing 'evidence' of an administrative agreement between the colonial authorities in charge of the Caprivi strip (precursor to modern Namibia) and the authorities in Bechunaland.[84] However, the document was not accepted as evidence of the adequate exercise of *colonial effectivités* over the territory,[85] and correspondingly the sovereignty claim was rejected.[86]

76 *Ibid.* 119–155.

77 *See* Land, Island and Maritime Frontier Dispute (*El Salvador v. Honduras*: Nicaragua intervening), *ICJ Reports* (1992) 351, 363–364; *Frontier Dispute* (*Burkina Faso v. Mali*), *ICJ Reports* (1986) 554, 568, 582; *Sovereignty over Certain Frontier Land* (*Belgium v. Netherlands*), *ICJ Reports* (1959) 218.

78 See, e.g., *Territorial Dispute* (*Libya v. Chad*), *ICJ* Reports (1994) 16; Frontier Dispute (*Burkina Faso v. Mali*), *ICJ Reports* (1986) 620–624.

79 *ICJ Reports* (1975) 12.

80 *Ibid.* 14.

81 *Ibid.* 40.

82 *Ibid.* 41.

83 *Ibid.* 586.

84 *Kasikili/Sedudu Island* (*Botswana v. Namibia*), *ICJ Reports* (1999) 1045, 1058. The ICJ emphasized the presence and activities of the Masubian people and their title-generating capacities. *See id.* at 1045, 1093.

85 *Ibid.* 1100.

86 *Ibid.* 1103–1105.

The Principle of Equity Infra Legem *and Reluctance towards* Ex Aequo et Bono

Article 38(2) of the statute of the ICJ states clearly:

> This provision [outlining the sources of law in article 38(1)] shall not prejudice the power of the Court to decide a case *ex aequo et bono*, if the parties agree thereto.

There is considerable judicial restraint in exploring the use of equity under the law (*equity infra legem*) and making of decisions according to what may be right and good (*ex aequo et bono*). Strict legal training around the world, especially in systems influenced by European law, instils deep loyalty to the written law, accompanied by institutional suspicion of these principles as highly subjective. Parties remain reluctant to make the request indicated above, and Article 38(2) remains mostly untriggered. Judicial benches repeatedly express reservations towards its use, best captured in Judge Weeramantry's Opinion in *Maritime Delimitation*:

> the heavy overtones of equity's corrective influence over law tend to spill over into international law, necessitating a constant vigilance against this tendency.[87]

Even in maritime delimitation cases where equity and use of equitable principles are more widely accepted, a distinction is made that such equity not be applied *ex aequo et bono*.[88] Instead, the insistence is that the rule of *equity infra legem* (fairness as determined within the law) carries the day. As leading ICJ commentator Rosenne states:

> It [the Court] has permitted the first steps to be taken towards creating a conception of international equity, not *contra legem* in the sense that it is sometimes said that a decision *ex aequo et bono* may be a decision *contra legem*; but *intra legem*, it being the substantive law, and not the agreement of parties, that calls for its application.[89]

The fear of overstepping its mandate and acting like a Roman Praetor in adjudicating disputes in *jus civile* appears to drive the Court's conservatism

87 *ICJ Reports* (1983) 191.

88 Judge Weeramantry cites the following support: *ICJ Reports* (1974), paras. 78, 69; *ICJ Reports* (1982), paras. 71, 133; *ICJ Reports* (1984), paras. 59, 112; *ICJ Reports* (1985), paras. 45, 56–57.

89 S. Rosenne, *The Law and Practice of the International Court*, Vol. II (Leyden: A. W. Sijthoff, 1965) 605.

with regard to making determinations based on equity.[90] Such decisions would only be possible with prior consent from parties. The room for equity has solidified more in cases concerning maritime delimitation where 'a degree of clarity and predictability' has emerged for its recognition as a 'fundamental norm operating within, and not outside, the law'.[91]

Equity does not feature among the nine factors Summers identified as relevant in adjudicating territorial claims. These were treaty law, geography, economy, culture, effective control, history, *uti possidetis juris*, elitism, and ideology.[92] Unsurprisingly, his jurisprudential study confirmed a greater emphasis on treaty law, *uti possidetis* and effective control. After all, treaty law determines the *uti possidetis* line, with effective control becoming the test through which the emerging post-colonial State spreads its territorial wings in transforming its inherited *de jure* situation into *de facto* reality. The three factors are thus locked in a symbiotic relationship which ultimately reinforces (mostly colonial) treaty law.

A moderated approach could consider *uti possidetis* and treaty law as starting points, establishing the colonial photograph of the territory, to use Judge Ajibola's words in Burkina Faso Mali, which, other things being equal, ought to be maintained. The Court could, however, go further taking an *ex aequo et bono* approach that heeds culture, history, economy, and prospects for cross-border cooperation to arrive at an equitable solution. Such an approach featured in *Qatar Bahrain* and equitable principles were also applied in a disguised fashion in *Frontier Dispute* between Burkina Faso and Mali, and in *Land, Island & Maritime Frontier Dispute* (*El Salvador v Honduras with Nicaragua intervening*). In the former the decision to divide the territory equitably was justified on the principle of *infra legem*,[93] and in the latter equity was applied *infra legem* (though equitable claims were rejected) when no other factors would assist a full legal determination.[94]

90 For more, see V. Lowe, 'The Role of Equity in International Law' 12 *Australian Yearbook of International Law* (1988–1989) 58–63.

91 B. Kwiatkowska, 'The International Court of Justice Doctrine of Equitable Principles Applicable to Maritime Delimitation and Its Impact on the International Law of the Sea' in *Forty Years International Court of Justice: Jurisdiction, Equity and Equality* [A. Bloed & P. van Dijk eds.] (Utrecht: Europa Institute, 1988) 158.

92 B. T. Sumner, 'Note: Territorial Disputes at the International Court of Justice' 53 *Duke Law Journal* (2004) 1779–1812.

93 *ICJ Reports* (1986) 570.

94 *ICJ Reports* (1992) 351, 356.

Defeating Arguments of Force, Harnessing Force of Arguments: Forum Conveniens?

One question at the heart of the future settlement of disputes is whether these are best regulated through politics or law. A caricature demonstration could portray *politics* on the basis of the ability to explore and articulate claims based on national interest, even if subtly disguised, or on long-term visions for peace and stability, which may be motivated by moral considerations or a longer vision of national interest. By contrast, the *Law* could concern the use of arguments based on pre-agreed rules designed to guarantee order and justice, heard by an objective party familiar with existing rules, sympathetic to the quest for justice and reparation, with the aim of achieving peace and stability. Both seem valid routes to the same objective: the final determination of stable sovereign frontiers.[95] Others explore how effective political processes may or may not be in the settlement of territorial disputes. This section focuses on the use of rules described above and on legal or *quasi* legal processes and institutions.[96] To explore this thoroughly the section is further subdivided into two parts. The first explores the means available for the pacific settlement of (territorial) disputes highlighting strengths and weaknesses. This subsection advocates the use of international adjudication as a potentially useful though not exclusive means for dispute settlement.[97] The second subsection advocates for the ICJ as the least problematic of existing fora, justifying this on negative (towards other regimes) and positive (towards the ICJ) grounds.

Pacific Settlement of Disputes

Bilateral Negotiations

International law provides for frontiers to be altered through the consent of parties who seek such a renegotiation. The original purpose of *uti possidetis juris* as described above enabled recognition of *de facto status quo* until later points when parties could renegotiate the boundary based on factors other than *de facto* possession. It was always assumed that such negotiations

95 Law may contribute to creating disputes that may not arise otherwise, e.g. the creation of the Exclusive Economic Zoneand Continental Shelf for Islands was considered as such via Article 121 of UNCLOS, which generated disputes that may not have existed without the potential of claiming extra territory.

96 These arguments are explored in greater detail by B. Simmons, 'See You in Court? The Appeal to Quasi-Judicial Legal Processes in the Settlement of Territorial Disputes' in *A Road Map to War: Territorial Dimensions of International Conflict* [P. Diehl ed.] (Nashville, TN: Vanderbilt University Press, 1998) 205–237.

97 I. Brownlie, 'The Peaceful Settlement of International Disputes' 8(2) *Chinese Journal of International Law* (2009) 267.

would occur bilaterally between parties since there are no global governance institutions that could compel, though good offices of multilateral organizations and mediators could be used. The 100th anniversary of the *Åland Islands* dispute between Sweden and Finland suggests this as a model for how agreements could be negotiated, verified, and evaluated.[98] Yet this has proved extremely difficult in the post-colonial phase.[99] While new boundaries have been arrived at through bilateral discussions recently, with the *velvet divorce* between the Czech Republic and Slovak Republic as the most classical, such negotiations have, more often than not, stalled (e.g. Kashmir, Palestine, Tibet, Abkhazia, Nagorno Karabakh) or resulted in new boundaries formed after considerable violence (Eritrea, South Sudan, Timor Leste).

The inexhaustive list of places where boundaries remain uncertain is growing: Crimea, Dagestan, Chechnya, South Ossetia, Transdniester, Nagaland, and Somaliland. It is difficult to imagine how or why bilateral negotiations will have any greater impact in the next few decades than they have had in the previous few decades. While such negotiations would be needed at some stage in the process of agreeing on settled frontiers, bilateral negotiations themselves do not have enough of a track record of success to warrant a conviction in such processes yielding more certain boundaries in the future. Bilateral agreements would be scrutinized closely in national circles, with the incumbent government that presides over the loss of sovereignty becoming unpopular, leaving both parties locked into a *zero-sum* game.[100] Bilateral negotiations also leave little room for sub-state actors. In many circumstances the insistence on bilateral solutions to territorial disputes has been nothing more than a stalling tactic for states who appear keener to have a reason to agitate than a genuine desire to arrive at a settlement.

Facilitation through Other Dispute Settlement Mechanisms

Mediation, conciliation, and the use of good offices have traditionally been considered among the various means used in the settlement of disputes.[101] This facilitation is best understood as any means using traditional diplomatic

98 More details are available on the website of the Government of Finland at https://um.fi/the-special-status-of-the-aland-islands.

99 According to a survey covering close to 3,000 disputes, bilateral negotiations were attempted in half of these. See P. R. Hensel, 'Territory: Theory and Evidence on Geography and Conflict' in *What Do We Know About War?* [J. A. Vasquez ed.] (Boulder, CO: Rowman & Littlefield, 2000) 57–84.

100 See L. Broers, 'Unrecognized Reality' in *Armenia and Azerbaijan: Anatomy of a Rivalry* (Edinburgh 2019; online edition, 21 May 2020) available at https://doi.org/10.3366/edinburgh/9781474450522.003.0009 [accessed 19 December 2023].

101 [Editors], *Approaches to Solving Territorial Conflicts: Sources, Situations, Scenarios and Suggestions* (Atlanta, GA: Carter Centre, May 2010).

methods to solve disputes other than adjudication through arbitration or judicial settlement. Such processes traditionally involve a third party and may or may not involve processes recognizable as mediation, conciliation, or good offices, but would, in essence, reflect discussions held between parties and/or other interested stakeholders, including non-state actors, with a view to arriving at the settlement of the dispute.[102] Unlike arbitration and adjudication in law, considered below, the means used here would not bind the parties to a settlement.

Mediation usually refers to processes where a third party takes an active role in bringing parties towards an agreement in a dispute. For such a role to work, the mediator needs to be agreed to by both parties, as does the form in which the processes would transpire. The practice of mediation varies tremendously, as does the manner through which the final settlement is hoped to be arrived at. Such processes have been in train for long-running disputes, including the Israeli–Palestinian conflict,[103] the eventually unsuccessful attempt in Qatar–Bahrain[104] and the successful post-judgment mediation between Norway and Iceland.[105] All three vastly different experiences show that mediation could run parallel to other developments. They have not been particularly successful as a means to settle a territorial dispute, especially where the demarcation and delimitation of boundaries is involved.[106]

Conciliation is usually considered to differ from mediation in that the facilitator, a third party, would be expected to consult with the parties separately and make suggestions to each of them as to how their dispute may be resolved. Like in mediation any process of conciliation starts from the premise that both parties wish to submit to the process and that they consent to the third party involved. While such measures may be useful in resolving a range of disputes, the extent to which they can delimit a boundary or agree on a territorial demarcation absent other features is hard to envision. The proposals for solutions submitted as non-binding recommendations could be discarded by both parties or at the very least by the one that feels aggrieved by the process and proposal. Conciliation may be effective in setting baselines for

102 For an insider view, see M. I. Kamil, *The Camp David Accords: A Testimony* (London: KPI Publishers, 1986).

103 See, e.g., J. Rynhold, 'Realism, Liberalism and the Collapse of the Oslo Process: Inherently Flawed or Flawed Implementation?' in *The Failure of the Middle East Peace Process?* [G. Ben-Porat ed.] (London: Palgrave Macmillan, 2008).

104 I. Fraihat, 'Superpower and Small-State Mediation in the Qatar Gulf Crisis' 55 *The International Spectator: Italian Journal of International Affairs* (2020) 79–91.

105 K. Ervasti, 'Past, Present and Future of Mediation in Nordic Countries' in *Nordic Mediation Research* [A. Nylund, K. Ervasti, & L. Adrian eds.] (Cham: Springer, 2018) 105–133.

106 For an exploration of such mechanisms through the prisms of specific disputes, see K. E. Wiegand, *Enduring Territorial Disputes: Strategies of Bargaining, Coercive Diplomacy and Settlement* (Athens, GA: University of Georgia Press, 2011).

negotiation, but the failure to impute values to these discussions also means that subsequent state parties and governments could contradict the proposed solutions unless signed into binding agreements and given the nature of a legally enforceable contract.

There have been significant efforts by multilateral organizations or senior diplomats with an international mandate to undertake processes of facilitating dispute resolution. These are often referred to as the use of *good offices* and fall within the remit of bodies such as the United Nations. Perhaps the most evolved processes for the use of good offices under a multilateral organization exist under the *Organization for Security and Cooperation in Europe*. It offers all of the advantages and suffers all of the disadvantages of mediation and conciliation, though the higher profile of having the backing of a multilateral organization and a more formalized process may assist in the quality of the outcome and the ability to 'sell' proposed solutions within the domestic polity. The advantage of good offices, such as used by the OSCE in a mandate analogous to this topic (the *Office of the High Commissioner for National Minorities*), is that it provides legitimacy and voice to sub-state actors who may otherwise be ignored in such processes. While the OSCE has had success in seeking to dampen conflict and de-escalate tensions, its sidelining from the issue concerning Russia's invasion of Ukraine simultaneously highlights the limitations and weaknesses in multilateral involvement in dispute resolution as it overemphasizes the power attributed to powerful nuclear weapon–owning sovereign States.

Arbitration

Located in The Hague alongside the ICJ, the PCA essentially consists of membership of over 100 States with a list of arbitrators who could adjudicate intergovernmental disputes. Its mandate is derived from the 1899 and 1907 Hague Treaties.[107] The original vision for the two world courts was akin to the bifurcation in English common law between equity and formal law. Thus, while formal law required determination of legal disputes based on established law, equitable considerations are at the forefront of attempts to settle disputes at the PCA. As a consequence, the PCA has developed into an institution that addresses disputes through arbitration, through procedures that are flexible, assisted by optional rules that serve to guide adjudicators

107 *Convention for the Pacific Settlement of International Disputes* (First Hague I), signed on 29 July 1899, 26 Martens Nouveau Recueil (Ser. 2) 720, 32 Stat. 1779, T.S. No. 342, entered into force on 4 September 1900, and the *Convention for Pacific Settlement of International Disputes* (Second Hague Conference, I) signed on 18 October 1907, Martens Nouveau Recueil (3d) 360, 36 Stat. 2199, T.S. No. 536, entered into force on 26 January 2010.

and parties in disputes between States,[108] and disputes between State and non-State actors.[109] While relying on similar sources to the ICJ, the PCA's flexibility with regard to the designation of arbitrators and mutual involvement of the parties in shaping the dispute, combined with a 'service-oriented' ethos, has seen its caseload grow steadily over the years.[110] While the vast majority of disputes that have arisen before the PCA concern commercial matters, its adjudication in territorial dispute cases has been significant, if understated. The *Island of Palmas* decision is perhaps among the most cited in the area of territorial disputes, where the adjudicator Judge Huber ruled in favour of the Netherlands, paying significant attention to the effective control exercised rather than the position in law.[111] This case built on less cited precedents, in *Boundaries in the Island of Timor*, determined through the application of equity *infra legem* in allowing Portugal to retain the enclave of Oecussi-Ambeno while eliminating other enclaves.[112] These earlier precedents have also spurred recent awards in *Sovereignty over Certain Red Sea Islands* (Eritrea v Yemen);[113] in the decision to make the PCA a registry for the *Eritrea–Ethiopia Boundary Commission*,[114] and with the *Abyei Commission* tasked with delimiting the frontier between Sudan and South Sudan.[115] The difficulty of arriving at the *Abyei settlement* eloquently illustrates the challenges associated with the legal determination of boundaries where formal historical and geographical records may be scant or non-existent. While the

108 PCA, *Optional Rules for Arbitrating Disputes between Two States* (The Hague: n.d.) available at https://docs.pca-cpa.org/2016/01/Optional-Rules-for-Arbitrating-Disputes-between-Two-States_1992.pdf

109 PCA, *Optional Rules for Arbitrating Disputes between Two Parties Only One of Which is a State* (The Hague: n.d.) available at https://docs.pca-cpa.org/2016/01/Optional-Rules-for-Arbitrating-Disputes-between-Two-Parties-of-Which-Only-One-is-a-State-1993.pdf

110 T. Van den Hout, 'Resolution of International Disputes: The Role of the Permanent Court of Arbitration – Reflections on the Centenary of the 1907 Convention for the Pacific Settlement of International Disputes' 21 *Leiden Journal of International Law* (2008) 643–661.

111 *Island of Palmas Case*, Award of the Tribunal, 4 April 1928.

112 *Boundaries in the Island of Timor*, Award of the Tribunal, 24 June 1914.

113 *Sovereignty over Certain Red Sea Islands* (Eritrea v Yemen), Award of the Tribunal, 3 October 1996 (including jurisdiction question, adjudicated upon first).

114 *Delimitation of the Border* (Eritrea-Ethiopia), 13 April 2002–7 November 2002 UN Reports of International Arbitral Awards.

115 *In the Matter of an Arbitration before a Tribunal Constitutes in Accordance with Article 5 of the Arbitration between the Government of Sudan and the Sudan People's Liberation Movement/Army on Delimiting Abyei Area, and the Permanent Court of Arbitration Optional Rules for Arbitrating between Two Parties of Which Only One is a State, between the Government of Sudan and the Sudan People's Liberation Movement/Army, Final Award.* PCA, Registry, (The Hague, 22 July 2009) 270pp. Also see *Land Reclamation by Singapore in and round the Straits of Johor* (Malaysia v Singapore) Award on Agreed Terms, 1 September 2005.

settlement is a validation of the credentials of determining awards *ex aequo et bono*,[116] it is not clear if adequate attention was paid to the aspirations and perspectives of the residents of Abyei.[117]

There remain questions as to whether the PCA can play a bigger role in adjudicating territorial disputes. When viewed through the lens of the importance of the pacific settlement of disputes, it ought not to matter to the international community how territorial settlements have been arrived at as long as they have the consent of the implementing parties and go some way towards guaranteeing peace, security, and justice. However, two criticisms of the PCA make it less suitable in the settlement of territorial disputes. First, the issue of confidentiality; and second, the fact that no safeguards exist to address instances where the two claimants can agree to demarcate territories based on equitable principles between themselves without necessarily consulting other potentially interested stakeholders, especially sub-state entities. Briefly addressing each in turn will allow further elaboration. The awards of the PCA can remain confidential if the parties wish this. While this is in the spirit of seeking to arrive at solutions, it has the negative effect of resolving a dispute within its specific context and not contributing to the development of international law. While the role of the court is to arrive at a judgment in a given dispute, ideally its decision ought to also advance the codification of international law.

In the case of the ICJ, Article 59 of its statute emphasizes the restriction of its judgments to the context in which they have arisen, another feature that respects the sovereignty of States by not binding them to precedent set elsewhere in a different dispute. Yet it is clear that parties, Courts commentators, and others look to previous judgments for guidance, and while they may not form 'precedent' in the manner of common law, they remain persuasive arguments that have been relied upon and that contribute to the codification of international law. By exercising restraint on the publication of awards (in the case of territorial disputes, as with all other forms of disputes), the PCA sets back the codification of law governing territorial disputes and reduces legal certainty for the outcome of territorial disputes. Thus, while the rationale for the Court's approach to arbitrators as *amiables compositeurs* (acting according to general principles of fairness) is commendable, permitting arbitrators to determine disputes based on legal principles *they* believe to be just, while not being limited to jurisdictions or legal technicalities, is dangerous. The historical tendency for such arbitrators to come from backgrounds very similar to those discussed in the previous chapter heightens the risk for outcomes that could be deemed just by others. That the manoeuvrings would

116 [Editors], *Approaches to Solving Territorial Conflicts* (2010), *op. cit.* 35.

117 See M. Parish, *Mirages of International Justice: The Elusive Pursuit of Transnational Legal Order* (Cheltenham: Edward Elgar, 2011) 63.

remain beyond public scrutiny if the parties sign confidentiality agreements only enhances this danger, often making it difficult to 'sell' the decision to the public as a just outcome. This becomes egregious in light of the lack of adequate safeguards for all stakeholders.

The brief glance into the history of boundary lines as viewed in the previous chapter, in conjunction with the predicted rise in disputes governing territory, suggests that any approach that relies overtly on arbitration may enable States to settle disputes without recourse to communitarian considerations. For instance, a scenario could arise where a community divided by a colonial boundary, living as a minority in both countries, discovers a natural resource. Rather than engaging with the principle of free, prior, and informed consent, States could seek settlement of a dispute through the PCA, reiterating fault lines where some are treated as objects and not subjects of law. For these and other reasons, including cost-effectiveness and the standing and experience of the ICJ, addressed below, it would seem preferable over the PCA, while imbibing techniques that have enabled the PCA to impact the settlement of territorial disputes to date. This criticism would also apply to arbitral awards made outside the PCA framework, which has yielded influential but rarely studied awards such as *The Taba Arbitration*,[118] the *Rann of Kutch Dispute*, and the *Beagle Channel Cases*.[119] The cases commonly showed greater willingness to apply the principle of *ex aequo et bono* and equity *infra legem* as advocated above, a capacity that the ICJ has but is reluctant to use.[120]

More often than not, the resolution of boundary disputes needs a combination of the approaches outlined, with evidence that the judicious use of different tools for the pacific settlement of disputes at different times may yield stable longer term solutions. The *Brasilia Agreement* of 1998 which ended the entrenched conflict between Ecuador and Peru, for instance, included mediation, conciliation, good offices, and arbitration, finally yielding an agreement that could be upheld in law.[121]

In Support of the World Court

As competition for resources intensifies further, the continued contestations around colonial boundaries will likely increase the propensity for conflict, against a backdrop of higher commodity prices set against scarcity, and the challenges of sustainable development. Uncertainties over boundaries mitigate against meaningful solutions and act as a brake on the world's economy.

118 *Case Concerning the Location of Boundary Markers in Taba between Egypt and Israel*, UN Reports of International Arbitral Awards (29 September 1988) Vol. XX, 1–118.

119 *Rann of Kutch Case*, UN Reports of International Arbitral Awards (29 September 1988) Vol. XX, 170.

120 For a clear articulation of this point, see the separate judgment of Weeramantry *op. cit.* 88.

121 [Editors], *Approaches to Solving Territorial Conflicts* (2010), *op. cit.* 18–21.

A fully functional judicial system with standing and technical capacity to resolve disputes would appear beneficial to short- and medium-term threats to peace and to longer term projects of sustainable development and environmental justice for *all,* but especially those in border regions. This brief subsection highlights why the ICJ could play a significant role in such disputes, given greater support and a few adjustments. Its prominence over the situation in Gaza that commenced in 2023 has also brought it further to the forefront of the imagination of the international community, even if the lack of bite for its opinions may have weakened its ability to resolve disputes.

The ICJ suffers from being taken for granted: first, when this organ needed to be reconstituted to continue the role played by the Permanent Court of International Justice under the *League of Nations* with minimal discussion about prospective operational changes.[122] In over seven decades, its load has been relatively light, though it is regularly scrutinized in terms of its operations, ethos, and judgments. In the aftermath of the *Nicaragua case* when it took on a superpower, many forecast its doom.[123] At the end of the Cold War, the Court benefited from greater optimism over internationalization, even attracting more African cases. However, with heightened concerns post–11 September, gloomy forecasts returned despite the Court's relatively full docket.[124] Posner suggests a 'decline' in relevance due to a drop in usage by great powers, relatively low usage by States, perceptions of judges' failure to apply the law impartially, and States' conflict of interest.[125] Each factor can be challenged from the lens of territorial disputes. As many as 56 of the 195 cases in the General List before the Court (upto April 2024) have territorial elements. Most arise between post-colonial States making it no surprise that so-called 'Great Powers' are not litigants to such disputes. The Court has had the greatest salience in two regions with the most egregious boundaries, i.e. in Latin America and sub-Saharan Africa where there is least overlap between political boundaries and pre-colonial ethnic, linguistic, and religious contours. The critique over judicial impartiality is skewed by the appointment of *ad hoc* judges by litigants, who rule in their favour. Yet these are contained within general judgments where their impact does not appear significant to the overall result. National interests determine whether or not a State may be willing to bind itself through compulsory adjudication to the Court, but

122 See G. L .Scott & K. D. Csajko, 'Compulsory Jurisdiction and Defiance in the World Court: A Comparison of the PCIJ and ICJ' 16 *Denver Journal of International Law & Policy* (1987–1988) 377–392.

123 K. Highet, 'The Peace Palace Heats Up: The World Court in Business Again?' 85(4) *American Journal of International Law* (1991) 646–654.

124 E. A. Posner, 'The Decline of the International Court of Justice' Issue 233 JM Olin Program in Law & Economics Working Paper, School of Law, University of Chicago, Chicago, IL, 2004.

125 *Ibid.*

this facet of State sovereignty impacts the development of *all* international law. The prominence of the Court's role in the context of the South African complaint against Israel over claimed violations of the Genocide Convention shows the utility of the Court in live conflicts. While the failure by State parties, not least the UN Security Council, to act meaningfully on its orders may seem to have weakened its efficacy, these failures may have done the reverse: show the contrast between the legal and political approaches to the most serious questions concerning breaches of the peace.

Territorial disputes are notoriously difficult to resolve in a manner that will endure. Adjudication on border issues has been unpredictable, less due to a lack of legal certainty or the quality of judgment, but because the nature of the evidence and scope of the determination is challenging. Political leaders, unwilling to accept the risks of losing territory, are ostensibly reluctant to submit disputes for international adjudication.[126] Despite this, a significant number of such disputes have been submitted for international adjudication, and the judgments delivered see compliance despite criticisms.

In adjudicating these disputes in a transparent manner, the Court has developed the law governing title to territory, building a track record with rules and providing legal certainty in difficult disputes. Many areas of international law have developed through treaty law or the emergence of international custom gleaned through domestic *opinio juris*. In issues concerning title to territory, the ICJ remains the lead player, adjudicating disputes based on unequal treaties, contestable evidence, and a host of different regimes of applicable law, providing a semblance of clarity and legal certainty. The standing of the Court has risen through its track record in such disputes, and the attention devoted to the hearings over Gaza in 2024 brought this into more public focus. With Great Power usage diminished, the Court has become attractive to other litigants, with its standing providing it with legitimacy and authority superior to regional courts. The clarity of submission rules, transparency of the proceedings, and gradually improving representation in the Court's composition are additional factors in overcoming negative perceptions (i.e. of 'western' bias) of the Court. A further factor compared to other forms of adjudication is the relatively lower cost of bringing a case to the ICJ, eliminating this from being a major impediment to access to justice.

Evidence suggests that ICJ judgments are accorded deference,[127] and as a consequence, cases of non-compliance remain rare.[128] This is significant

126 [Editors], *Approaches to Solving Territorial Conflicts* (2010), *op. cit.* iii.

127 J. I. Charney, 'Disputes Implicating the Institutional Credibility of the Court: Problems of Non-Appearance, Non-Participation, and Non-Performance' in *The International Court of Justice at a Crossroad* [Lori Fisler Damrosch ed.] (New York: Transnational Publishers, 1987) 288.

128 C. Paulson, 'Compliance with Final Judgments of the International Court of Justice since 1987' 98 *American Journal of International Law* (2004) 434.

despite the slightly lower compliance in cases concerning territorial disputes and boundary delimitations, in comparison with other topics.[129] In a survey of cases that have arisen since 1987, Polter found that four of the five cases where there was some form of non-compliance concerned issues of land boundaries, with three having a history of armed conflict. He distinguishes these issues from those concerning maritime boundaries, where judgments in six of the seven disputes were respected, including in Libya Chad, where the maritime components received compliance.[130]

In *Sovereignty over Pulau Ligitan & Pulau Sipadan* (*Indonesia v. Malaysia*)[131] the Court awarded both islands to Malaysia, with Indonesia accepting and agreeing to abide by the judgment despite its disappointment. The judgment in *Kasikili Sedudu Island Dispute* (*Botswana v. Namibia*) met with a similar response from Namibia after the Court awarded the island to Botswana, while providing equal access to the channels around the island to both parties.[132] The judgment on *Territorial Questions between Qatar & Bahrain* (*Qatar v. Bahrain*) was potentially difficult, since it included a dispute over the Hawar islands – a third of Bahrain's total land area.[133] The reasoning in the judgment negated previously accepted doctrine concerning arbitral awards and settled points of maritime delimitation.[134] The Court showed sensitivity and deft handling of delicate political questions, dispensing justice mindful of the potential impact of the judgment on Bahrain. The success of the judgment lies in the dispute being considered definitively settled, with subsequent statements and actions taken by the governments, including with regard to the reallocation of oil and gas rights, pointing to the emergence of a 'new era of understanding' between the parties.[135] *The Arbitral Award of 31 July 1989* (*Guinea-Bissau v. Senegal*) concerned an attempt by Guinea-Bissau to declare the nullity of an arbitral award between itself and Senegal, which the Court rejected, upholding its valid and binding nature on both parties.[136] The impact of the tensions concerning the maritime boundary had spilt over to tensions along the uncontested land boundary between the two States. While Guinea-Bissau contested the judgment for many years, its behaviour since 1995 signals compliance despite continued

129 *Ibid.* 457.
130 *Ibid.*
131 *ICJ Reports* (2002).
132 *ICJ Reports* (1999) 1045.
133 *ICJ Reports* (2001).
134 G. Plant, 'Case Report: Maritime Delimitation and Territorial Questions Between Qatar and Bahrain (Qatar v Bahrain)' 96 *American Journal of International Law* (2002) 198, 200–201.
135 R. Saad, 'Gulf Emirates Settle Debate' 526 *Al-Ahram Weekly Online* (March 22–28 2001).
136 Arbitral Award of 31 July 1989 (Guinea-Bissau v. Senegal) *ICJ Reports* (1991) 53, also available 86 *American Journal of International Law* (1992).

dissatisfaction.[137] The judgment concerning maritime delimitation between Denmark and Norway was complied with to the extent that it was subsequently renegotiated by parties in good faith after *Maritime Delimitation in the Area between Greenland and Jan Mayen* (*Denmark v. Norway*).[138] Thus, the ICJ delivered a judgment that spurred parties back to negotiation that had failed in the eight years leading up to the case, eventually yielding a mutually acceptable solution.

One key motivating factor in the submission of territorial disputes to the Court's adjudication is the ostensible cover such adjudication may provide domestic politicians faced with an adverse judgment. When a situation concerning a contested boundary risks spilling into violent confrontation and other means of bilateral and multilateral negotiation have failed, submitting a dispute to the Court becomes a logical next step. With enhanced standing, the Court could formulate solutions that, even if unpalatable for one of the parties, could be justified in the domestic arena as an international action, moving 'blame' away from the government of the day.

An Agenda for Change?

This chapter has argued that (i) international boundary disputes are likely to grow; (ii) an established set of rules has emerged that while problematic and in need of some modification, have created a framework for judicial determinations of title to territory; and that (iii) the ICJ may be the best forum for the resolution of such disputes. This final section will focus on how this could be achieved, focusing on technical and practical implements that merit attention if the efficacy of the Court in becoming the focal point for territorial disputes is to grow.

Technical Impediments

(i) Lack of Compulsory Jurisdiction

As an organ adjudicating interstate disputes, the ICJ ought to be available to all States within the United Nations. Yet the principle of State sovereignty dictates that because States are free to decide how to resolve their disputes (an attribute of their sovereignty), they cannot be brought before the ICJ (or any other third body) unless they consent to it. Without express consent, the ICJ is prevented from addressing contentious disputes between States. There

137 M. Bendi, *Guinea-Bissau: Oil & Gas Industry* available at http://www.mbendi.co.za/indy/oilg/af/gb/p0005.htm.

138 *Agreement Concerning the Delimitation of the Continental Shelf in the area between Jan Mayen and Greenland and Concerning the Boundary Between the Fishery Zones*, 17 December 1995, Nor.-Den., 1903 UNTS 171.

are a number of ways in which consent can be gauged: nearly 73 States have accepted jurisdiction via express declaration under Article 36.2 of the Statute of the ICJ. This declaration is normally subject to reciprocity (i.e. a similar acceptance by the opposing party), but States can also conditionally accept jurisdiction, or through a compromissory clause (a provision within the treaty establishing recourse to the Court, provided the State has no reservation to this clause). States may also express consent to bring a dispute before the ICJ through Special Agreements signed for that specific purpose, often drafted immediately before submission of a dispute (as in *Qatar v. Bahrain*).

The ICJ may also gain jurisdiction if the State brought before the Court accepts proceedings even if it had not manifested previous consent (*forum prorrogatum*). France is, to date, the only State to have agreed to this procedure (in a case raised by Djibouti). Many powerful States including 11 of the 19 State members of the G20 are beyond the compulsory reach of the Court. Besides France, Argentina, Brazil, China, Indonesia, Russia, Saudi Arabia, South Africa, South Korea, Türkiye, and the United States may subject themselves to ICJ jurisdiction on an *ad hoc* basis through a special agreement over a given matter, but have not given the Court automatic jurisdiction over disputes concerning themselves. Interestingly, of the remaining eight G20 States that are subject to compulsory jurisdiction, four have made the requisite declaration within the last decade (Germany, Italy, Japan, and the UK), while the remaining four (Mexico, India, Canada, and Australia) accepted jurisdiction for a considerably longer period. If the Court is to become the focal point for the settlement of disputes concerning title to territory, significantly more attention would need to be paid to the extent to which States are willing to subject themselves to compulsory adjudication. The growing stature of the Court can be gleaned in that nearly a quarter of the States that have accepted compulsory jurisdiction (17 of 73) have done so since 2000. This is not due only to acceptance by new States that have emerged in that time period since, in addition to the powerful States listed above, others who accepted compulsory jurisdiction include Cote d'Ivoire, Cyprus, Djibouti, the Commonwealth of Dominica, Ireland, Lesotho, Lithuania, the Marshall Islands, Peru, Portugal, Slovakia, and Timor-Leste.

Locus Standi

As an interstate body created to adjudicate disputes between States, the ICJ restricts jurisdiction to States or to questions concerning international law that arise in the operation of an intergovernmental organization. This narrows the scope for its use in territorial disputes to those between States concerning questions of possession, occupation, delimitation, or demarcation. In such disputes, the role of non-State actors is considered only if raised by Parties. The Court has pronounced on questions of contested sovereignty, including over Palestine, Kosovo, and the Chagos Islands,[139] though these remain the exception rather than the rule, usually requiring significant political mobilization for the matter to arrive at the Court. There is little possibility that a case could be raised in the name of indigenous peoples or non-state claimants to territory, though South Africa's advocacy on behalf of the Palestinians, which builds on the different example of the Gambian attempt to seek justice for the Rohingya, may provide new possibilities where norms of *jus cogens* are involved. Although some States may be willing to sponsor territorial claims through advisory opinions (as in the *Wall, Kosovo* or *Chagos* cases), the nature of the process and the determination of admissibility operate to prevent potential claims. Thus, peoples who claim self-determination, including title to territory, have no option but to seek relief within State structures, with the lesser offer, perceived or real, of territorial autonomy often considered a viable option.[140] This often fails to address claimants' title to territory[141] offering a negotiated political settlement to the governance of the territory at best.[142]

Strict Application of Rules

The doctrine of the separation of powers plays an important role in setting judicial limits, and Courts around the world interpret their roles conservatively to avoid accusations of judge-made law, following the maxim that courts uphold and interpret law rather than frame it. Courts remain reluctant to deviate from rules established and agreed upon. In title to territory cases, this means that the rules discussed above are applied by the court in

139 *ICJ Reports* (1975) 12; *Legal Consequences of the Construction of a Wall in the Occupied Palestinian Territory*, Advisory Opinion, *ICJ Reports* (2004) 136; *Legal Consequences for States of the Continued Presence of South Africa in Namibia (South West Africa) Notwithstanding Security Council Resolution 276*, Advisory Opinion, *ICJ Reports* (1971)16. See also J. Dugard, 'Namibia (South West Africa): The Court's Opinion, South Africa's Response, and Prospects for the Future' 11 *Columbia Journal of Transnational Law* (1972) 14; *International Status of South-West Africa, Advisory Opinion, ICJ Reports* (1949) 270.

140 See G. Gilbert, 'Autonomy and Minority Groups: A Right in International Law?' 35 Cornell International Law Journal (2002) 307; J. Wright, 'Minority Groups, Autonomy, and Self-Determination' 19 *Oxford Journal of Legal Studies* (1999) 605, 606.

141 The status of self-determination as a right in modern international law is highly dependent on the respective state's political perspective. In applying self-determination to federal states, there is even less information available than in the international domain. The definitive case on the subject is the secession of Québec that came before the Canadian Supreme Court: *Reference re Secession of Québec*, [1998] 2 S.C.R. 217. Nevertheless, the court expressed concern about the safeguards necessary to protect the rights of indigenous Canadians within Québec. See *Ibid.* at 261–263 (addressing protection of minorities).

142 See generally A. Buchanan, *Justice, Legitimacy, and Self-Determination: Moral Foundations for International Law* (Oxford: Oxford University Press, 2004) 248–262.

every circumstance within a limited margin of interpretation. The hostility to applying *equity* or *equitable principles*[143] is mainly due to its perceived 'vagueness' which may

> open the door to making subjective and therefore arbitrary evaluations, instead of following the guidance of established general principles and rules of international law in the settlement of disputes submitted to the Court.[144]

In his separate opinion on equity in *Maritime Delimitation*, Judge Weeramantry addressed some of the issues around equity but was keen to stress that 'there has been no resort to equity *ex aequo et bono*'. As he highlights, 'Nearly every decision applying equity to maritime delimitation has stressed that the species of equity employed is not *equity ex aequo bono*'.[145]

The Court has strived to remain within the remit of the law even in instances where a more thorough contextual exploration may have yielded a different outcome (see the argument pertaining to sovereignty in Nigeria–Cameroon), or taking into account the context in which judicial determination was sought (see Western Sahara). This approach signals that Courts may not seek modification to rules that may be necessary in the pursuit of perpetual peace. Disputes concerning title to territory usually centre around the processes of decolonization and the integrity, justice, and validity of territorial units left behind. Strict application of rules governing title to territory reify 'solutions' derived during transition but fail to examine whether preserving these for posterity serves the interest of order or justice. Perhaps it is appropriate that judges do not determine answers to that question but rely instead on the rules. Yet this means that they are unable to address the consequences of broken rules in the acquisition of the territory by colonial rulers, providing a lopsided (if predictable and therefore safe) quality of justice. Any change in approach requires State consent, but States seem content with judicial determination of titles to territory, which is unsurprising since these reify the State as the fundamental actor in a specific space over every other contestant.

Heightened Value of Evidence

A more scientific approach is needed to determine the value of evidence. The Court has pronounced itself cautiously on the value of maps, which are

143 G. Ripert, 'Les regles du droit civil applicables aux rapports internationaux' 44 *Recueil des Cours de l'Academie de Droit International* (1933-II) 575.

144 *ICJ Reports* (1969) 166.

145 *ICJ Reports* (1983) 184.

known in many instances to be drawn from specific perspectives, with cartography often commandeered to reflect those perspectives. It makes sense to endorse the approach advocated by Donohue, Otte, and Smith, who suggest that not only the content but even the technique through which disputes could be approached should be rethought in light of changes to the quality and efficacy of modern standards of evidence. They advocate an 'ontology-based strategy,' which would offer

> a cumulative, integrated, and continuously updated resource providing information about such disputes in an easily accessible form...[which] would...benefit... intelligence analysts, military strategists, political scientists, and...historians and others concerned with international disputes.[146]

This would entail accessing, understanding, interpreting, and where necessary and possible, verifying narratives based on a fuller reading of human history than that documented through the limited lens of colonial documents. In pleadings, States often offer complex cultural context-specific information, which can now be assessed and verified in far greater detail than ever before. For any enhancement in the quality of decision-making, such opportunities must be embraced.

Reducing the Ambient Noise

Through the history of the Court, there has been a consistently high number of additional opinions appended to judgments. The last 20 completed judgments (on merits) came with an additional 139 opinions (not distinguishing between separate, dissenting opinions and additional declarations). While this compares less favourably than the judgments in the first 20 cases (104 additional opinions), it is less in volume than the next 20 cases (which peaked at 145 additional opinions appended). These opinions, when they dissent from the main findings, are important in clarifying the interpretation of key points of law but undermine the overall efficacy of the decision. The proliferation of separate opinions, dissenting opinions, and declarations dilutes legal certainty and confuses the public. It makes the international adjudication of disputes seem like a more complicated process than it needs to be. Self-restraint on the part of judges in issuing such judgments could contribute to an enhanced belief in the value of seeking judicial pronouncements, would streamline legal pleadings (which draw on these additional statements), and promote greater legal certainty.

146 B. Donohue, J. N. Otte & B. Smith, 'An Ontological Approach to Territorial Disputes' available online at http://ncor.buffalo.edu/mil/STIDS-2014-Territorial-Disputes.pdf [last accessed 3 May 2015].

Some Practical Impediments

The explosion of academic research in the context of history, geography, sociology, anthropology, religion, and culture provides greater insight into communities and processes in various parts of the globe than ever before. Today's experts comment with a degree of authority and concrete evidence to back arguments about lost and denied histories. Pleadings are more likely to rely to a greater extent on these testimonies, and the Court ought to have the ability to seek more effective research on such matters. As viewed in the first part, the domination of literature and materials from the perspective of colonial powers formed the basis for many decisions concerning boundaries. Wider participation by others dictates a contrite approach that reaches for new sources of information.

In comparison to others, the cost of litigation at the ICJ is relatively low. To garner greater access, other processes, notably the Dispute Settlement Mechanism at the WTO, have created a service to enable States that feel burdened by costs to access good quality legal advice. Ensuring a strong *pro bono* culture among practitioners at the Court may enhance accessibility and serve to further reduce costs, potentially leading to greater use.

Many states and commentators operate under the belief that all international systems serve exclusive Western interests and are, by their nature, biased against smaller, poorer States. There is evidence underpinning this: the double standards in international law have been documented many times over. With the ICJ, however, the argument since *Nicaragua* has been that the Court is biased towards smaller States and against big Western superpowers.[147] There is also a more general point made by Posner about the propensity of the *ad hoc* judge, when appointed by a State, to vote in favour of that State, which is advanced as evidence of bias. Yet the transparency over such appointments mitigates this, as does the fact that these *ad hoc* judges often append lone dissenting statements. The issue of judicial bias needs to be under vigilance since justice needs to be seen to be done as well as done, and accusations of bias act against the integrity of the individual judges and undermine the collective decision-making of the world's apex court.

If the composition of the Court is scrutinized over time, it becomes clear that the great powers have maintained a constant presence on the bench, albeit through individuals who notionally sit in their individual capacity. Such a process, where the powerful are better represented on judicial bodies, is a direct consequence of colonial societal structures but calls for greater vigilance to appointment processes and their impact on the composition of the Court.

147 E. A. Posner & M. F. P. de Figueiredo, 'Is the International Court of Justice Biased?' 34(2) *Journal of Legal Studies* (2005) 599–630.

Criticisms concerning the Euro-centricity of the ICJ appear outdated when viewed from positions adopted in terms of the doctrine of *uti possidetis juris*. The rule-based reliance of the Court could be ascribed to rules and lines drawn under Europe's hegemony, which may mitigate against the quality of justice. However, to use this as an argument of Western bias in such cases would be unfair: the parties before the Court have almost unanimously insisted on the strict application of such rules and the Court has merely respected this. So, rather than Euro-centricism imposed from Europe, this may instead be a reflection of the impact of Europe-trained political elites. It would be fair to endorse Aman McHugh's perspective:

> The ICJ is well equipped to handle African boundary disputes in particular because the ICJ is experienced in resolving them and has an exemplary overall record of compliance from African governments. In fact if the past in any indication, African governments will continue to comply with the Court's findings, in part because of a fear of being foreclosed from bringing future claims.[148]

While in some ways better than the International Criminal Court, which seems to have mainly African States in its sights, significant improvements are still needed, including in the heavy Western bias of the judicial training and the significant domination of white and Western-trained lawyers practising before it.[149] Such criticism needs to be tempered against the fact that States in the developing world have begun to feel increasingly comfortable in approaching the Court and are, in general, compliant with its findings.

Conclusion

More than half a century has passed since the end of widespread European colonial domination. As indicated in previous chapters, the process of transition from colonial rule occurred along lines drawn on maps from afar. This chapter has sought to demonstrate the role that international law played in that transition. This consisted of framing and upholding rules based on the ostensible quest to ensure that decolonization could occur in an orderly manner, and then adjudicating subsequent disputes in a manner that reiterated those rules. Yet it could be argued that the quest for order that was so cherished has, to a large part, been frustrated. Wars have been persistent, and

148 A. M. McHugh, 'Resolving International Boundary Disputes in Africa: A Case for the ICJ' 49 *Howard Law Journal* (2005–2006) 209.

149 See G. Odentun, 'Africa Before the International Court: The Generational Gap in International Adjudication and Arbitration' 44(4) *Indiana Journal of International Law* (October–December 2004) 701–748.

post-colonial States that emerged have not, in general terms, consolidated the legitimacy of their authority even if they may have firmly established their power over the territory. Sustainable peace has proved beyond reach, and the development agenda may have strengthened the hegemony of an extractive, exploitative economic model resulting in the climate crisis. If conflict provided a regular drumbeat in the post-colonial period, scarcities caused by a combination of the climate crisis and the solidification of wealth in a few hands have made that drumbeat more frenzied, raising the potential of increasingly violent conflict that is enabled by significantly more brutal technologies than before.

The call for system change may be loud in some circles, but it often proves merely rhetorical as power shifts to accommodate this demand, rather than generating forces for abdication whereby new kinds of power motivated by other goals can emerge. It is against this backdrop that new thinking is vital to understand how the quest for perpetual peace can be galvanized. Engaging in the blame game, attributing the ills of post-colonial States to their colonial demarcation is becoming an intellectual pursuit of dubious value. This chapter has focused instead on the importance of winning the peace over the coming decades against new challenges posed by climate change and the unaddressed need for sustainable development. When the *Cairo Resolution* was passed in 1964, the governing sentiment within the *Organization of African Union* was that there were bigger questions at stake than narrow identity constraints, and in this spirit, the freezing of boundaries was accepted as a necessary evil in pursuit of development. The argument, made most vehemently by Western-trained elites, benefited them, but may well have been sensible at a time of transition. The post-colonial States' track record in development has, since then, been at best mixed. Wider questions concerning development have become subsumed in the quest for determinate frontiers, which are sometimes hampering the ability of States to cooperate across contested boundaries.[150] This legal uncertainty is providing grounds for separatists and identity entrepreneurs to further their aspirations. The situation is exacerbated by a permissive climate concerning the use of force and the proliferation of weapons, which brings questions concerning territorial disputes into ever sharper focus.

The current agenda accentuates the need for interstate cooperation, which will likely be mutually beneficial, even against the backdrop of heightened competition within the global economy.[151] One authoritative report on territorial disputes states:

150 B. Simmons, 'Rules over Real Estate: Trade, Territorial Conflict and International Borders as Institution' 69(6) *Journal of Conflict Resolution* (2005) 823–848.

151 [Editors], *Approaches to Solving Territorial Conflicts* (2010), *op. cit.* v.

> Competition for contested or shared resources has become more intense in recent years due to economic developments, such as high commodity prices, and environmental changes, such as overutilization of agricultural land, overgrazing, and desertification, as well as regional and global climate change. It is unlikely that increasing stresses among states resulting from these factors can be successfully resolved using traditional legal methods, particularly adjudication.[152]

While this assessment is to be endorsed as accurate, the conclusion concerning the resolution of the disputes is unduly pessimistic. It would seem instead that the growing contemporary challenges make it imperative that international dispute settlement mechanisms are reiterated as ideal fora for solutions, with changes made to ensure an enhancement of their efficacy. This will require a changed emphasis, greater flexibility, and fidelity to the underlying importance of justice, rather than to rules articulated to promote such justice in a vastly different era.

152 *Ibid.* vi.

Chapter 4

Decolonization

The Quest for Peace, Not Justice?

Introduction

Having discussed the range of rules governing title to territory that are in operation, this chapter returns to the period during which those rules were crystallizing to identify the specific regional customs that could have featured more strongly in the drawing of boundaries at a time of transition. This chapter focuses on the impact of how territory was returned in each geographical part of the globe, arguing that this contributed to the contemporary state of boundaries and a sense of insecurity and tension.

The Americas

No study on the drawing of boundaries would be complete without a review of Latin American contributions to the development of the guiding principles that have become central to how international law treats questions concerning title to territory. The first transposition of Roman norms such as *uti possidetis* and *terra nullius* into international law emerged in Creole action[1] that claimed to 'liberate' Latin American territories from the aegis of Imperial Spain.[2] Until this action European powers had become accustomed to acquiring territory abroad, augmenting their wealth and influence, while successfully suppressing all dissent towards their occupation of such territory. The strident opposition that existed was nullified by a combination of

1 For a general reading about the Creoles motivations, see David A. Brading, *Classical Republicanism & Creole Patriotism: Simon Bolivar (1783–1830) & the Spanish Revolution* (Cambridge: Cambridge University Press, 1983).

2 For general reading on the subject of the colonization of Latin America, see Mariano Picon-Salas, *A Cultural History of Spanish America from Conquest to Independence* (Berkeley, CA: University of California Press, 1962); Beatrice Pastor Bodmer, *The Armature of Conquest: Spanish Accounts of the Discovery of America 1492–1589* [Lydia Longstreth Hunt trans] (Stanford, CA: Stanford University Press, 1992); S. Whittmore Boggs, *International Boundaries: A Study of Boundary Functions and Problems* (New York: Columbia University Press, 1980).

DOI: 10.4324/9781003503279-5

force and subterfuge and deliberately excluded from historical records that were being disseminated as education. As a consequence the opposition to occupation that galvanized the peoples coming under its yoke did not filter into the global public imagination. With challenges to European possession of land through lawfare, argumentation, and forceful means non-existent in written records, the actions engaged upon by or on behalf of communities seeking self-governance were ignored, and instead European acquisition of such lands was presented as being welcomed.

The Latin American challenge to Europe was different from the others that will be examined here in that it came from within the European family: literally, the offspring of colonial settlers, steeped in European Enlightenment values and armed with their own neo-colonial desires to seize control of the vast territories and wealth of the continent for themselves rather than being forced to repatriate it to Europe. Their ability to maintain effective control and resist Spain (and Portugal) drawing on existing legal tools enabled the emergence of practices that impacted the doctrine of *uti possidetis*, the view of territory, and the notion of *terra nullius*. This remains the fulcrum through which these Roman law concepts were transposed into modern international law. Already early in the twentieth century, the substantiation of the notion of *terra nullius* was attributed as one of the biggest contributions of Latin American States to the development of international law.[3] Yet this ostensible substantiation, around the early to mid-1800s, had little impact on the *Scramble for Africa*, which commenced towards the end of the century. So any odes to Latin American contributions need to be put into sharper perspective, as does the absolute disregard of the Creoles in acknowledging or accepting that the lands they claimed as *terra nullius* were the long-established ancestral domains of communities, nations, and peoples whom they dismissed as uncivilized and subhuman.

Writing in 1909, international lawyer Alvarez distinguished Europe, formed of 'men of a single race', from the admixture of races in Latin America, who were 'in great part illiterate and ignorant'.[4] This racial superiority mindset invited European intervention in Latin America in the name of emancipation: a process still prevalent in the marginalization of indigenous populations who are viewed as 'primitive' and in need of development. The Creoles, born of European descendants, drove the independence movement as a quest to separate from their European parents, without acknowledgement or concession to the rights of indigenous communities. Instead they viewed themselves as forming an intellectual elite that had the entitlement and duty to thrust for independence. For Alvarez, this responsibility flowed naturally,

3 Fiore 'Il Diritto Internazionale Codificato' a.541 as quoted in Alejandro Alvarez, 'Latin American and International Law' 3 *American Journal of International Law* (1909) 286, 321.
4 *Ibid.* 271–272.

since he identified them as the 'only thinking part of the population'.[5] The failure to include indigenous peoples and Afro-descendants transported as slaves has left a deep structural legacy in many of the Inter-American States.[6]

The prime motivation that was declared for Creole independence was the apparent injustice of the mother country towards its colonies, which was curated to germinate revolution.[7] Influenced by the philosophical writings of the eighteenth century, the Creoles seized on Spain's embarrassment in the Napoleonic Wars to launch their quest.[8] Their action proved decisive in recreating a French Revolution style process[9] resulting in a form of independence for Latin American 'countries'.[10] This was accompanied by the emotive generation of a supervening identity to overthrow colonial governance with 'legitimate governance' forged through consent.[11] However, the active segment of the subject population involved was restricted to the Creoles, excluding nations, tribes, and others living on the same territory.

On seizing power the Creoles consolidated republican, liberal, and democratic constitutional regimes.[12] However, the practice of democratic values floundered in the first period of independence, characterized by continent-wide civil wars, the emergence of dictatorships, and regular modifications of the fundamental ordinances of those countries.[13] Despite continuous unrest and boundary skirmishes, a fraternal spirit existed among the first 'Latin Americans': the sense born from the continuation of the fight against the common colonial enemy – the large indigenous populations – was a shared problem for those of an inherited European cultural background. This fraternity was stoked by shared insecurities around the settler colonial State-building

5 *Ibid.* 274.

6 See Yanoamani Indian Case, Case 7615 IACHR 24, OEA/Ser.L/V/11.66, doc. 10 Rev.1 (1985). For this and other cases concerning indigenous peoples in the Americas, see Shelton H. Davis, *Land Rights and Indigenous Peoples: The Role of the Inter-American Commission on Human Rights* (Cambridge, MA: Cultural Survival Report v 29, 1988).

7 This fits with Charles Tilly's classic four factors for revolution, which were all prevalent in Latin America. See Tilly C. 'Revolutions' in *Handbook of Political Science* [Fred I. Greenstein & Nelson W. Polsby eds.] (Reading, MA: Addison-Wesley, 1975) 521

8 Brading (1983) *op.cit.* 1, 16

9 See Joshua Castellino, 'Liberté, Fraternité, Egalité: The Dubious Fruits of 'National' Self-determination in International Law' 1(1) *Turku Law Journal* (1999) 1–32.

10 Jack Hayward, *After the French Revolution: Six Critiques of Democracy and Nationalism* (London: Harvester Wheatsheaf, 1991) 1.

11 Neuberger likened this to the actions of Marsilus of Padua in the Renaissance Period. See Benjamin Neuberger, *National Self-Determination in Postcolonial Africa* (Boulder, CO: Lynne Reinner, 1986) 4–5. Also see Kurt Rabl, *Das Selbstbestimmungsrecht der Völker – Geschichtliche Grunlagen und Umriss der gegenwärtigen Bedeutung* (Köln: Böhlau, 1973) 5.

12 Alvarez (1909) *op.cit.* 3, 273.

13 *Ibid.*

processes within the continent,[14] factors that remained central to the growth of the independent States in Latin America throughout the nineteenth century. Similar to fifteenth and sixteenth-century European jurists, the developing regime governing territory was subsequently applied as international legal principles.

Legal Impact of the Creole Action

To safeguard the new regimes against renewed European conquest (*Reconquista*), the Creoles buttressed themselves using legal justifications against European interest in what they viewed as their lands. This involved compromise over inherited boundaries: they accepted colonial boundaries temporarily to prevent infighting and forceful renegotiation. The geographical parameters of the new States were built into constitutions to forestall territorial disputes, coupled with attempts to foster interstate cooperation through regional defence pacts.[15] The inevitability of such disputes was the *prima facie* cause for the establishment of continent-wide arbitration procedures, which have since become a legitimate form of boundary adjudication in international practice.[16] The doctrine of *terra nullius* was invoked, preventing further European acquisition of territory in the Americas. This rebutted the argument that there was any territory anywhere on the continent that was still *terra nullius*. In other words all territory in the Americas would now be deemed occupied and under the jurisdiction of an existing sovereign irrespective of whether they exercised effective control over it, making it ineligible for occupation. While *terra nullius* as a concept was not new to international law, it had not prevented dominant powers in consolidating overseas Empires, as can be noted by the spread of the Ottoman Empire from the seventh century onwards, the Mongol acquisition of territories in the thirteenth century, or Russian expansion in the nineteenth century into Asia. While 'unfair' occupation of occupied territory was not deemed acceptable in law, it remained subject to power dynamics and the interpretation of the rules by expansionists. Instead it was always justified on the basis that the

14 Similar sentiments led to the creation of the International Union of American Republics of 1890 and subsequently the Organisation of American States in May 1948. For more on the Inter-American system of human rights, see David Harris & Stephen Livingstone (eds.), *The Inter-American System of Human Rights* (Oxford: Clarendon Press, 1998).

15 This can be seen in numerous Latin American constitutions: see the Constitution of El Salvador 1981. Referred to in the El Salvador/ Honduras Case (Nicaragua Intervening) *ICJ Reports* (1992).

16 Most notably, in the Opinions of the Badinter Arbitration Commission that was created by the European Community Conference on Yugoslavia: see Malcolm Shaw, 'People, Territorialism & Boundaries' 8 *European Journal of International Law* (1997) 478–508.

lands occupied were ones with no 'recognizable' form of government or by governments that were not strong enough to defend their physical realms.

Though the new States maintained territorial claims against each other, there was an explicit belief that the Spanish and Portuguese lines were to be considered sacrosanct and that disputes could only be resolved through arbitration set up under the aegis of a regional pact.[17] The first element validated the *uti possidetis de jure* boundaries established under Spanish colonial administration. The war of succession between Brazil as successor to the Portuguese Empire and the former Spanish States cast doubt on the validity of this principle, but only to the extent that the parties disputed whether the lines to be sanctified and preserved were *de jure* or *de facto* lines at the time of the creation of the independent States.[18] It left the principle that the line itself (*de facto* or *de jure*) should remain sacrosanct and uncontested. In cases that proceeded to arbitration, the question to be determined was the location of the original line rather than its legitimacy.[19] Thus, the contemporary principle of the sanctity of boundaries can be ascribed to post-colonial Creole statecraft.

While it was relatively easy to agree on a moratorium on boundary changes between different former Spanish colonies emerging from decolonization, the discussion with Brazil involved discussions with a different sovereign. The delimitation of Brazil's borders with its neighbours had the added complication of the boundaries being contested between the colonial powers, not least from 1801 when Spain and Portugal were still at war. Also unlike in the case of Latin American States, which emerged at distinct points between 1810 and 1825, Brazil did not have a moment when the boundaries could be deemed to have crystallized, i.e. a critical date. In this sense the emergence of a Brazilian interpretation of *uti possidetis* was closer to its Roman law origin, meaning it required effective *de facto* possession rather than a mutually agreed, *de jure* right to possess territory.[20]

17 See, for instance, [Editorial] 'In the Matter of the Arbitration of the Boundary Dispute between the Republics of Costa Rica & Panama Provided by the Convention between Costa Rica and Panama of March 17th 1910' in 8(4) *American Journal of International Law* (1914) 913–941.

18 Malcolm Shaw, 'The Heritage of States: The Principle of *Uti Possidetis Juris* Today' 67 *British Yearbook of International Law* (1996) 75–154.

19 See P. K. Menon, 'International Boundaries – A Case Study of the Guyana – Surinam Boundary' 27 *International & Comparative Law Quarterly* (1978) 738–768; Georg Maier, 'The Boundary Dispute Between Ecuador and Peru' 63 (1) *American Journal of International Law* (1969) 28–46.

20 Ramos Acevedo, Jairo, 'El "Uti Possidetis" un principio americano y no europeo' 5(5) *Misión Jurídica* (2012) 145–163, 155 and 156.

Denial of *terra nullius* as early as 1824[21] formed a significant buttress in the diplomatic history of nineteenth-century Latin America against European expansion.[22] This was accompanied by efforts to form a Confederation,[23] first articulated in 1810,[24] with five objectives: reiteration of the sovereign autonomy of each State;[25] collective addressal of the fear of external domination through collective self-defence; determining the courses of domestic or foreign policies; harmonizing interests;[26] and establishing a conflict resolution system. The spur for confederacy came from Simon Bolivar, labelled the great liberator, who as President of Colombia was devoted to establishing such a confederacy.[27] His vision included a Congress in Panama and the articulation of the treaties of *Union, Alliance and Confederation*, which he signed with several countries in 1825.[28] A subsequent pact, *Union, Alliance and Perpetual Confederation*[29] was agreed upon by Mexico, Central America, Colombia, and Peru to augment the confederation, identifying salient features on the issue of territory and boundaries that became significant to the development of regional custom in Latin America. Primarily a defensive pact to support fledgling sovereignty and territorial integrity, it addressed the delimitation of boundaries in Article 22. This article reinforced the notion of *uti possidetis*, obliging States to delimit, guarantee, and secure boundaries under the protection of the Confederation.[30] It reified the notion that the inherited colonial boundaries were sacrosanct.[31]

The practical significance of the Treaty remained incidental since only Colombia ratified it – a trend that plagued confederacy processes throughout the nineteenth century. While the treaties are not part of codified international law, their negotiation contributed to the development of legal opinion on such matters, as evidenced by events leading up to another Congress

21 See generally Josef L. Kunz, 'Guatemala v Great Britain: in Re Belice' 40(2) *American Journal of International Law* (1946) 383–390; also see 'The First Pam-American Scientific Congress' 2(3) *American Political Science Review* (1908) 441–443.

22 See e.g. Charles G. Fenwick, 'The Third Meeting of Ministers of Foreign Affairs at Rio de Janeiro' 36(2) *American Journal of International Law* (1942) 169–203.

23 See William Manger, 'The Pan American Union at the Sixth International Conference of American States' 22(4) *American Journal of International Law* (1928) 764–775.

24 Alvarez (1909) *op.cit.* 3, 276–279.

25 For early writing on the European Union see Herbert W. Briggs, [Editorial Comment] 'The Proposed European Political Community' 48(1) *American Journal of International Law* (1956) 110–122.

26 Alvarez (1909) *op.cit.* 3, 276.

27 *Ibid.* 277.

28 *Ibid.* 277–278.

29 *Ibid.* 278–280.

30 Article 22 *Union, Alliance and Perpetual Confederation, 1826.*

31 For this literature on *uti possidetis*, see Shaw (1996) *op.cit.* 18, 105.

in 1847.[32] Impetus was generated by the threat of a planned expedition supported by Spain, led by the Ecuadorian General Flores, that had, as its expressed purpose, his recovery of the government of Ecuador.[33] The mission was perceived as orchestrated by Spain to recapture power through a Spanish proxy. A Congress was convened in Lima in 1847 to unify responses.[34]

The Lima Congress was attended by New Granada, Ecuador, Peru, Bolivia, and Chile,[35] all of whom perceived themselves threatened by the return of Flores and the Spanish agenda. It yielded two treaties and two conventions. The *Treaty of Confederation of February 1848*[36] highlighted the importance of what came to be known as the Monroe Doctrine[37] unifying signatory powers in repelling attacks against their independence or territorial sovereignty.[38] Articles 1 and 2 mirror statements enunciated by President Monroe of the United States a few years earlier. Article 7 created a system to regulate conflict arising amongst members of the confederacy with regard to boundaries.[39]

Negotiation of the *Treaty of Union of the American States* presented another opportunity for discussions around title to territory. Two treaty mechanisms emerged, signed in Santiago and Washington in 1858, with different States promoting relations between the northern and southern continents[40] while highlighting consensus on issues pertaining to the treatment of territory. While its prime purpose was the generation of allegiances against European interference, it also sought to regulate the influence of the United States in Latin America. The US–Mexican war of 1848 had provided impetus for this move, emphasizing the new threat emerging from within the continent. In strengthening opposition to hostile takeovers of territory (less likely in the north than the south), Article 13 of the Pact stipulated:

> each one of the contracting parties binds itself not to cede nor to alienate to another State, under any form, any part of its territory, nor to permit any nationality foreign to... dominat[e]... to establish itself within its

32 See 'Arbitration Convention between the United States and Ecuador' 4(4) *American Journal of International Law* (1910) 347–348.
33 Alvarez (1909) *op.cit.* 3, 280.
34 See Simeon E. Baldwin, 'The International Congresses and Conferences of the Last Century as Forces Working towards the Solidarity of the World' 1(3) *American Journal of International Law* (1907) 808–829.
35 Alvarez (1909) *op.cit.* 3, 281.
36 Quincy Wright, 'The Constitutionality of Treaties' 13(2) *American Journal of International Law* (1919) 242–266.
37 For basic reading on the Monroe Doctrine, see Charles E. Hughes, 'Observations on the Monroe Doctrine' 17(4) *American Journal of International Law* (1923) 611–628.
38 Alvarez (1909) *op.cit.* 3, 281
39 Article 7, *Treaty of Confederation 1848*
40 Alvarez (1909) *op.cit.* 3, 284.

> boundaries, and promises not to recognise in this character, any that stand in the way of any cession that may be made by the interested States for the purpose of regulating their geographical boundaries or in fixing their natural limits or in determining with mutual advantage their frontiers.[41]

Article 13 explicitly permitted negotiation between two or more States to regulate or demarcate existing frontiers between themselves to gain the best advantage. In 1862 Argentina objected on the grounds that Article 13 imposed unacceptable limitations on State sovereignty.[42] Not party to the earlier treaty that provided veto powers to the Confederacy in matters considered prejudicial to the security of the Confederation, Argentina believed that the nature of sovereignty ought to include the power to determine the destiny of its own territory.

Consensus within the Congress was strengthened in the face of Spanish attempts to reoccupy the Chincha Islands belonging to Peru.[43] Meeting in Lima in 1864 to strengthen and codify relationships between the States,[44] the Congress also adopted principles to end boundary disputes within the continent and create arbitration mechanisms to regulate all disputes. Two pacts were signed in 1865: the *Union and Defensive Alliance*[45] and the *Preservation of Peace*,[46] both providing significant insights into the settlement of boundary disputes within the continent.

Despite these developments, boundary disputes between States plagued their ability to form meaningful relationships with their immediate neighbours.[47] This was exacerbated by disagreements about river navigation – often the traditional route to facilitate commerce – and by civil wars relating to these and other disputes.[48] While attempts at initiating regional foci had greater moral than legal force, in terms of title to territory in international law, these developments had far-reaching consequences.

41 Article 13 *Treaty of Union of American States 1858*.

42 Alvarez (1909) *op.cit.* 3, 285. Also see the Drago Doctrine in Elihu Root, 'The Real Monroe Doctrine' 8(3) *American Journal of International Law* (1914) 427–442.

43 Alvarez (1909) *op.cit.* 3, 285. Also see 'The Chaco Dispute' 28(4) *American Journal of International Law* (1934) 137–208.

44 Alvarez (1909) *op.cit.* 3, 285.

45 Article 2, *Pact of Union and Defensive Alliance 1865* states it becoming operational if any of the High Contracting Parties under a Protectorate or force it to sell or cede territory or to establish or impair the free and complete exercise of its sovereignty and independence.

46 This pact established the process of arbitration to settle boundary disputes. See Alvarez (1909) *op.cit.* 3, 287.

47 *Ibid.* 290.

48 *Ibid.*

The Doctrine of Uti Possidetis

On claiming independence one of the first actions the new republics undertook was the drafting of a 'fundamental law/political chart' (a precursor to a constitution) for self-governance in a particular territory. Instead of describing the territory in question in geographical terms, they opted to refer to the inherited political and administrative realms. Therefore, the transfer of sovereignty towards self-governance was assumed within a pre-established territory. The parameters of the unit cross-referenced existing political and administrative divisions within Spanish rule (*Virreinatos en las Indias Occidentales).* The subsequent transfer of sovereignty was described as occurring through regions that were already geographically delimited and organized for administrative and military purposes through the existence of the Viceroyalties in the West Indies (*Virreinatos en las Indias Occidentales).*[49] Thus, the *Ley Fundamental de Venezuela 1919* signalled the unification of the Republics of Venezuela and New Granada to form the Republic of Colombia, with reference made to the existing vice royalties.

The *Ley Fundamental de la República de Colombia* of 1810 enunciated the doctrine of *uti possidetis juris* for the first time,[50] which was subsequently endorsed in Article 6 of the *Cúcuta Constitution* of 1821 and then the *Mexican Constitution* of 1824. The rule by which the new independent territories decided to adopt territories already demarcated by the Spanish Crown was described by the Latin term *uti possidetis*, but its interpretation then and how it came to be used later differ significantly from its origin in the Roman interdict with that name.[51]The constitutional convergence among the diverse American States, all of whom used the same formula to determine their territories, resulted in the most immediate consequence of serving as the basis for the treaty on borders that followed, namely *los Tratados de Unión*, and also for the arbitral awards that were then agreed to resolve border conflicts in the Americas.[52]

It is worth noting that the Roman law derivation of *uti possidetis* had been applied previously in international law to adjudicate upon possessions

49 Personal translation from Ramos Acevedo (2012) *op.cit.* 20, 150.

50 The 'Uti possidetis of 1810', according to the Colombian writer Alfredo Vázquez Carrizosa, was 'a bold and positive formula to open the inevitable border differences between the new republics of the continent. It provided a strict principle of justice for all; it did not break the tradition of the Ancient Law represented by the titles of the colonial demarcations; and spared the American Continent from the chaos it would have ensued, had there not been any rule to adjust border issues'. Personal translation of Alfredo, Vasquez Carrizoza, *Relatos de historia diplomática de Colombia*, 2nd ed., T. I y II (Bogotá: Pontificia Universidad Javeriana/ Ministerio de Relaciones Exteriores, 1996) 509.

51 John Bassett Moore, *Costa Rica-Panama Arbitration: Memorandum on Uti Possidetis* (London: Commonwealth Company, 1913) 9–11.

52 Acevedo (2012) *op.cit.* 20, 152–153.

acquired by a State as a consequence of war. The first recorded precedent for this is in the *Treaty of Breda*, between the Dutch and the British in 1667. On that occasion the application of the principle enabled the Dutch to retain Surinam while the British had their possession of New Amsterdam (New York) legitimized. At that time it was used to confirm the fate of conquered territories in the aftermath of war, rather than in a governance succession concurrent to self-determination.[53] Of course, that earlier meaning of *uti possidetis* in public international law has been subsumed by its current use – as the principle that settled borders of entities emerging from decolonization – a practice that stems from the emergence of Latin American States as discussed here, independent of the laws of war. While the doctrine of *uti possidetis* required adherence to colonial boundaries, numerous surrounding issues still required resolution. The biggest of these remained the actual agreement of the line and its validation and demarcation, all of which occurred in a context of nationalism and confusing historical trends. For example:

> At the time of the struggle for emancipation, there were four vice royalties in Spanish America (Mexico, New Granada, Peru and Buenos Aires) and seven *Capitanias Generales* (Yucatan, Cuba, Puerto Rico, Santo Domingo, Guatemala, Venezuela and Chile). Bolivar formed of New Granada, Venezuela and Northern Peru, the United States of Columbia, which fell away in 1830 into three States: New Granada, Venezuela and Ecuador. The old vice royalty of Buenos Aires became sub-divided into four States: Bolivia (which was separated from the vice-royalty by Bolivar in 1825), Uruguay, Paraguay, and the United Provinces of the River Plate. The United States of Central America, founded in 1823 split up into five separate States in 1839.[54]

The transition yielded unitary alliances, mergers, and groupings of States which fragmented the old colonies along predetermined administrative boundaries. Despite discussions around confederacies, evidence from documents such as the *Additional and Explanatory Convention of 1833* appended to the *Treaty of Peace, Friendship, Commerce and Navigation 1832* signed between Chile and the United States, suggests that the new States could only be formed by dismemberment of the old: contradicting the purpose of *uti possidetis*.[55] With doubt surrounding inherited boundaries, the emergent States agreed to adhere to *uti possidetis*. However, the concept of 'critical

53 See Shavana Haythornthwaite, 'Sovereignty and Early Modern Private Property Rights' in *Early Modern Sovereignties* [Erik De Bom, Randall Lesaffer & Werner Thomas eds.] (Leiden: Brill Nijhoff, 2020) 152–166.

54 Alvarez (1909) *op.cit.* 3, 289.

55 *Ibid.*

date' became crucial and was agreed upon around 1810, though it remained contested, and was only mutually established in other contexts by 1821.[56] The lack of geographical awareness, especially of secluded non-contact interior areas, created further complications. The Brazilian interpretation of the doctrine and the practical difficulties of resolving border disputes according to *uti possidetis juris* resulted in the need to resort to complementary formulas, including the application of *uti possidetis de facto* for former Spanish colonies.[57]

Adherence to *uti possidetis* lines privileged the destiny of the territory above that of the people,[58] with boundary demarcation and delimitation relying exclusively on claimed occupation of land by the State – colonial then by its post-colonial successor. The arbitral proceedings used to resolve the disputes focused on questions concerning titles of occupation, possession, and prescription, none of which engaged the situation facing indigenous peoples, nor of communities living in frontier regions or those in more interior impenetrable territories.[59] This disenfranchised communities whose deep spiritual connection and existence were linked closely to a symbiotic relationship with their territory, replacing this instead with a culture where territory was viewed and claimed based on agreed frontiers between hegemons as a means for generating and acquiring wealth. In this equation, nature, flora, or fauna were not seen as rights holders to be respected.[60] Even notwithstanding this marginalization of original inhabitants, serious disputes arose between rival claimants leading to war, such as over 'Provincia Cisplatina' eventually resolved through the emergence of Uruguay.[61] Others, such as the simmering dispute over the Malvinas/Falkland Islands, even led to cross-continental wars without clear resolution. There were also 'Old' World versus 'New' World disputes such as between Venezuela and Holland with regard to the possession of the island of Aves,[62] and North versus South disputes such as between the United States and Haiti over the island of Navassa (1856).[63]

56 In subsequent cases, this date is later (e.g. El Salvador/ Honduras) but this has to do with the break-up of the alliances that originally gained independence from the Spanish. See *ICJ Reports* (1992).

57 This is illustrated by Jairo Ramos Acevedo with the treaties between El Salvador and Honduras in 1895, Arbitral Treaty between Peru and Bolivia in 1902, and the dispute between Colombia and Venezuela, resolved by arbitral award of 1922, Ramos Acevedo (2012) *op.cit.* 20, 153–154.

58 Contrast this with the statement of Judge Dillard in the Western Sahara Case [Advisory Opinion] *ICJ Reports* (1975) 116–126.

59 See Pleadings in the El Salvador/Honduras Case *ICJ Reports* (1992).

60 *Yanomani Indian Case*, Case 7615 IACHR 24, OEA/Ser.L/V/11.66, doc. 10 Rev.1 (1985).

61 Alvarez (1909) *op.cit.* 3, 293.

62 See R. Floyd Clarke, 'A Permanent Tribunal of International Arbitration: Its Necessity & Value' 1(2) *American Journal of International Law* (1907) 342–408.

63 Alvarez (1909) *op.cit.* 3, 298.

When looked at in greater granularity, it was thus questionable as to the extent to which order was maintained by the decisions taken around that time.

Despite these failures in the search for perpetual peace, which were conveniently glossed over, developments in Latin America contributed significantly to the development of laws governing the title to territory, including the articulation of the doctrines of *uti possidetis* and *terra nullius*, development of boundary settlement arbitration processes,[64] and the enunciation of the Monroe Doctrine. It also emphasized continent-wide Congresses as a forum for articulating and collectively resolving grievances.

The Middle East and North Africa

The notion of the emergence of wider confederate units visible in Latin America in the early 1800s was echoed in the aftermath of the colonial adventures in the 'Middle East'. Much discussion and engagement took place among Arab scholars, policymakers, and those deeply concerned about how the wider region might regenerate in the aftermath of the disastrous period of European colonization. Heikal, for instance, advocated for the emergence of 'one nation having common interests and security priorities distinct from those of the West'.[65] The emergence of a Pan-Arab area may have lessened the valence of discussions around boundary lines, though negotiating its contours from the Persian world in the east, Russian influence in the north, and Pan-African interests in the Maghreb may have proved equally complex. In any case, faced with lines drawn by colonial powers that were deemed to solidify in the very short period of their existence based on a selective reading of the Latin American experience, Pan-Arabism was also doomed to failure.

A range of shrewd divide-and-rule policies were perpetrated by European powers in complicity with specific ethnic groups and influential families to hasten this failure. This persists even in the determination of the geographical contours of the region. Dessouki and Matar sought to overcome the failure of Pan-Arabism by advocating an 'Arab regional order' to replace the contested concept of the 'Middle East'.[66] Such an order envisaged comprising Algeria, Bahrain, Djibouti, Egypt, Iraq, Jordan, Kuwait, Lebanon, Libya, Mauritania, Morocco, Oman, Palestine/PLO, Qatar, Saudi Arabia, Somalia, Sudan, Syria, Tunisia, Yemen, and the United Arab Emirates. Instead the term 'Mediterranean' was used to classify many of the States, though its

64 *Ibid*. 344. Also see *Treaty of Arbitration of 1890*.

65 Mohammed Heikal, 'Egypt's Foreign Policy' 56 *Foreign Affairs* (1978) 714–727, 719.

66 Abdel Aal (AMSA), 'The Superpowers and Regional Security in the Middle East' in *Regional Security in the Third World: Case Studies from Southeast Asia and the Middle East* [M. Ayoob ed.] (London: Croom Helm, 1986) 196–213, 197–198.

obvious exclusion of the Gulf and inclusion of the European Mediterranean countries by default made it less appealing.[67] The privileging of the lines on the map trace to the much discussed *Sykes–Picot Agreement*, which as a claim for demarcation of territory, was never concerned with communities in the region. Tensions on the Arabian Peninsula had grown considerably as the centuries-old Ottoman Empire began to crumble at the turn of the twentieth century, but this also came at a time of the discovery of oil concessions on which the global economy would come to be based, and which has hastened the crisis of climate change while continuing the expropriation of wealth from the region.[68]

Unraveling three distinct complexities will provide an understanding of the intertwining between the peoples and territory in the wider region. Firstly, issues related to the territory itself. European interest in the region commenced with the fall of Constantinople in the fifteenth century, which deprived Europe of a land passage to the perceived wealth of India. Rather than interest in the Arabian Peninsula or 'Asia Minor' as the region was designated in colonial maps, control of it was considered necessary to access this wealth. This was reflected upon at the turn of the twentieth century by US Naval Captain Alfred Thayer, attributed with coining the term 'Middle East'.[69] Secondly, the populations within the wider region have always been diverse as swathes of communities and cultures have passed through what was historically a meeting point for trade. Ancient communities of Hittites, Jews, and others intermingled with Venetians and other Europeans in proximity to the Silk Route, which linked China to the region in a relationship far more engaged than it had with Europe. The spread of Islam in the seventh century unified many communities, but also birthed new schisms between Shia and Sunni, along more ancient identity crossroads between Persia and the rest of the region. In a 'normal' course of history, these identity fault lines would have probably tussled with war and bloodshed, and, if other regions serve as examples, new entities and communities may have been born, who would create myths to establish or consolidate governance systems. In the

67 This is evidenced by a number of EU dialogues and Agreements with Arab States, including bilateral cooperation agreements under the Neighbourhood Policy; multilateral relations with all Arab states via the Euro-Arab dialogue (established in 1973); multilateral agreements with regional organizations in the Middle East (Arab Maghreb Union; Gulf Cooperation Council; Arab League); to the Conference of Security and Cooperation in the Mediterranean (CSCM), and the Euro-Mediterranean process established by the EU at the European Council Meeting in Barcelona in 1995.

68 For the extent to which this colonial crime impacted the contemporary push towards the climate crisis, see Joshua Castellino, *Calibrating Colonial Crime* (Bristol: Bristol University Press, 2024).

69 See W. D. Puleston, *Mahan: The Life and Work of Alfred Thayer Mahan* (London: Jonathan Cape, 1939).

region this could not happen because of a third factor: the discovery by Western explorers of oil, first in Persia early in the twentieth century and then later in Saudi Arabia, in an area that historically had loose and decentralized governance. This prompted companies backed by colonial regimes to use their superior technology and bargaining power to make deals and enter agreements to ensure comparative advantages in terms of resources. Treating the populations as objects rather than subjects of law, Britain and France decided, over a hundred years ago, to come up with the *Asia Minor Agreement*, more familiar to most by its more recognized name as discussed above, the *Sykes–Picot Agreement*. As discussed this agreement was concerned mainly with establishing clear proprietary lines between the powers, guaranteeing 'peace' between them as they sought to develop their ability to benefit from the spheres of influence gained.

While accounts of European involvement in the region dominate recent narratives, this sometimes has the impact of overshadowing the significant Ottoman impact on the wider region. GE Hubbard's book,[70] essentially a travelogue of the journeys of the *Turco-Persian Frontier Commission* as it sought, nearly 70 years after the *Treaty of Ezerum* (1847), to delimit the frontier between the Ottoman and Persian Empires, highlights the practical challenges to be overcome in such a mission. Hubbard himself can also be considered a boundary-maker, having contributed alongside Lieutenant-Colonel C.H.D. Ryder (Chief Surveyor) to the drawing of the 1914 line that demarcated the legal basis of Iran's territorial sovereignty from that of Türkiye and Iraq. In his book, Hubbard emphasized that line drawing was not solely a Western pursuit and how it was important to understand local factors such as race, tradition, and religion in delimitations. The work is also important in showing how the emerging frontiers were being justified in London.[71] In his introduction to a new edition of the 1916 classical text 100 years later, Schofield, while accepting the devastating consequences of the boundary lines drawn by Britain and France, comments:

> The lines laid down as borders by Britain and France in the aftermath of World War I were by no means purely arbitrary and many reflected vague and putative former Ottoman divisions, but they had little to no tradition or function as political boundaries, frontier zones of border marches. Except, that is, for the Ottoman-Persian border margins which, by any reckoning, constituted classical historical borderlands.[72]

70 See Richard Schofield, 'Foreword' in *From the Gulf to Ararat: Imperial Boundary Making in the Late Ottoman Empire* [G. E. Hubbard ed.] (London: I. B. Tauris, 2016) xv.

71 G. E. Hubbard, *From the Gulf to Ararat: Imperial Boundary Making in the Late Ottoman Empire* (London: I. B. Tauris, 2016).

72 Schofield (2016) *op.cit.* 70, xiii–xiv.

In terms of scope and vision the reach of the Ottoman Empire was among the most impressive. As Isom-Verhaaren and Schull highlight:

> The Ottomans established one of the longest lived, most powerful, and largest empires in history, lasting for over six centuries and ruled by one continuous dynasty from the end of the thirteenth century to the early twentieth. Their empire left its mark on the regions known today as southeastern Europe, the Middle East, and North Africa. It stretched from the eastern gates of Vienna to the borders of contemporary Iran in the east, Morocco in the west, north to the Black Sea, and south to the tip of Arabia.[73]

But in addition to the territorial reach, Ottoman influence spread further:

> The Ottomans exercised soft power through diplomacy, alliances, trade, patronage of the arts and sciences, and the movements of large numbers of people, extending their influence beyond the territory they controlled politically and militarily. Throughout its existence, the empire was the epitome of connectivity between East and West, a crossroads of Eurasia, Africa and the Indian Ocean basin.[74]

The extent to which rigid boundary lines derived in European minds with little familiarity with other cultures, driven by a quest to capture others' resources may be able to capture the fluidity of history and the consequences of the flow of history on identity, is an important consideration in assessing the utility of boundaries. This example of the changing frontiers between the Byzantine and Ottoman empires at the commencement of the rise of the Ottomans is worth reproducing:

> The dynamic conquest policy, to which the frontier society owed its very existence, created a high degree of physical mobility, with a moving frontier that set people in motion and displaced and resettled them at an astonishing pace. Accordingly, the way the people of the frontier envisioned their political and cultural environment kept changing requiring new terms of defining self and others.[75]

Heywood characterizes the Ottoman frontier as a region where colonization and settlement involved military action as well as religious proselytization,

73 *Living in the Ottoman Realm: Empire and Identity, 13th to 20th Centuries* [Christine Isom-Verhaaren & Kent F. Schull eds.] (Bloomington, IN: Indiana University Press, 2016) 1.

74 *Ibid.* 1.

75 *Ibid.* 30.

forming at once a zone of interaction and passage as well as a political barrier.[76] This led Aydogan to distinguish between the traditional classification of frontiers and boundaries by geographers and political scientists and the application of these concepts to premodern frontiers. Thus:

> Geographers and political scientists consider frontiers and boundaries as belonging to distinct categories: frontiers are zones evolving organically between states or societies; boundaries, on the other hand, are state-defined artificial lines of separation. Although this definition of 'frontier' is of considerable importance for modern conceptualizations, it cannot be easily applied to premodern frontiers.[77]

Instead of seeking to assess Ottoman conceptions of frontiers, Heywood highlights how this conception changed over time. Thus from 1300 to 1700, the Ottoman Empire viewed itself as a 'frontier polity' with an active and expanding frontier. This period ended around 1700 when the Ottomans accepted a more European-style demarcated frontier through the *Treaty of Karlowitz* (1699).

During the fifteenth and seventeenth centuries the expansionist approach of the Ottomans was relentless, and under Selim's short reign (1512–1520) continued into eastern Anatolia while simultaneously conquering Syria, Egypt, and the Arabian Peninsula. This created identity schisms, with the Sunni and Shia religious divide becoming a factor. As Isom-Verhaaren and Schull narrate:

> This complicated Ottoman identity because, as a result, many Muslims in the empire were distinctly different ethnically and linguistically from the Turkish-speaking Muslims of Anatolia and the Balkans.[78]

Selim's son Süleyman (1520–1566), in his much longer reign, moved the Empire further into European and African lands, acquiring territory in modern Hungary while also using his growing naval prowess to assert Ottoman sovereignty over Mediterranean lands, including North Africa as far as Algiers.[79] Süleyman worked to consolidate Ottoman rule by introducing

76 Colin Heywood, 'The Frontier in Ottoman History: Old Ideas and New Myths' in *Frontiers in Question: Eurasian Borderlands, 700–1700* [Daniel Power & Naomi Standen eds.] (New York: St. Martin's Press, 1999) 228–250, 231.

77 Zeynep Aygoğan, 'Changing Perceptions along the Frontiers: The Moving Frontier with Rum in Late Medieval Anatolian Frontier Narratives' in *Living in the Ottoman Realm: Empire and Identity, 13th to 20th Centuries* [Christine Isom-Verhaaren & Kent F. Schull eds.] (Bloomington, IN: Indiana University Press, 2016) 29–41 at 30.

78 *Ibid.* 91.

79 *Ibid.* 91.

laws and decrees that were designed to create good governance in what were lands, communities, and cultures that were very different from each other and from the Ottomans.[80]

The Ottoman Empire reached its territorial zenith by the seventeenth and eighteenth centuries, and with other European hegemons seeking to expand their own powers, the *Treaty of Karlowitz* became an important marker in an attitudinal change to territorial expansion. As the Ottoman Empire sought to consolidate the territories it had acquired, the challenge turned to the expansion of administrative measures to govern the vast territory under Ottoman sway.[81] This came at a time of significant internal challenge and external turbulence caused by European and Asiatic expansionism, the Hundred Years' War, and even a climate change–oriented change referred to as the Little Ice Age.[82] The impact of the various 'global' crises had signalled the end of the Ming and Safavid dynasties in China and Persia, respectively, but the Ottomans held on and consolidated their empire through reform of their administrative, social, cultural, fiscal, diplomatic, and political realms.[83]

The need to modernize the challenges of governing vast territories and the emerging internal pushes for forms of autonomy and self-governance led to widespread reform as the empire sought to transition towards a modern imperial State between 1839 and 1918. While the overarching goal of these reforms was to preserve the empire, this was becoming more difficult in the face of the growing appetite of European powers for Eurasian lands, in conjunction with a rising thirst for the accommodation of nationalisms amongst the diverse populations that constituted the Ottoman Empire. The latter forces 'engendered mass political activity that led to a simultaneous push for constitutionalism, local autonomy, and secession by different groups'.[84]

The end of the Empire was violent, characterized by

> a constitutional revolution, massive territorial loss, two *coups d'état*, a war with Italy, the Balkan Wars, World War I and subsequent uprisings and wars of independence. By the end of this period, all southeastern European, Arab Middle Eastern, and North African territories were severed from the empire, and the empire itself ceased to exist. The population, economy, infrastructure, and political system of the former Ottoman Empire were devastated as a result of wars, disease, famine, ethnic cleansings, population transfers and multiple genocides. The events of the final years of the empire had an enormous impact on creating and shaping the

80 *Ibid.*
81 *Ibid.* 167.
82 *Ibid.*
83 *Ibid.*
84 *Ibid.* 256.

> modern Middle East, North Africa, Caucasus, and southeastern Europe as inheritors of an Ottoman legacy for good and ill.[85]

As Peacock states in his introduction to a collected work that examines life on the Ottoman frontiers:

> For every modern state, its frontiers constitute a vital part of its identity, marking – in theory at least – the extent of its government's authority and serving as a barrier or bridge to the world beyond... Thus the modern understanding of frontiers and borders relies largely on relatively recent or specific technology and concepts: precise maps, only really sufficiently developed for exact border delineation in the nineteenth century... Some historians have wondered whether the concept of frontiers is valid at all for the pre-modern world, at least until the development of a reasonably sophisticated cartography in the Renaissance.[86]

Seeking to summarize the differences in the extent to which the borders of the Ottoman Empire were in line with modern conceptions of borders and frontiers, Peacock states:

> Ottoman frontiers were constantly shifting as the empire expanded and contracted over its history. They also varied radically in their nature, according to geography, local circumstances, and the nature of the powers contesting Istanbul's authority. In Europe, on the front line with the Hapsburgs, something akin to a modern frontier had developed by the sixteenth century, if not before, with the two powers confronting each other across a delineated border from behind a network of fortifications, even if this frontier line was not always taken particularly seriously in practice. In sixteenth to seventeenth century Iraq, the border with the Safavids of Iran was more ambiguous, with numerous tribes of fluctuating loyalties inhabiting the no-man's land between the two empires, but for merchants and pilgrims clearly defined stations nonetheless marked the transition from one political jurisdiction to another. In Africa, on the other hand, it remains unclear how far the empire's reach stretched up the Nile, and it

85 *Ibid.* 257.

86 *The Frontiers of the Ottoman World* [Andrew C. S. Peacock ed.] (Oxford: Oxford University Press for the British Academy, 2009). Peacock cites the following works in addition: Daniel Power & Naomi Standen (eds.), *Frontiers in Question: Eurasian Borderlands 711–1700* (Basingstoke: Palgrave Macmillan, 1999); Charles R. Whittaker, *The Frontiers of the Roman Empire: A Social and Economic Study* (Baltimore, MD: Johns Hopkins University Press, 1994); Hugh Elton, *The Frontiers of the Roman Empire* (Bloomington, IN: Indiana University Press, 1996); and Thomas J. Barfield, *The Perilous Frontier: Nomadic Empires and China, 221 BC to AD 1757* (Oxford: Blackwell, 1989).

> seems more likely that rather than there having been a direct frontier with the Ottomans' rivals… the authority of both sides simply petered out in the Middle Nile, leaving the intervening space to be ruled by local rulers who may pay nominal allegiance to one power or another.[87]

While the exogenous definition of the region is direct proof of intense outside involvement that has yielded a host of pacts, agreements, conventions, secret deals, and subterfuge, the document that receives the most attention is the *Sykes–Picot Agreement* of 1916, which divided what some, though not all, saw as the 'Arab nation' into spheres of influence. Within the 'French' side of the line, encompassing modern Syria and Lebanon, the French sought to interpret the Ottoman *millet* system, carving out autonomous territories (for the Alawites, for instance) and building a Christian State in Lebanon. French regional interests date to the *Promise St. Louis* made in 1250, which was renewed twice. This established France as protector of Christians in the Middle East.[88] Since the Grand Patriarch of the Maronites took refuge in Mount Lebanon (seventh century), it served as a beacon for fleeing Christians around the region.[89] Had the French vision for Lebanon been achieved, there may have been two religious homelands in the midst of the Middle East: a Christian homeland north of Tyre and Sidon, to rival the contiguous Jewish homeland of Israel to its south. As it happened the physical dimensions of the territory of Lebanon changed, and in the political bargaining over additional coastal regions, a significant Druze population was added, making the State one of the region's most diverse.[90]

The denial of a Kurdish homeland on the basis of exogenous line-drawing shows the direct impact of how such ventures effectively erase traditional identity-based fault lines from regional maps.[91] The decision to create a Jewish homeland in the wider region as a reparation for European atrocities against Jews stands in sharp contrast to European decisions to deny Kurdish recognition of their homeland, with both decisions cloaked in a *faux* legality that barely masks the absolute arrogance towards history and peoples. A promise for such a homeland was made by the ruling British within their sphere of influence in a manner not dissimilar to the one made by Arthur Balfour for a Jewish homeland.[92] However what were described as 'changing geo-political realities' (i.e. British interests) were attributed to submerging this nation and

87 Peacock (2009) *op.cit.* 86, 2.

88 Joshua Castellino & Kathleen Cavanaugh, *Minority Rights in the Middle East: A Comparative Legal Analysis* (Oxford: Oxford University Press, 2013).

89 *Ibid.* 339

90 *Ibid.* 334–350.

91 *Ibid.* 160–165.

92 For a discussion at its 50th anniversary see Mayir Vereté, 'The Balfour Declaration and its Makers' 6(1) *Middle Eastern Studies* (1970) 48–76.

scattering its population. The ostensible reason given was the British need to counterbalance Shia Iran, a historic heavyweight in the region, whose dominance was deemed a threat to peace. In reneging on its promise for a Kurdish homeland, the British consigned a community with a legitimate claims to being 'a people', to live as minorities due to *their* boundary-drawing enterprises. The Kurds remain scattered in four States: neither considered a minority nor enjoying political autonomy in Türkiye;[93] recognized as a minority but emerging as a powerful autonomous region in the midst of the chaos of Iraq post the US–UK led invasion of 2003;[94] denied recognition and citizenship in Syria until the uprising against Assad, who sought an inter-ethnic bargain to hold power;[95] and denied an autonomous State in Iran.[96] Historical documents attesting to Kurdish claims for statehood are strong, but decisions in international law governing title to territory, i.e. maintenance of colonial boundaries with change only possible through the consent of State parties, mean their claim is negated based on whimsical grounds.

The treatment of Kurdistan underscores why a rigid rules-oriented system reliant on flawed boundaries drawn on the basis of vested interests is unlikely to yield meaningful peace. Instead it venerates a cunning self-serving decision taken at a time of transition by illegal occupying powers, ostensibly to guarantee peace and regional stability as defined by the colonial interests who contributed to such division, and who then took action, including through sponsorship of specific sovereigns and their arming to maintain this new imposed reality into perpetuity. These decisions were validated among the small community of occupying States who reified each other as 'the international community' and claimed legitimacy in making such decisions, congratulating themselves on the validity of that decision based on the supposed maintenance of a precarious peace. Kurdish history documents a litany of problems instead: from ethnic cleansing and genocide, denial of citizenship, systematic and widespread discrimination, and systematic barriers to propagate their identity.

No commentary on boundaries in the region could be complete without the inclusion of Israel. This one will be brief in view of the extent to which these issues dominate the annals of public international law literature. The 1948 boundaries, guaranteed on behalf of the British by Arthur Balfour, may already have been problematic in giving precedence once again, as in colonial

93 Joost Jongerden, *The Settlement Issue in Turkey and the Kurds* (Leiden: Brill, 2007).

94 Ofra Bengio, *The Kurds of Iraq: Building a State within a State* (Westport, CT: Lynne Rienner, 2014).

95 Harriet Allsop & Wladimir van Wilgenburg, *The Kurds of Northern Syria: Governance, Diversity and Conflicts* (London: I. B. Taurus, 2019).

96 Abbas Vali, *Kurds and the State in Iran: The Making of Kurdish Identity* (London: I. B. Taurus, 2014).

rule, to territory over people.[97] Rather than negotiating space in which expelled Jewish communities could cohabit with incumbent Arab populations, a decision was made, as in previous eras, to treat existing populations as objects, supplanting a State around Jewish sacred places, albeit with a religious community with a legitimate historical presence within the region. The immediate attack by its neighbours on Israel and its ability to defend itself by acquiring territory and the means to defend it beyond its own borders is well documented.[98] It demonstrates the extent to which seeds of conflict were sowed through an increasingly aggressive settler colonial project that continues to germinate to this day with devastating consequences for Palestinians. Whether these are driven by purely racial superiority combining with a lack of imagination and foresight, or a simple disregarding of the future fate of the territory will never be known for certain. What is clear is that once again lines on a map drawn in a previous era, based on interests other than those of the people living in the region, have created a legacy of bloodshed and destruction that has given the new State and wider region an infamy in public international law which continues to grow. The width, depth, and callousness of the systematic and widespread State violence that followed the brutal Hamas attack of the 7 October 2023 have emphasized how small the distinction is between the various wielders of violence. The ICJ's interim findings of the plausibility of genocide committed by the Israeli government signalling the possibility that this has the intent to destroy Palestinians[99] has also brought into question the entirety of the post–World War II order as most post-colonial States aligned behind the Palestinians – recognizing the Israeli behaviour as synonymous to what transpired in their own histories – while former colonial powers failed to match their behaviour to the rules-based order they readily took credit for creating in the justification that it would create the blueprint for perpetual peace.[100] It is instructive to note that among widespread calls for ceasefire, two hegemons, the United States and United Kingdom, already with the most destructive history in the region, but who

97 Bernard Regan, *The Balfour Declaration: Empire, Mandate and Resistance in Palestine* (London: Verso Books, 2018).

98 Gershon Shafir, *A Half Century of Occupation: Israel, Palestine and the World's Most Intractable Conflict* (Oakland, CA: University of California Press, 2017).

99 *Application of the Convention on the Prevention and Punishment of the Crime of Genocide in the Gaza Strip* (South Africa v. Israel), Order of 26 January 2024.

100 J. Agnew, 'The Language of Intractability and the Gaza War: Conflating Anti-Semitism and Anti-Zionism is Historically Problematic and Misses How Much Contemporary Israel Has Become a Role Model for Ethno-Nationalists Worldwide' *Human Geography* (2023) https://doi.org/10.1177/19427786231220046

were central to the development of the so-called quest for perpetual peace, actively repudiated the means to bring the violence to an end.[101]

Post-colonial history has revealed how unsuccessful the imposition of a Western-style sovereign State in the region has been in the pursuit of peace. This specific imported form of territorial governance, with its only antecedent being the short colonial rule that preceded it, has been unable to deliver regional stability. In terms of historical antecedents to statehood and potential contributions to international law governing title to territory, the system of independent emirates trading with each other in a broader and looser confederation is one that has never fully been admitted into European-dominated works of public international law or politics. Even the much-cited commentary by Crawford on Statehood is restricted to discussing writings of jurists such as Grotius, Vittoria, and Vattel narrating its impact on 'state practice'.[102] While this classical approach to public international law has merits in documenting the richness of European ideas, its complete exclusion of other forms of governance impacting the emergence of statehood, including boundary-making and how this was transmitted around the world, leaves it incomplete at best. Crawford's historical narrative stems from antecedents predating Grotius, through examples of Lithuania (1385) and Aragon (1479), and the emergence of the Netherlands (1559–1648) which formed the backdrop to Grotius's writing.[103] It is notable in its absence, however, of any discussion around emirates as a legitimate form of governance that may be the precursor to sovereign statehood in many parts of the world, or to indigenous peoples' governance systems which maintained effective control over territory. The conspicuous absence of references to jurists who offered commentary on the efficacy of such governance models also makes the work typical of the limited Europeanized lens through which the world of international law, and the world itself, has been shaped.

Even in the Western Sahara case before the International Court of Justice, where the open-ended nature of the question posed to the Court allowed exploration of the *Bilad Shinguitti* (ostensibly the precursor to modern Mauritania), this was not recognized as an exercise of measuring effective sovereignty, with pleadings and judgments referring to it as an amorphous 'entity'.[104] Writing about the turn of the century, Andrews came up with

101 'UN Security Council Again Fails to Adopt Resolution Demanding Immediate Humanitarian Ceasefire in Gaza on Account of Veto by United States', UN *Press Release* SC 155/95 (20 February 2024) UN Security Council 9552nd meeting (AM).

102 James Crawford, *Creation of States in International Law*, 2nd ed. (Cambridge: Cambridge University Press, 2007, Oxford Online Resources).

103 *Ibid.* Chapter 1.

104 Hugh Thirlway, *The Law & Procedure of the ICJ: Fifty Years of Jurisprudence*, Vol. 1 (Oxford: Oxford University Press, 2013) 543.

an interesting list of categories of antecedents to the State;[105] however, once again, emirates merited little attention and remain worthy of further study for those interested in formulations of territorially based governance options outside Western-style statehood and boundaries. The impact of emirates in the wider region could not be overstated despite its relative erasure from documented international legal history, as manifest in the many that emerged, survived, disappeared, and were replaced by others over centuries.

Questions of territory and identity clearly remain at the forefront of historical events in the wider region. This has resulted in violent contestations between States exercised at the behest of hegemonic interests of powerful actors within (notably Iran, Saudi Arabia, and Türkiye) and from States outside the region (the United States, Russia, Britain, France, and, of late, China). Masquerading as the region's only democracy, Israel has been a persistent violater of international law and a regional bully, stealing land and resources through cloaks of *faux* legitimacy while steadily increasing settlement of Palestinian lands. The devastation it has visited upon the region in the war on Palestinians in Gaza signals a return to an era when the use of force by hegemons gave them a blank cheque to do as they please. Its stain on international law may well prove an existential threat to the idea of international law itself. This comes in a region where the Cold War, the Gulf Wars, and the attempts to mediate between the Arab world and Israel, and then between Palestine and Israel, alongside the neglected war in Yemen, have created a recurrent backdrop to what are portrayed as games for territory and resources in the region, played with devastating human loss. Against this backdrop the settler colonial politics in Israel that have driven its government to react in the genocidal manner it has to the terrorist attack of 7 October 2023 is indicative of contemporary quests for territory in the twenty-first-century modern world. These events inevitably impact the political map of the region and will deepen fragmentation and discord along 'national', ethnic, and religious lines. Economic and trade ties, built through careful negotiation over time and a source of more open dialogue and cooperation through bilateral agreements, are decimated by conflict and distrust attendant to the significant presence of arms in the hands of externally and internally armed militia and paramilitary groups.

The illegal US/British invasion of Iraq in 2003 had already played a significant role in hastening regional destruction, inundating the region with weapons and creating a conducive environment for male-determined violence while reducing sophisticated societies to feudalism and barbarism. The impact of transnational actors such as *Al Qaeda* seeking to undermine States through the mass mobilization of individuals committed to using violence to

105 J. A. Andrews, 'The Concept of Statehood and the Acquisition of Territory in the Nineteenth Century' 94 *Law Quarterly Review* (1978) 408–427.

overthrow governments further hastened destruction while generating new enmities and alliances based on flawed readings of historical hatreds.

This bloodied history suggests strongly that the imposed regime based on the sanctity of boundaries has failed to achieve peace and prevent conflict. Instead conflict has flared regularly, which could be classified into taking three distinct forms:

(i) Interstate disputes between Israel and Lebanon, Iraq and Iran, Iraq and Kuwait, Saudi Arabia and Yemen, Bahrain and Qatar, Egypt and Libya, Morocco and Mauritania, and Jordan and Syria.
(ii) Intrastate disputes within Lebanon, Iraq, Syria, Algeria, Jordan, Yemen, and Oman.
(iii) The various attempts by the State of Israel to flex its territorial reach by eliminating Palestinians not only from within its internationally agreed borders, but also from territories it has since occupied, claimed, and continues to settle.

The emergence and subsequent defeat of Daesh in its violent attempt to erase the *Sykes-Picot* line displayed manifestations of all three forms of conflict, making it a *quasi*-interstate conflict through non-state actors, manifesting itself as an intrastate conflict spread across two States, and using overwhelming force and brutality driven by hatred to subjugate those deemed its enemies.[106] The roots of these conflicts clearly lie in colonialism, failed statecraft, and the creation of clientelist alliances to exploit the region's natural hydrocarbon resources. These interests have chimed, intersected, and morphed into ethno-nationalist and sectarian conflicts, irreparably fragmenting the *ulemma* in the region, while germinating contestations between the large Muslim communities and smaller non-Muslim minorities. The naked objectives of colonial powers, reverberated strongly in the 2023–2024 annihilation of Palestinians in Gaza, have left an indelible impact on indigenous groups who fell within these artificially created borders. The legacy of Arthur Balfour may have been the most potent reminder of the catastrophic legacy of British intervention in the region, but it may yet be overtaken by the US/British invasion of 2003 or the 2023–2024 annihilation of Gaza by Israel in terms of its disruption and devastation. Every one of these initiatives was taken in the name of peace, and each involved the use of sustained violence. Meanwhile the multiple contested geographies of the region and the borders that remain less than fixed continue to fester at the heart of the Arab–Israeli dispute, the Palestinian question, Kurdish struggles for self-determination,

106 Matthew Bamber-Zryd 'Cyclical Jihadist Governance: The Islamic State Governance Cycle in Iraq and Syria' 33(8) *Small Wars & Insurgencies* (2022) 1314–1344.

demarcations that may be sought and even won on the basis of sectarianism, and potentially between the Persian and Arab worlds.

Closer scrutiny of boundary issues would be more accurate if the enquiry treats the region as being divided into distinct regions. The ideal typology in seeking to study questions of territory and identity lies in classifying the States that came under wide Ottoman and Arab influence, including through religion, along five distinct fault lines: (i) the oil-producing countries on the Saudi Peninsula of Bahrain, Kuwait, Saudi Arabia, Oman, Qatar, and the United Arab Emirates alongside Yemen, dominated by ancient systems of Islamic and tribal governance that appear to have survived through the externally sponsored patronage of selected royal families; (ii) the Fertile Crescent region of Israel/Occupied Territories, Jordan, Lebanon, Syria, and Iraq, where boundary disputes continue to be generated by indigenous and exogenous interests; (iii) the North African countries of Algeria, Egypt, Libya, Morocco, and Tunisia, which manifest a combination of tribal rule alongside the creation of sophisticated State machineries and are classified as African countries based on their geography and indigenous populations; (iv) sub-Saharan States who are members of the League of Arab States like Sudan, Mauritania, Djibouti, Somalia, and the Comoros Islands where religion, tribe, and ethnicity have been ignored in the establishment of colonial boundaries, and which are subject to the African Union's attitude to boundaries explored below; and (v) the outlying non-Arab States of Iran, Afghanistan, and possibly Tajikistan, Turkmenistan, Kyrgyzstan, Kazakhstan, and Uzbekistan, where the territories of all, including albeit to a much lesser extent Iran, have been the creation of external powers.

This analysis would, if carefully fostered through regional discussions, provide clarity to the myriad of boundary disputes that simmer and blaze in the wider meta-region, and which create tension through the presence of kin communities straddled by them. As elsewhere, the contemporary governing imperatives remain the same: urgently mitigating climate change, addressing the challenge of economic growth that is not fossil fuel–reliant, challenging deepening inequality, and finding regional solutions for the desperation of populations fleeing human insecurity *en masse* due to a combination of scarcity and violence.

Africa

The history of contemporary boundaries and a significant proportion of the global literature on the subject is devoted to the period in history referred to as the 'Scramble for Africa'.[107] Fuelled by the 3Cs – Commerce, Christianity,

107 J. D. Hargreaves, 'The Making of the Boundaries: Focus on West Africa' in *Partitioned Africans* [A. I. Asiwaju ed.] (London: Hurst and Co. 1985) 19–27.

and Civilization – European Powers sought to gain a territorial foothold in sub-Saharan Africa in a race against each other to win prosperity.[108] In return, the narratives of the time suggest that African entities were to be 'welcomed' into the Family of Nations as equals under classical tenets of *jus gentium*.[109] This 'bargain' was initially affected through treaties made with African rulers: treaties of dubious validity due to serious questions regarding form, substance, and consideration, but also in view of their long-term ramifications for colonization. The European acquisition of African territory at the end of the nineteenth century was driven more by a sense of competition between the powers who sought to establish title against each other for exclusive access to resources,[110] rather than any desire to extend sovereignty over peoples. Their actions remain material to contemporary boundaries of modern African States.

European self-belief in their superiority meant that they could not accept the premise that Africans were capable of the art of government,[111] and thus the perceived burden[112] of bringing the 'blessings of civilisation' to the continent served to mask the nature of European interest.[113] In the quest to open new markets, the costs of colonial administration were deemed prohibitive[114]

108 See generally Gann & Duignan (1969), *op.cit.*

109 See generally Charles H. Alexandrowicz, 'The Juridical Expression of the Sacred Trust of Civilization' 65 (1) *American Journal of International Law* (1971) 149–159.

110 See generally, Prosser Gifford & William R. Louis, *France and Britain in Africa: Imperial Rivalry and Colonial Rule* (New Haven, CT: Yale University Press, 1971); Gann & Duignan (1969), *op.cit.* 108; L. H. Gann & Peter Duignan, *The Rulers of British Africa 1870–1914* (Stanford, CA: Stanford University Press, 1978); John D. Hargreaves, *West Africa Partitioned*, Vol. 1 (London: Macmillan, 1974).

111 For example, see John Westlake, *International Law*, Vol. 1 (Ann Arbor, MI: The University Press, 1910) 07. Also see L. H. Gann & Peter Duignan, 'Introduction' in Gann & Duignan (1969) *op.cit.* 108, 1–26, 6–7 & 24.

112 John Flint, 'Chartered Companies and the Transition from Informal Sway to Colonial Rule in Africa' in *Bismarck, Europe, and Africa* [Stig Förster, Wolfgang J. Mommsen & Ronald Robinson eds.] (Oxford: Oxford University Press, 1988) 69, 73.

113 These phrases are taken from Article VI of the Final Act of the Berlin West Africa Conference 1885. Edward Hertslet, *The Map of Africa By Treaty*, Vol. 2 (London: Harrison & Sons for HMSO, 1909) 473.

114 As imperial municipal law would be automatically applied to the territory of a new colony, such acquisitions were potentially costly. This issue was of paramount concern to the British government at the Berlin West Africa Conference (1884–1885) where it was suggested that acquisition should take the form of annexation as a matter of course. Lord Chancellor Selbourne was anxious to avoid the creation of such a rule of law, not least for the consequences of such a rule for British colonial policy outside Africa. See William R. Louis, 'The Berlin Congo Conference' in Gifford & Louis (1971) *op.cit.* 110, 167–220, 210–214. The importance of this point was not lost on the Foreign Secretary, Lord Salisbury, in the context of the governance of the Oil Rivers Protectorate, which was reconsidered in 1888–1889. When formal annexation was recommended, Salisbury, aware of the difficulty of enforcing anti-slavery laws, ensured that the territory remained a protectorate,

and free trade imperialism, to be achieved through chartered companies,[115] was preferred in an early manifestation of a public–private partnership.[116] However, gaining the foothold to trade exclusively (rather than in a consortium with other European powers) nonetheless required intra-European conversations about sovereignty, which heralded a new imperialism towards the end of the 1870s, provoking conflict between the European powers in Africa,[117] leading to the 'Scramble'.[118] Chartered companies – state-backed private entities that acted in lieu of the State in many functions but where the acquisition of wealth from the activities was allowed to flow to private hands – operated with wide commercial privileges, exercising delegated sovereignty rights enabling the conclusion of treaties with African rulers,[119] resulting in the acquisition of territorial sovereignty on behalf of their States.[120] This outsourced colonial operation to private investors willing to undertake risks to generate revenue and profit.[121] Presented as 'milomania'[122] the chartered company became the symbol of African colonization,[123] in sharp contrast to the reality where many of these companies were loss-making.[124]

---

see John E. Flint, *Sir George Goldie and the Making of Nigeria* (Oxford: Oxford University Press, 1960) 235–236.

115 This as usually achieved through flag-bearing 'Chartered Companies': see Flint (1988), *op .cit.* 112 also see, in an Indian context, William Dalrymple, *The Anarchy: The Relentless Rise of the East India Company* (London: Bloomsbury, 2020).

116 The 'Standard' Newspaper, 11th October 1884, cited in Louis, 'The Berlin Congo Conference' in Gifford & Louis (1971) *op.cit.* 110, 167–220.

117 The participation of a unified Germany in the Scramble led to conflicts with Britain, for example, in the Cameroons and Angra Pequena in 1884.

118 See Thomas Pakenham, *The Scramble for Africa* (London: Little Brown Book Group, 1991); John Fage, *A History of Africa* (London: Routledge, 1995) 213–388; H. L. Wessling, *Divide and Rule: The Partition of Africa 1880 1914* (London: Praeger Westlake, 1996).

119 Charter companies held sway over nearly 75% of British territory in sub-Saharan Africa, demonstrating their importance to the British colonial venture. See Flint (1988) *op.cit.* 112, 71.

120 These privileges and monopolies were less common after the Berlin Conference 1885. See the struggle of the National Africa Company (later the Royal Niger Company) for its charter in Flint (1960) *op.cit.* 114, 68–87. Also see Hertslet (1909) Vol.1 *op.cit.* 113, 125–127.

121 See generally Flint (1960) *op.cit.* 114; Basil Williams, *Cecil Rhodes* (London: Constable, 1921); William T. Stead (ed.), *The Last Will and Testament of Cecil J. Rhodes* (London: "Review of Reviews" Office, 1902).

122 'Milomania' was a term coined to describe the imperialist policy of acquiring territory for its own sake. See John Atkinson Hobson, *Imperialism: A Study* (London: J. Nisbet, 1902) cited in Gann & Duignan, 'Introduction' in Gann & Duignan (1969) *op.cit.* 108, 9. More generally for a discussion of the antics of King Leopold of Belgium, see Victoria Brittain, 'Colonialism and the Predatory State in the Congo' 236 *New Left Review* (1999) 133.

123 See Gann & Duignan, 'Reflections on Imperialism and the Scramble for Africa' in Gann & Duignan, *op.cit.* 108, 100–129.

124 While this was obviously a negotiating figure arrived at for the purposes of securing a charter, the claim was accepted in principle by the British government, see Flint (1988), *op .cit.* 112, 79–85.

Classical international law held that only *terra nullius* was open to acquisition,[125] and lessons learnt from Latin America dictated that African territory could not be deemed as such. Instead consensus grew that such territory could only be acquired through treaties of *cession* with the inhabiting sovereigns. These were considered to constitute legitimate transfers of African territory, showing greater respect for the subjecthood of African inhabitants than had been afforded to Latin American indigenous peoples, even though the end result was European acquisition of territory in both cases.[126] The notion of a 'protectorate'[127] was established to consolidate such acquisitions, in which external sovereignty was vested in the 'protecting' State while internal sovereignty remained with the 'protected' entity.[128] Colonial rhetoric justified this as allowing the Powers to gain continental footholds.[129] Another classical practice developed was the instrument of 'jurisdictional capitulations'[130] ensuring that foreign communities established in a foreign State be granted self-government privileges, with jurisdiction vested in the head of that community.[131]

125 See generally, Oppenheim *International Law* (1992) 677–718. Robert Jennings, *The Acquisition of Territory in International Law* (Manchester: Manchester University Press, 1963) 1–35 also see Malcolm Shaw, *Title to Territory in Africa: International Legal Issues* (Oxford: Clarendon Press, 1986) 1–26.

126 For example, see the cession of the Port and Island of Lagos by King Docemo to Britain in 1861, Hertslet (1909) Vol. 1 *op.cit.* 113, 93–95.

127 Hall described a protectorate as 'somewhat indefinite, or rather perhaps it may be said to have different meanings in different circumstances in the mouths of different people'. W. E. Hall, *A Treatise on the Foreign Powers and Jurisdiction of the Crown* (1894) 204 quoted in H. F. Morris, 'Protection or Annexation? Some Constitutional Anomalies of Colonial Rule' in *Indirect Rule and the Search for Justice: Essays in East African Legal History* [H. F. Morris & J. R. Read eds.] (Oxford: Clarendon Press, 1972) 41–70, 42. A question around the meaning of the term was raised by King Ja Ja of Opoboland (1885), but dismissed. In 1886, the British Colonial Office released a statement where 'protection' was deemed to mean the promotion of the welfare of the natives of all the territories *taken as a whole* by ensuring the peaceful development of trade and facilitating their intercourse with Europeans (superseding any contrary obligation). Roseberry to Hewett, 15th April 1886, quoted J. C. Anene, *International Boundaries of Nigeria* (London: Longman, 1970) 74. Also see Oji Umozurike, *Self-Determination in International Law* (Hamden, CT: Archon Books, 1979) 44. For a fuller account of Ja Ja's actions see pp. 232–235.

128 See Charles Alexandrowicz, *The European-African Confrontation* (Leiden: A. W. Sijthoff, 1973) 54–60. Also see Oji Umozurike, *International Law and Colonialism in Africa* (Lagos: Nwamife Publishers, 1979).

129 Alexandrowicz, *Ibid.* 51.

130 See C. H. Alexandrowicz, 'The Role of Treaties in the European-African Confrontation in the Nineteenth Century' in *African International Legal History* [A. K. Mensah-Brown ed.] (New York: UNITAR, 1975) 27–68, 61–63.

131 Schwarzenberger (1962) *op.cit.* 55.

While acquisitory treaties are often presented as demonstrating a level of consent to the acceptance of European sovereignty in Africa,[132] the Powers did not formally question their right to colonize Africa. The history of the period is dominated instead by questions of *how* such colonization could occur, not whether it was justified. The decision to use acquisitionary treaties cloaked colonization with an aura of legality – a reflection of growing norms of democracy at home rather than compliance with international legal thought and philosophy. While acceptance of African sovereignty could be considered a step forward from the treatment of indigenous peoples in the Americas, its sole benefit in acknowledging such sovereignty lay in it being considered to legitimize the transfer of this sovereignty to European Powers.[133]

While there may have been grounds for believing African rulers wished to establish friendly relations with European agents, there is little clarity about the nature of such relations. Blood pacts and symbolic expressions of friendly relations were slyly interpreted as the basis for the conclusion of acquisitory treaties.[134] Lugard even conveniently argued that blood pacts were the African equivalent of the *jus civile* notion of the law of contract sealing agreements in international law.[135] There is no evidence to show that blood pacts were intended to surrender territorial authority; however, the ceremonial presentation of unequal, standardized, and predetermined treaties requiring acknowledgement was deemed European gesture of friendship[136] rather than act of territorial acquisition. This in reality amounted to the wide-scale deceitful transfer of territorial sovereignty,[137] though in form and substance these processes varied, depending on the size of the entity and the nature of

132 See Alexandrowicz (1973) *op.cit.* 128, 96–97. Also see Shaw (1986) *op.cit.* 125, 37.

133 According to Judge Huber, '[S]overeignty in the relation between states signifies independence. Independence in regard to a portion of the globe is the right to exercise therein, to the exclusion of any other state, the function of a state'. See the *Island of Palmas Arbitration* (1928) 875. In the circumstances, such a limited interpretation of the concept of territorial sovereignty cannot be justified under international law.

134 M. Mwa Bawele, 'Afro-European Relations in the Western Congo Basin 1884-5' in Förster, Mommsen & Robinson (1988) *op.cit.* 112, 469–489.

135 *Pacta sunt servanda* states that every treaty in force is binding on the parties and must be performed in good faith. See Alexandrowicz (1973) *op.cit.* 128, 50–54 see Frederick John Dealtry Lugard, *The Rise of Our East African Empire*, Vol. 2 (London: Blackwood & Sons, 1893).

136 See Hertslet (1909) Vol.1 *op.cit.* 113, 137–153. This source provides a number of standardized forms used in the conclusion of treaties of protection between the National African Company (later Royal Niger Company) and African entities in the area of Nigeria.

137 See Mwa Bawele (1988) *op.cit.* 134, 471.

the colonial power.[138] One of the lowest points of the acquisitory process was expressed by the account of an agent in Uganda:

> A ragged untidy European, who in any civilised country would be in danger of being taken up by the police as a vagrant, lands at a native village, the people run away; he shouts out after them to come back, holding before them a shilling's worth of beads ... the so-called interpreter pretends to explain the treaty to the chief. The chief does not understand a word of it, but he looks pleased as he receives another present of beads; a mark is made on a printed treaty by the chief, and another by the interpreter, the vagrant, who professes to be the representative of a great empire, signs his name. The boat sails away, and the new ally and protégé of England or France immediately throws the treaty into the fire.[139]

The lack of true consent severely invalidates these treaties[140] and their central misrepresentations amount to bad faith and fraud. By the late nineteenth century, the Powers were aware that unsubstantiated territorial claims deprived them of their imperial ambitions. Vague or fictional protectorates served to intensify demands for an international regime to determine territorial claims, leading to the *Berlin West Africa Conference of 1884–5* to agree on legal principles to regulate and legitimize actual territorial acquisition. Grounded in principles of free trade imperialism,[141] the Conference sought to create continent-wide criteria for territorial acquisition through the lens of West Africa.

Bismarck as Chair intended to secure effective occupation as mandatory for territorial acquisitions, ending the practice of 'paper protectorates'. The British, concerned about the costs of occupation and administration, especially of what they deemed as interior hinterlands, argued that since indigenous sovereignty was retained, protectorates could not amount to acquisition of title under international law, making effective occupation unwarranted.[142]

138 Notable examples here include the protectorate over the territory of *Opoboland* concluded between Britain and King Ja Ja and British negotiations with King Lobengula of Mashonaland and Matabeleland and the Sultan of Zanzibar.

139 A. B. Thruston, *African Incidents* (London: John Murray, 1900) 170–171.

140 According to Vattel, freedom of consent was held to be sacrosanct in the cession of territory in modern *jus gentium*. See *Le Droit des Gens*, Vol. 2, ch.12 para.163, cited in Alexandrowicz (1975) *op.cit.* 130, 46.

141 According to Bismarck at the first session of the Conference, the aims of the Conference were (1) freedom of commerce on the Congo; (2) freedom of navigation on the Congo and Niger; and (3) agreement about the formalities of valid annexation of territory in the future. See generally, Louis (1971) *op.cit.* 110.

142 *Ibid.* 208–214.

The compromise under Article XXXV allowed the signatories of the Berlin Final Act to:

> recognise the obligation to insure the establishment of authority in the regions occupied by them on the coasts of the African Continent [as] sufficient to protect existing rights, and, as the case may be, freedom of trade and of transit under conditions agreed upon.[143]

The Conference thus accepted the practice of paper protectorates facilitating *de jure* territorial acquisition to continue unabated. Attention was focused exclusively on the Coast, since no European powers had means to effectively occupy the interior regions they claimed as protectorates.[144] The Conference touched on consent, raised by the American delegate who stated:

> Modern International Law steadily follows the road which leads to the recognition of the right of native races (African communities) to dispose freely of themselves and their hereditary soil. Conformably to this principle my Government would be willing to support the more extended rule – one which should apply to the said occupation (of territory) in Africa, a principle looking to the voluntary consent of the natives of whose country possession is taken (by treaty) in all cases when they may not have provoked an act of aggression.[145]

The refusal of the United States to ratify the Final Act is indicative that this principle was ignored among others by the European delegations.[146] While the Berlin Conference legitimized the actions of the Powers during the Scramble, it failed to establish an effective framework for the process.[147] In any case, the Powers simply ignored emerging territorial regimes, preferring to rely on spheres of influence and protectorates to achieve each of their colonial objectives. The impact of the treaties on contemporary African boundaries and their continued material importance in the settlement of disputes means that

143 Hertslet (1909) *op.cit.* 113, Vol. 1, 485 the requirement of notifying other signatories of a territorial acquisition did, however, apply to protectorates see art. XXXIV.

144 Shaw (1986) *op.cit.* 125, 49.

145 Declaration of John Kasson, head of the US delegation, which he asked to be included as a Protocol of the Berlin Final Act, quoted in Alexandrowicz (1975) *op.cit.* 130, 47.

146 Alexandrowicz draws on Lugard's view that the Conference tacitly supported this principle; see *Ibid.* 47. Shaw, however, believes this view to be rather optimistic: (1986) *op.ci t.* 125, 42. For the text of the General Act of the Conference of Berlin 1885, see Hertslet (1909) *op.cit.* 113, Vol. 2 468–487 and extensive compilation of documents in R. J. Gavin & J. A. Betley (eds.), *The Scramble for Africa* (Ibadan: Ibadan University Press, 1973).

147 See Sybil Eyre Crowe, *Berlin West-African Conference* (New York: Longmans, Green and Co, 1942).

they have to be attributed to some legal valence. Judge Huber touched on this in *Island of Palmas*, emphasizing their political import and concluding that

> contracts of this nature are not wholly void of indirect effects on situations governed by international law; if they do not constitute titles in international law, they are nonetheless facts which the law must in certain circumstances take into account.[148]

This appears pragmatic in view of difficulties concerning the absence of African parties during the Berlin Final Act, which would make the Act invalid under the rule of *pacta tertiis nec nocent nec prosunt*. In other words, any provisions imposing obligations on third parties in their absence from the agreement would be nullified, as explained in the *Las Palmas* Case.[149]

The absence of unambiguous territorial boundaries made decolonization problematic. Topographical mistakes effected by ignorance of demographic and ethnographic factors resulted in arbitrary haphazard boundaries.[150] Statistical analysis found that 44% of modern African boundaries are astronomical lines (meridian parallels), 30% mathematical lines (arcs, curves, etc.), and only 26% based on geographical features.[151] Neither geography nor the identity of African communities was deemed material in the Powers' continental carve-up. Instead their prime purpose was conflict avoidance – ostensibly perpetual peace – between themselves as they violently sought to acquire African territories and subjugate Africans.[152] At independence post-colonial Africa was thus faced with the tough choice of whether to embark on fundamental revisions of colonial boundaries or to acquiesce to their predecessors' boundary regimes. The former raised the spectre of chaos overemphasized by the departing colonial powers, which also enabled a sale of arms to mitigate the threat; the latter missed the opportunity to establish representative States based on shared history, culture, and imagination. Trained in

148 *Island of Palmas Arbitration* (1928) 897–898.

149 The nullifying of provisions imposing obligations on third parties in their absence from the agreement. For modern application of this principle, see the Island of Palmas Arbitration (1928). Also see the Free Zones of Upper Savoy and the District of Gex *PCIJ Reports* (1932) Series A/B, No. 46, p. 141.

150 This cavalier approach was compounded in some instances by representatives of the Powers encouraging African Chiefs to make exaggerated claims about the extent of their territorial authority which of course could then be claimed as against other Powers. See J. C. Anene, *International Boundaries of Nigeria* (London: Longman, 1970) 15.

151 Calculated approximately by K. M. Barbour, 'A Geographical Analysis of Boundaries in Inter-Tropical Africa' in *Essays in African Populations* [K. M. Barbour & R. M. Prothero eds.] (London: Brown, 1961) 305. See Ravi L. Kapil, 'On the Conflict Potential of Inherited Boundaries in Africa' 18 *World Politics* (1966) 656–673, 660.

152 Jeffrey Herbst, 'The Creation and Maintenance of National Boundaries in Africa' 43 *International Organization* (1989) 673–692, 682.

Western political thought, African leadership accepted colonial boundaries at national independence, a decision incorporated into the Charter of the Organisation of African Unity[153] with its juridical basis founded in the classical principle of *uti possidetis*.[154]

Uti possidetis was once again called upon to protect the territorial *status quo* in State succession by recognizing the sanctity of existing boundaries.[155] This facilitated the transformation of internal administrative lines developed by colonial powers into international frontiers delimiting the jurisdiction of emerging States. Deemed to help maintain territorial integrity when fledgling States were vulnerable to threat, this interpretation of *uti possidetis* also reinforced the territorial basis of Statehood – restricting questions of legitimacy and recognition by rating territoriality above other legitimizing principles such as ethnicity, tradition, linguistics, religion, and ideology. Instead of seeking territorial settlement, *uti possidetis* sought to 'settle' people within fixed territories, with territorial 'order' deemed more important than the 'identity' of people. The *All African Conference* of 1958 called for readjustment of boundaries at the earliest opportunity but was primarily concerned with a piecemeal process of revision as opposed to a latter-day Scramble in Africa.[156]

153 Article 3(3) of the OAU Charter (1963) provides that states must show 'respect for the sovereignty and territorial integrity of each State and for its inalienable right to independent existence'. While support for *uti possidetis* was originally implied in the Charter by Article 3(3), the principle was expressly affirmed by resolution 16(1) of the OAU Assembly of Heads of State and Government at Cairo in July 1964. This provided that 'all Member States pledge themselves to respect the borders existing on their achievement of national independence'. See generally, Jon Woronoff, *Organising African Unity* (Metuchen, NJ: Scarecrow Press, 1970); Samuel Chime, 'The Organization of African Unity and African Boundaries' in *African Boundary Problems* [C. G. Widstrand ed.] (Uppsala: Scandinavian Africa Institute, 1969) 65–78; Saadia Touval, 'The Sources of *Status Quo* and Irrendentist Policies' also in Widstrand 101–118.

154 The adoption of *uti possidetis* was affected by Pan-African ideology. The influence of Pan Africanism was clearly evident at the All-African Peoples Conference (1958) with its commitment to the early abolition and readjustment of existing boundaries and in the *OAU Resolution on Border Disputes*, 1964, that proclaimed that the borders constituted 'a grave and permanent factor of dissension' Ian Brownlie, *African Boundaries: A Legal and Diplomatic Encyclopaedia* (London: C. Hurst, 1979) 360. See generally, Colin Legum, *Pan Africanism: A Short Political Guide* (New York: Preager, 1965) and Ali Al'Amin Mazrui A., *Towards a Pax Africana: A Study of Ideology and Ambition* (London: Weidenfield & Nicolson, 1967).

155 See generally, Stephen Ratner, 'Drawing a Better Line: *Uti Possidetis* and the Borders of New States' 90 *American Journal of International Law* (1996) 590. Also see Gino J. Naldi, 'The Case Concerning the Frontier Dispute (*Burkina Faso/Republic of Mali*): *Uti Possidetis* in an African Perspective' 36 *International & Comparative Law Quarterly* (1987) 893–903.

156 See generally Saadia Touval, 'Africa's Frontiers–Reactions to a Colonial Legacy' 42 *International Affairs* (1966) 641. Also see Charles Riziki Majinge, 'Uti Possidetis and State Secession in International Law: An Examination of the Evolving Legal Practice in Africa'

The difficulties confronting the modern African State when advancing claims for territorial revision were amply demonstrated in *Libyan Arab Jamahiriya/Chad*, where the ICJ reinforced non-recognition of the doctrine of unequal treaties in modern international law.[157] The Court was unwilling to accept the validity of a submission regarding Libya's diplomatic inexperience (and therefore inequality) in relation to the conclusion of a post-colonial treaty with France.[158] It is at least arguable that Libya's naivety in the conduct of its international relations could be likened to that of the African signatories to acquisitory treaties in the late nineteenth century. While the process of concluding a postcolonial treaty in 1951 was significantly different from that of a treaty of 'protection' concluded during the Scramble, the difference was perhaps a matter of degree rather than kind. In any event, the case raised questions regarding the continuing ramifications of colonial subordination for fledgling States within international society.

Acquisitory treaties in Africa clearly failed to comply with international legal standards of even the nineteenth century. The Powers were prepared to acknowledge classical modes of territorial acquisition and principles of the customary international law of treaties between themselves but were unwilling to extend such membership of the human family to Africans on the basis of equality to what they deemed the Family of Nations. Thus, the Powers relied on illusory institutions, third-party political conventions, and jurisdictional measures to legitimize territorial gains during the Scramble. This reticence of the existing international regime to provide effective means of redress against the international boundaries forged by the Powers remains damaging to pre-colonial territorial and ethnographic parameters.

The value of maintaining existing territorial boundaries as a fundamental contributor to present-day international peace and security cannot be underestimated. Modern international law continues to reflect its significance by adhering to the presumption of the continuity of existing boundaries.[159] The primacy of this norm was expressed in *Libyan Arab Jamahiriya/Chad Case* where the ICJ held that

> once agreed, the boundary stands, for any other approach would vitiate the fundamental principle of the stability of boundaries, the importance of which has been repeatedly emphasised by the Court.[160]

18(1) *African Yearbook of International Law Online/Annuaire Africain de droit international Online* (2010): 81–119.

157 Libyan Arab Jamahiriya/Chad Case *ICJ Reports* (1994) para.36.

158 France was the colonial Power with regard to the territory of Chad.

159 See generally, Kayan Kaikobad, 'Some Observations on the Doctrine of Continuity and Finality of Boundaries' 49 *British Yearbook of International Law* (1983) 126–127 also see Touval (1966) *op.cit.* 156.

160 *ICJ Reports* (1994) para.37.

It remains unsurprising that international law would deny States pre-colonial territorial integrity on the basis of the actions of colonial Powers that have gained legitimacy with the passage of time. This approach, initially based on a short-term solution to questions of order, was perhaps somewhat justifiable: the failure to design a new system of adjudication is, however, far from satisfactory against the backdrop of an international regime struggling to resolve the contradictions between competing norms of territorial sovereignty and self-determination. A territorial regime that does not countenance the evaluation of the legitimacy of claims for readjusting colonial boundaries in a bid to reflect its constituent societies sacrifices the values of enduring stability, cultural identity, and national development in favour of momentary and fragile peace.

The Pacific and Island States[161]

As the world's largest ocean, the Pacific covers a third of the earth's surface and, at 165,384,000 square kilometres, it is more than twice the size of the Atlantic.[162] The vast Pacific expanses have over 5,000 islands – more than the rest of the world combined.[163] In human history, distance has been among the most important variables, and the Pacific was the last marine basin to be brought into the reach of a global system.[164] The term 'Pacific' as a geographic and subject delineator is another European construct: the change of name from the equally European 'Mar del Sur' to 'Pacific Ocean' occurred in 1520 – the former having persisted for the previous two centuries.[165] While 'Mar del Sur' or 'South Sea' initially applied only to the Bay of Panama, it remained in usage among European mariners sailing far to the south to enter its waters. The term 'Pacific' came into usage as shifting nineteenth-century trade patterns made the northern Pacific an important area of global commerce.[166] 'South Sea' faded as a descriptive term only after World War II.[167]

161 This section of the chapter has benefitted from the research undertaken primarily by David Keane as part of his contribution to the book *Minority Rights in the Pacific* [Joshua Castellino & David Keane eds.] (Oxford: Oxford University Press, 2009).

162 Gerard Segal, *Rethinking the Pacific* (Oxford: Clarendon Press, 1990) 6.

163 *Ibid.* 7.

164 Paul Blank, 'The Pacific: A Mediterranean in the Making?' 89(2) *Oceans Connect* (1999) 265–277, 267, 275.

165 Oscar Hermann Khristian Spate, '"South Sea" to "Pacific Ocean": A Note on Nomenclature' 12(4) *Journal of Pacific History* (1977) 205–211. Also see Kerry R. Howe, *Nature, Culture and History: The 'Knowing' of Oceania* (Honolulu, HI: University of Hawai'i Press, 2000) 60.

166 Spate (1977) *op.cit.* Also see Martin Lewis, 'Dividing the Ocean Sea' 89 *The Geographical Review* (1999) 188–214.

167 Martin (1990) *op.cit.* 208. Micronesia, lying almost wholly north of the equator, is still often popularly located in the 'South Pacific', perhaps a reflection of the continuing influence of the 'South Sea' concept.

Inter-island exchanges and marriages created regional sub-identities in the human geography of the region, cemented through mythological and genealogical ties. These reveal important interconnections that predate Magellan's arrival.[168] The Pacific Island Countries (PIC), one of six distinct zones in the Pacific basin, are located in the south and centre of the ocean. Almost all the people, plants, and animals in the Pacific originated from Asia about 50,000 years ago, moving through what is now Indonesia and New Guinea.[169] The modern Pacific is ethnically diverse with its island nations made up of numerous minority groups and indigenous peoples, as well as resettled peoples and internal migrants from different regions.[170] The islands are, of course, far more than dots of land as they are treated in European histories and geography. The surrounding seas, with their resources and mythological associations, form vital parts of islanders' consciousness of territory. When configured alongside the 200-mile exclusive economic zone, many of the island States are significantly bigger than many European countries, and if undersea mineral wealth is accounted for, they are potentially as wealthy.[171]

The islands fall into three categories, based on human rather than physical geography: Melanesians, Polynesians, and Micronesians.[172] The terms were coined by the French explorer Dumont d'Urville to describe perceived racial differences between peoples of the Pacific Islands in 1832, with Melanesia meaning 'dark islands', Polynesia 'many islands', and Micronesia 'little islands'.[173]

Melanesia, the largest area, contains 97% of the land and 75% of the Pacific Islands' population.[174] It includes New Guinea, Papua New Guinea and Irian Jaya, Solomon Islands, Vanuatu, and New Caledonia.[175] Diversity is an essential characteristic of the region, boasting an array of ethnic groups, social organization, and topography and languages. Most of the 1,200 or so Melanesian languages belong to the Austronesian language family, with non-Austronesian languages found in New Guinea and some in the Solomon Islands.[176] Papua New Guinea, with around 840 distinct living languages,

168 Rainer Buschmann, 'Oceans of World History: Delineating Aquacentric Notions in the Global Past' 2(1) *History Compass* (2004) 1–10, 2.

169 Ron Crocombe, *The South Pacific: An Introduction* (Auckland: Longman Paul, 1987) 3.

170 Jon Fraenkel, 'Minority Rights in Fiji and the Solomon Islands' United Nations Doc. E/CN.4/Sub.2/AC.5/2003/WP.5, UN Sub-Commission on Promotion and Protection of Human Rights, Working Group on Minorities, 5 May 2003, Executive Summary.

171 Howe (2000) *op.cit.* 165, 61.

172 Segal (1990) *op.cit.* 162, 8.

173 Ann Gibbons, 'The Peopling of the Pacific' 291(5509) *Science* (2001) 1735–1737, 1735.

174 Australia is not considered as part of the Pacific Islands even though it is adjacent to Melanesia

175 Crocombe (1987) *op.cit.* 169, 17.

176 Ian C. Campbell, *A History of the Pacific Islands* (Christchurch: University of Canterbury Press, 1989) 18, 23.

is the world's most ethnically diverse State, while Vanuatu, with approximately 109 languages amidst a far smaller population, has the highest number of languages *per capita* in the world.[177] *Polynesia*, the eastern part of the ocean, includes Hawai'i in the north, Easter Island, the Marquesas Islands, Society Islands, Tuamotu and Austral Islands in the east, New Zealand in the south, the Cook Islands in the centre, Tonga and Samoa in the west, and Tokelau and Tuvalu in the north-west.[178] The languages spoken in the region are closely related and form a distinct group within the Austronesian language family.[179] Polynesian societies generally retain the idea of hierarchical social and political distinctions and rank, manifest in ruling chiefs. As in other regions discussed above, there is some overlap: e.g., Fiji could be regarded as part of Melanesia or Polynesia or both.[180] *Micronesia* is a series of small islands lying mainly to the north of the equator, including Kiribati, Nauru, the Marshall Islands, the Federated States of Micronesia (formerly the Caroline Islands, comprising Yap, Truk, Pohnpei, and Kosrae), Palau, Guam, and the Mariana Islands.[181] Micronesian languages are more diverse than Polynesian but less than Melanesian, representing one or more branches of the Austronesian language family.[182] The smaller islands of Polynesia and Micronesia are relatively ethnically homogeneous, with small migrant or settler communities.[183] The intricate network of human relations across the regions[184] has made the Pacific Islands a significant draw for anthropologists, resulting in significant literature in that domain of the cultures, languages, and peoples of the region.[185]

In relation to title to territory it is worth noting that Polynesia is probably the last global area of the world to have been settled by people.[186] In other words it could have well been the last genuine *terra nullius* to be occupied through human settlement. In seeking to understand the populating of the islands, geneticists and linguists proposed an 'express train to Polynesia' model of migration,[187] wherein Polynesian ancestors emerged from Taiwan, setting sail 3,600–6,000 years ago, bypassing indigenous Papuan-speaking

177 Fraenkel (2003) *op.cit.* 170, 3.
178 Campbell (1989) *op.cit.* 176, 14.
179 *Ibid.*
180 Crocombe (1987) *op.cit.* 169, 18.
181 *Ibid.* 17.
182 Campbell (1989) *op.cit.* 176, 26.
183 Fraenkel (2003) *op.cit.* 170, 3.
184 Campbell (1989) *op.cit.* 176, 26.
185 *Ibid.* 27.
186 Gibbons (2001) *op.cit.* 173, 1735. This statement excludes Antarctica.
187 The 'express train' metaphor is attributed to Jared Diamond in a 1988 article in *Nature* magazine (*Ibid.* 1736). See also Jared Diamond and Peter Bellwood, 'Farmers and their Languages: The First Expansions' 300 *Science* (2003) 597–603.

people of Melanesia.[188] Diamond notes that when Polynesians got to Hawai'i and New Zealand, 'ancient China's occupation of the Pacific was complete'.[189] The trail of archaeological evidence for this includes distinctive pottery and shell ornaments known as the 'Lapita' culture that first appeared 3,500 years ago in the Bismarck Archipelago in Papua New Guinea, spreading eastwards to arrive in Fiji some 3,000 years ago.[190] From there the migrants continued east, using the islands as stepping-stones to Tonga and Samoa.[191] Genetic analyses of Pacific rats support the theory that Lapita mariners from Southeast Asia may have moved across the region in a series of migrations, from 6,000 to 3,000 years ago.[192] Doubt exists over the archaeological basis for Taiwan being the original homeland,[193] backed by genetic studies revealing dissimilarities between Taiwan and Polynesia.[194] This led to a growing consensus in a 'slow boat' model that believes that Polynesian ancestors

> were Austronesians who moved out of Southeast Asia – not necessarily Taiwan – whose population expanded along the coast of New Guinea, intermingled, and then moved out into Polynesia. But it was not an express train, because as they moved through Melanesia, they moved slowly enough to mix extensively with Melanesians.[195]

Pacific trade in early modern times was significant, with transpacific silver flows to China equalling or exceeding those that crossed the Atlantic and the Eurasian land mass.[196] During the sixteenth century, the expanding reach of Europe, driven by a quest for land and improving seafaring technologies, began to impact the Pacific basin, integrating it into an emerging global

188 Gibbons (2001) *op.cit.* 173, 1735.

189 John Edward Terrell, Terry L. Hunt & Chris Gosden, 'The Dimensions of Social Life in the Pacific: Human Diversity and the Myth of the Primitive Isolate' 38(2) *Current Anthropology* (1997) 155–195, 172.

190 Gibbons (2001) *op.cit.* 173, 1735.

191 *Ibid.*

192 Society for Science and the Public, Bruce Bower, 'Rat DNA Points to Pacific Migrations' 166(2) *Science News* (2004) 30. The research obtained mitochondrial DNA from 100 Pacific rats. The DNA exhibited three geographically distinct patterns, one of which appears only on islands just off the Asian coast, reflecting interaction among people who probably didn't migrate elsewhere. A second pattern extends from the islands into Oceania's western half, probably mirroring human migration along that path.

193 Stephen Oppenheimer, 'The Express Train from Taiwan to Polynesia: On the Congruence of Proxy Lines of Evidence' 36(4) *World Archaeology* (2004) 591–600, 593.

194 *Ibid.* 596.

195 Mark Stoneking, Max Planck Institute for Evolutionary Anthropology, quoted in Gibbons (2001) *op.cit.* 736, 1737.

196 Blank (1999) *op.cit.* 164, 267.

economy.[197] Although Pacific trade fell in relative terms with the Industrial Revolution and its integration into the Atlantic economy, trans-Pacific flows caught up again with the 'opening' of Japan, the settlement of Australia and New Zealand, the opium trade, and the colonization of Southeast Asia. The process was abetted by new transportation and communications developments.[198] The colonization and settlement of Europeans into Australia and New Zealand, itself a fascinating story, remains out of the remit of this book since it does not engage boundary issues.[199]

As in the other regions discussed, European culture played an important role over the last 200 years, which remains a short period relative to the 50,000 years of Pacific history.[200] The beachcombers were the first Europeans to settle on the Pacific islands, followed by traders, missionaries, and administrators associated with the formal establishment of colonies.[201] By 1900, all Pacific Islands had fallen under the authority of foreign powers.[202] Despite prolonged and intense influences, Pacific island cultures do not resemble those of the majority settler populations in New Zealand or Australia.[203] Instead, Crocombe predicted in 1987 that European influence would wane and be replaced by a resurgence of Pacific cultures against the cultural dominance from Asia.[204]

The Pacific islands offer a spectrum of sovereignty landscapes from fully independent nations to incorporated territories. In its 1989 proposal for a *Pacific Charter of Human Rights*, *Law Asia*, classified the States on the basis of suitability for inclusion in a proposed regional body. This division is an interesting benchmark for assessing the political status of the Pacific Islands and highlights the colonial legacy. Thus a distinct group would consist of fully independent Pacific Island nations including Fiji, Kiribati, Nauru, Papua New Guinea, Solomon Islands, Tonga, Tuvalu, Vanuatu, and Western Samoa.[205] A second group would include the two dominant and former metropolitan powers in the Pacific: Australia and New Zealand.[206] A third group

197 Marks and Engels had believed that the Pacific would replace the Atlantic as the centre of trade, as quoted by Ravi Palat, 'Pacific Century: Myth or Reality?' 25(3) *Theory and Society* (1996) 303–347, 303.

198 Blank (1999) *op.cit.* 164, 267.

199 See Joshua Castellino & David Keane, *Minority Rights in the Pacific: A Comparative Legal Analysis* (Oxford: Oxford University Press, 2009).

200 Crocombe (1987) *op.cit.* 169, 22.

201 Patrick Nunn, 'Recent Environmental Changes on Pacific Islands' 156 (2) *The Geographical Journal* (1990) 125–140, 127.

202 Campbell (1989) *op.cit.* 173, 136.

203 Crocombe (1987) *op.cit.* 169, 23.

204 *Ibid.* 22.

205 [Editors] 'Report on a Proposed Pacific Charter of Human Rights, prepared under the auspices of LAWASIA, May 1989' 22 *Victoria University Wellington Law Review* (1992) 103.

206 *Ibid.* 104.

consists of newly independent States emerging from trusteeships with associate status, including the Federated States of Micronesia, the Marshall Islands, and Palau.[207] The three States associated with New Zealand – Cook Islands, Niue, and Tokelau, would potentially form another distinct group. Although part of Micronesia, their decision to stay as a self-governing territory within the United States would make the Commonwealth of the Northern Mariana Islands a further distinct case, while Guam in Micronesia and American Samoa remain unincorporated territories of the United States, administered through the country's Department of the Interior. The islands incorporated into France – Wallis and Futuna, New Caledonia, and French Polynesia – remain modern-day outposts where *territoires d'outre-mer* remains in force,[208] though persistent tensions in New Caledonia may lead to change. This leaves four *sui generis* islands: Norfolk Island, in the south-west Pacific, is part of Australia; Hawai'i is a fully-fledged State of the United States; Rapanui (Easter Island) is a province of Chile; and the British dependency of the Pitcairn Islands.

Many of the varied sovereignties in the region are worthy of study in a bid to unearth governance systems that could replace the winner-takes-all approach of the sovereign State, especially in places in other parts of the world where the territorial dimensions are highly contested. In terms of the Pacific basin overall, climate change is likely to alter the territorial dimensions of the islands, with the likelihood that the imminent risk of the submergence of Kiribati will spread wider. The continued question of European and American sovereignty remains an issue through the potential for further testing of nuclear weapons[209] and the creation of law-free zones beyond scrutiny, such as in the so-called *War on Terror*.

207 Ibid.

208 Catherine Giraud-Kinley, 'The Effectiveness of International Law: Sustainable Development in the South Pacific Region' 12 *Georgetown International Environmental Law Review* (1999) 125–176, 129, n.7. In New Caledonia, the *Accords de Noumea* (5 May 1998) replaced the *Accords de Matignon* (1988), after a majority of New Caledonians voted in favour of the former in a referendum held on 8 November 1998. They provide for the progressive transfer of jurisdiction from France to New Caledonia, such as jurisdiction over its Exclusive Economic Zone. See *Law No. 7302 of 5 May 1988*, J.O., 11 June 1998 (New Caledonia) or Noumea Accords. The third in a series of referenda on independence was held on 12 December 2021, which rejected independence (96.5%).

209 Law of the Sea Institute, 'Oceans in the Nuclear Age' (University of California, Berkeley) http://www.law.berkeley.edu/centers/ilr/ona/pages/testing.htm. Also see *Nuclear Tests (Australia v. France)* (Interim Protection) ICJ Rep. 1973, 99; *Nuclear Tests (New Zealand v. France)* (Interim Protection), ICJ *Reports* (1973), 135; *Nuclear Tests (New Zealand v. France)* Judgment, *ICJ Reports* (1974) 457.

Contested Boundary Lines in Asia

Unlike other continents which can be so determined by the presence of clearer geographical factors, the landmass of Eurasia is often portrayed in a manner where Asia, in the words of Said, appears to be a mere stage appended to Europe, despite Europe (defined as extending to the Ural Mountains) forming the smaller proportion of the landmass. Asia also has ancient, well-established, and clearly documented civilizations. When the Middle East is factored in, this includes the area attributed as the 'cradle of such civilization' and the birthplace of the largest number of recognized global religious systems. Inevitably with such a range of human history many forms of governance have evolved through its history, and with there being no significant barriers to the movement of peoples, this has led to significant cross-fertilization of ideas. To further complicate matters, Asia (not including the Middle East and Persia[210]) is home to the Empire with the world's longest documented history (China), a rival empire of nearly as long standing that is an important player in global commerce over centuries (Japan), and a country that has made significant contributions to philosophy and science (India). In today's classificatory terms, Asia has nearly 60% of the world's population, making it significantly bigger, in these terms, than all the other continents put together. Yet when viewed from the perspective of the contribution made to rules governing title to territory, Asian territory and its peoples have been treated as *objects* rather than *subjects* of law lumped together in one mass.

It is most useful to think of Asia as consisting of four distinct regions: East Asia, Southeast Asia, South Asia, and Central Asia. This classification already ignores the fact that the vast majority of the landmass of the world's largest State (Russia) lies in Asia, and that 90% of one of Europe's biggest States (Türkiye) lies within the continent. While the classification of Russia as a European State is beyond the scope of this discussion, it is worth considering the extent to which Russia has continued to operate as an Empire rather than a State, with headquarters in Europe and attendant Asian landmasses governed in a manner that fits Said's analysis of European actors on an Asian stage. By similar analogy Australia and New Zealand's European identity in the midst of the Pacific has also seen them classed as being part of Western society despite lying at a significant distance from Europe.

Russian Expansion into Asia

Lieutenant-General Von Alten's account, written in 1905, provides a clear flavour of the extent to which *Central Asia* was treated as a game between

210 For this dimension, see Firuz Kazemzadeh, *Russia and Britain in Persia, 1814–1914: A Study in Imperialism* (New Haven, CT: Yale University Press, 1968).

European powers.[211] Serving in the German army, Von Alten explains how Russian influence in the region was spreading towards India, capturing the vast plains of Central Asia, in 'an irresistible movement towards the extension of frontiers!'[212] Describing these lands between China and the Caspian Sea as inhabited by tribes over centuries, he highlights that '[T]hey were governed by their own Khans and Ameers, and had probably never heard of Europe or the White Tsar in St. Petersburg'.[213] Of course Russian expansionism included the seizure and settlement of Siberia, and a significant move forward 'in the sixth decade of the nineteenth century, the stretches of land to the east and southeast of the Aral Sea'.[214] This included annexations such as Tashkent, which became the Russian province of Turkestan, and the creation of vassal States such as Bukhara. There was also a Sino-Russian dimension to this competition in the seizing of Khokand (between Tashkent and the Chinese Empire), which was appended to a strip of land from the Chinese Empire to form what is known as the Ferghana Valley today between Uzbekistan and Kyrgyzstan.[215] In all of this schema Afghanistan was viewed as discussed above, not as an inhabited territory per se, but as a 'buffer zone' between the Russian and British Empires. The civilizing mission discussed in Chapter 2 was never far from expressed rhetoric and practice, and Lieutenant-General Von Alten, while critical of Russian expansionism, nevertheless voiced admiration for General Skobeleff, who was dispatched by Tsar Alexander II to consolidate Russian interests in Central Asia. Von Alten describes Skobeleff as 'brilliantly qualified for the process of transforming the half-savage Asiatic natives on his (sic!) borders into Russian subjects'.[216] Interestingly however, Skobeleff's approach appeared to have been significantly more progressive than that of his commentator:

> He makes no attempt to superimpose on them an alien civilization. He permits them to retain their customs and their religion, lives with them as one of themselves, and demands practically nothing more than recognition of the sovereignty of the Tsar and military obedience.[217]

This is reported as having important effects in subjugating once-proud tribes, enabling cooperation in the building of an impressive railway line primarily for military purposes but which it was hoped would eventually assist in trade

211 Von Alten, 'The Powers in Asia' 181 (589) *The North American Review* (December 1905) 834–844.
212 *Ibid.* 835.
213 *Ibid.*
214 *Ibid.*
215 *Ibid.*
216 *Ibid.*
217 *Ibid.* 836.

and the spread of Russian influence to the region. In this sense the Chinese Belt and Road Initiative has strong precedents in the region.

The essay 'The Asiatic Problem and Its Relation to the United States', written in 1903 by Jameson Reid, commences by outlining that 'the problem' alluded to in the title is not so much Asia or Asian tribes and peoples,[218] but rather that Russia was engaging in extraordinary political activity in Manchuria, 'playing fast and loose with the other great powers in the settlement of affairs in China'.[219] The arrogance behind this expression shows how subjecthood, sovereignty, and rules governing territorial acquisitions were used in *post-facto* justifications at home, rather than as guiding principles in international relations. This arrogance also offers a scathing critique of the time period when blatant power politics were dressed up as 'civilizing missions' at home for a restive domestic audience. Thus, Reid continues:

> If for the altruistic though misleading professions by which the civilized nations of the West have sought to explain their various attitudes in China, such as the spreading of 'civilizing and Christianizing influences', 'the safeguarding of subjects', and the thousand and one stock virtuisms in the diplomatic catalogue, we substitute the never-ending struggle for political and commercial supremacy in Asia, we have the whole question in a nutshell.[220]

He unmasks the real reasons as consisting of the need for strategic frontiers, ice-free and ice-bound ports, spheres of concession and influence, rather than any betterment of China. In a pointed critique, he states:

> How misleading and fatuous are these shallow claims is patent to anyone familiar with Asiatic political conditions. It is too probable, - more's the pity,- that China will be the next unfortunate victim of the abused name of civilization, the modern diplomatic euphemism for the generally accepted policy of 'every nation for itself, seize what you can get, and the devil take the hindmost'. And in this struggle for supremacy, -although the entire civilized world has had a more or less active finger in the pie, - the question of mastery, when sifted down to matter-of-fact and concrete conditions,

218 Usually at the time it appeared that the 'Asian Problem', or 'Chinese imbroglio' referred to contestations between Japan and China over Manchuria. However, the author is keen to state that this is mere manifestation of the quest for territorial supremacy by the great powers. W. C. Jameson Reid, 'The Asiatic Problem and Its Relation to the United States' 18(2) *Political Science Quarterly* (June 1903) 181–196, 182.

219 *Ibid.* 181.

220 *Ibid.* 182.

> is, politically at least, of vital concern to but two nations, Great Britain and Russia.[221]

While Reid is scathing towards all the so-called great powers, he highlights the spread of Russian influence in Asia through territorial expansion:

> In Afghanistan, in Central Asia, and in Persia, Russian dominance is day by day more boldly unmasking. It is an open secret that in Persia the power of the Czar is greater than that of the Shah. The entire country is surveyed for a network of Russian railways, some of which are now being built, so that Teheran and St. Petersburg will soon be connected by them. So secretly and gradually has this all been done, that even now British statesmen have not ceased rubbing their eyes and questioning the evidence of their own senses. Another dream that has been as ruthlessly shattered is the historic theory of a 'buffer state' between India and Russia's Asiatic possessions. The futility of this project, and the real disaffection of Russia toward such a condition, can hardly be more fully exemplified than in her unconcealed attempts to embrace Persia in the ramifications of her campaign of expansion. And what is true of China, what is true of Persia, is but an indication of what Russia purposes to do throughout Asia.[222]

While the historical assessment of Russian expansionism is underexplored by public international law jurists, it is striking for scholars of the acquisition of territory. David Moon offers an intriguing account of how these frontiers expanded from 1550 when 6.5 million peasants lived in what was described as the 'forest-heartland of Muscovy', to around 1897 when the population had swelled to 50 million, stretching across vast Asian lands.[223] Moon tracks this expansion with reference to four facets of what was considered the frontier of expansion itself: (a) the political expansion of the Russian State; (b) the environmental frontier between the forest and the steppe; (c) the 'lifeway' frontier between settled peasant agriculture and pastoral nomadism; and (d)

221 *Ibid.*

222 *Ibid.* 186.

223 For general reading on the historical and colonial expansion of Russia, see Vladimir O. Klyuchevskii, *Russya Istoriya: Polnii Kurs Lektsii v Trekh Knigakh*, 3 vols. (Moscow: Nizni, 1993). English texts that comment on this over time include Donald W. Treadgold, *The Great Siberian Migration: Government and Peasant in Resettlement from Emancipation to the First World War* (Princeton, NJ: Princeton University Press, 1957) and J. L. Wieczynski, *The Russian Frontier: The Impact of the Borderands upon the Course of Early Russian History* (Charlottesville, VA: University of Virginia Press, 1976); Milan Hauner, *What is Asia To Us Today: Russian Heartland Yesterday and Today* (London: Unwin Hayman, 1990);

the hierarchical frontier between Russian authorities and the peasantry.[224] These, notably (a) and (d), are of greatest political significance in understanding issues concerning territoriality and sovereignty. Russian political expansion enabled the acquisition of territory through acquiescence and subjugation of other actors; while the notion of its ethnic superiority generated a sense of entitlement for the emerging power to justify extending rule to populations that came with the acquired territories.

Originating from the territory referred to as Muscovy, consisting of 1.1 million square miles between the Oka River and the Ural Mountains, the Russian State emerged as an Empire under Peter the Great (1682–1725). [225] By 1897 the Russian Empire stretched from the Baltic Sea to the Pacific Ocean, the Arctic to the Steppes of Central Asia, and covered 8.5 million square miles.[226] While contemporary Russia, successor to the Soviet Union, is smaller,[227] this is the result of the dissolution of that Union and the emergence of independent States with the issues already discussed above.

At its zenith the Russian Empire was constituted of multiple nationalities, with Russians accounting for half the population. The rest consisted of 'nations', nomadic groups, and indigenous peoples, significant numbers of whom were peasants. The frontiers and geography were impacted by three and a half centuries of peasant migration and resettlement of ethnic Russians into more distant territories. Despite other cleavages, the overwhelming majority of the population were described as peasants (*soslovie*), accounting for around 90% in the mid-sixteenth century to around 77% by the end of the nineteenth century. The rest of the population were often referred to as *inorodtsy* or 'aliens'. Describing Russia's frontier as the 'middle ground' for its expansion, Moon explains:

> It was an intermediate zone of interaction and mutual accommodation between the Russian state and neighbouring state structures, Russian peasant-migrants and the environment, and agricultural peasants and pastoral nomads and other native peoples. In the wake of the expansion of Russia's political frontier, Russian peasant-settlers eventually overcame

224 David Moon, 'Peasant Migration and the Settlement of Russia's Frontiers 1550-1897' 40(4) *The Historical Journal* (1997) 859–893.

225 *Ibid.* 859.

226 *Ibid.*

227 This theme is discussed by R. Taagepera, 'An Overview of the Growth of the Russian Empire' in *Russian Colonial Expansion to 1917* [M. Rywkin ed.] (London/New York: Mansell, 1988). Also see Matthew C. Jamison, *Weakness, Expansion and Disobedience: The Beginning of Russian Expansion into the Heart of Central Asia 1864–1854* (Oxford: Oxford University Press, 2007).

> the environmental and lifeway facets of the frontiers, in part as a result of interaction with the state and elites across the hierarchical frontier.[228]

Moon traces the expansion of the Russian frontier by classifying Pre-Petrine Russia into three zones. The forest heartland includes the 'central non-black earth region' encompassing Moscow, the north-western region including St. Petersburg, the northern region with provinces such as Archangel and Vologda, and northern Urals region including the province of Perm. Second, the Steppes region, divided into two belts and four subregions; with the third and largest being the sparsely populated but vast territories of Siberia.[229] In tracking peasant migration across the zones, Moon stresses it was accompanied by natural population increases due to higher birth rates in regions other than the forest heartlands.

The original Muscovy political frontier expanded eastwards before connecting with the westernmost region (Golden Horde) of the empire built by Genghis Khan in the thirteenth century. As Genghis Khan's influence began to wane, the Golden Horde came apart in the mid-fifteenth century, leaving the principality of Russia bounded by the Tartar khanates of Kazan and Astrakhan to the south and east. These were conquered quickly by Tsar Ivan (The Terrible) in 1533–1584, though the subjugation of the Tartars was more drawn out – taking close to a century. By the sixteenth century, Muscovites sought active conquest of the Steppes, using various means of warfare: shifting allegiances between rulers, and activating differences between them to weaken their resolve to act collectively. The elite played an important role in this quest:

> One way in which the Russian state achieved this was by co-opting the elites of people in the borderlands into Russian service. The Russian state preserved and supported the elites' privileged status in their societies in return for their swearing allegiance and paying tribute to the tsar. This policy was carried out among steppe peoples such as the Tatars and Kalmyks and, later, in other frontier regions in Siberia and the western borderlands.[230]

Mindful of rebellions, especially from Muslim populations that fell under their sovereignty, Russia built fortified lines to protect themselves from raids by nomadic tribes. Despite this, rebellions occurred often, and populations and tribes of the North Caucasus fought an almost century-long war against the Russian State until the 1860s, with defeats in these wars leading to formal

228 Moon (1997) *op.cit.* 224, 862.
229 *Ibid.* 866–868.
230 *Ibid.* 871.

conquest and incorporation of the acquired lands behind the ever-expanding frontier.[231] Russian conquest of Siberia commenced in the late sixteenth century with Cossack crossings of the Urals in 1581 to defeat the Tatar khanate of Siberia.[232] Similar techniques (elite privilege, divide and rule, shifting allegiances) were used, though resistance offered by some of the sparsely populated indigenous tribes of Northern Siberia could not be compared to the robust defence by Turkic and Mongol tribes in the south. The building of fortifications consolidated the expansion of the empire, finally restricting Russian expansion when confronted with Manchu China in the Pacific Far East. Faced with defeat they were forced to acknowledge Chinese rule over the Amur River Basin under the terms of the *Treaty of Nerchinsk* (1689), only finally gaining access to the Pacific in 1858–1860.[233]

The Ebb and Flow of Chinese Territorial Ambitions

Writing in 1950, Lattimore highlights that while Russia was expanding into Central Asia, arriving at the 'backdoor' of the British Empire in India (sic!), they gained the 'sympathy of the Americans… who regarded them as benevolent and competent empire builders'.[234] The author argued that Sinkiang (Xinjiang in China) was likely to become a key pivot and a new centre of gravity since it sat at the 'whirlpool in which meet political currents flowing from China, Russia, India and the Middle East'.[235] While that analysis is yet to bear fruit, Lattimore's description of the centrality of the region remains important in contemporary trends that lie at the heart of Asia, especially in reflecting how political frontiers struggle to capture multiple fragments of identity.

> There are linguistic and cultural frontiers between Mongols, Chinese, Tibetans, Indians, Afghans, the people who speak one or another of the Inner Asian Turkic languages, and the Russians.
>
> There are religious frontiers between Mohammedans, Buddhists, followers of primitive (sic!) religions, Orthodox Christian Russians

231 See M. Atkin, 'Russian expansion in the Caucasus to 1813' in *Russian Colonial Expansion* (1988) *op.cit.* 227,154–167. Also see M. Gammer, *Muslim Resistance to the Tsar: Shamil & the Conquest of Chechnia & Daghestan* (London: Routledge, 1944).

232 For more, see Bruce Lincoln, *The Conquest of a Continent: Siberia and the Russians* (New York: Random House, 1994).

233 This quest is captured coherently in James Forsyth, *A History of the Peoples of Siberia: Russia's North Asian Colony 1581–1990* (Cambridge: Cambridge University Press, 1992).

234 Owen Lattimore, *Pivot of Asia: Sinkiang and the Inner Asian Frontiers of China and Russia* (Boston: Little, Brown and Company, 1950) vii.

235 *Ibid.* 3.

> intermingled with consciously atheistic Russians, and predominantly unreligious Chinese.
>
> There are frontiers between the recently industrialized economy of the Soviet Union, the rapidly changing pastoral economy of the Mongolian Peoples' Republic, the traditional nomad economies of the Kazakhs and Mongols of Sinkiang, the ancient agricultural practices of China, partly infiltrated by such new agencies of transformation as the railroad and the factory, the oasis economy of Inner Asia, the Alpine economy of the Kirghiz of the Tien Shan, and the high plateau economy of such peoples as the Sarikolis of the Pamirs…[236]

Xinjiang has historically occupied the important crossroad between the Persian Empire, the Arab conquest, Chinese imperialism, Russian expansionism, and British designs on maintaining safe trade routes into India through Afghanistan. In terms of sovereignty and China's expansion westwards, as Lattimore emphasizes, while Xinjiang has been within the Chinese political horizon for more than two centuries, it has only 'intermittently been under Chinese influence, control or sovereignty'.[237] The relatively recent delimitation of the frontier between China and Russia was crucial to Xinjiang, which finds itself definitively within the Chinese realm. This delimitation, with subsequent militarization of the border and establishment of the *Shanghai Cooperation* countries, has been a crucial element in solidifying Asian boundary lines, not least because it has the acquiescence of all potential State claimants.

The defeat and demise of the Mongolian empire in the mid-fourteenth century had already led to contestations over territory that had come under this influence, including Russia, China, and 'Inner Asia' as referred to in history books. This period also saw the emergence of several strong small Muslim States in Inner Asia around the oases, ruled by Moghuls, described as warriors of Mongol descent who had adopted Turkish languages and Islam.[238] These were the same Moghuls, originally raiders then empire builders, who turned to India from the sixteenth century onwards.

Commenting on Russian Empire building, Lattimore stressed that 'it was in the great land mass between Europe and Asia that the Russians created a nation and made that nation the master of an empire'.[239] In describing how the empire was consolidated, he stated:

236 *Ibid*. 4.

237 *Ibid*. 5.

238 For more see Dmitri D. Pokotilov, *History of the Eastern Mongols in the Period of the Ming Dynasty 1368–1634* (St. Petersburg, 1893) – translated into English from Russian by R. Lowenthal (Chengdu: China Studies in History & Civilization, 1947).

239 Lattimore (1950) *op.cit*. 235, 21.

> Centuries of interpenetration with nomadic peoples on the steppe frontier made class warfare and politics as familiar as national warfare to both Russians and non-Russians. When nomad Khans had the upper hand, some of the Russian nobility became their vassals, and continued as a ruling class, through a subordinate ruling class. When the Russians, in turn, conquered the steppe, they took the steppe nobility into their service, and continued some of their privileges.[240]

The British meanwhile viewed Russian expansionism into Asia with alarm. Pratt, with his long association working in the Foreign Office in the Far East, stated:

> Throughout the nineteenth century the expansion of Russia into Asia was the favourite bogy of British statesmen of all schools of thought. Occasionally a voice would be raised to point out that a sprawling, loose-knit and somewhat slack and inefficient empire such as that of Russia was not really capable of embarking on and carry out through so desperate an enterprise as the invasion and conquest of India, but it was always a voice crying in the wilderness. We continued to persistently overrate the offensive capacity of Russia as much as later on we underrated that of Japan. Nevertheless, it is difficult to understand why, when our chief fear was the threat to India, we should from the earliest times so persistently have thrown ourselves across Russia's path in the Far East.... We interfered [in other parts of the world] only when a threat to British interests gave us definite *locus standi*, but it is difficult to see what important British interest was threatened by Russian expansionism in northeastern Asia in the middle of the nineteenth century.[241]

Meanwhile, the Chinese expansion into Xinjiang probably best reflects the ebb and flow of that empire. Until its definitive integration as a Chinese province in 1884, the date significant for colonial expansions elsewhere, the Chinese referred to the region as *Hsi Yu* (the Western region) with whom it had maintained trade relations tracing back to 115 BC.[242] Regular representations were made by the Han to rulers of the kingdoms in *Hsi Yu* and history records that by 36 BC there was a limited recognition of their suzerainty to the Chinese Emperor. This period lasted until the fall of the Han dynasty in the third century AD. Following a period of independence, Chinese sovereignty was restored through conquest from 657 under the T'ang Dynasty. The Tangs were eventually defeated by the Prince of Tashkent with Arab

240 *Ibid.*
241 John Pratt, *War and Politics in China* (London: Jonathan Cape, 1943) 94.
242 *Ibid.* 45.

help in 751, liberating the kingdoms of Inner Asia from Chinese rule. They remained independent until the Manchu conquest of the region in the second half of the eighteenth century, with formal incorporation of the region as a Chinese province at the end of a rebellion by Yakub Beg at that time.[243] In contrast to Russian expansionism into Asia, Chinese rule in Central Asia was maintained through means similar to European colonial government in Asia and Africa. Thus, a minority of Chinese were in charge and ruled indirectly through lower administration-oriented strata of political life while traditional Uighur, Kazakh, and Mongol feudal structures were left relatively undisturbed.[244] Yang Tseng-hsin, a key Chinese administrator, respected in the literature, for his role in governing the region, wrote in 1936:

> It is a pity that what is called the five races in one family [Chinese, Manchus, Mongols, Moslems, and Tibetans] has been only nominal and has not become a reality. Chinese officials, without a sense of moral obligation but full of ideas or selfish gain are rarely talented in administration. There are too many bad officials and too few good ones. This is why there have been more days of trouble and fewer of tranquillity. This is true of all provinces, but it is worse on the frontier. It will be impossible for the Chinese officials to control the Moslems permanently unless administration is greatly improved.[245]

In examining the diversity of Xinjiang in the mid-1940s, Lattimore highlighted how there were, in addition to the Uyghurs who formed the majority, other nationalities with a territorial base in close proximity, including Kazakhs, Kyrghiz, Mongols, Iranians (Sarikolis and Tajiks), Uzbeks, Chinese, Manchus, Russians, and Tartars.[246] Xinjiang in the latter half of the nineteenth century was described as a political vacuum under intense competition from Russia, China, and (British) India. However, the emergence of a large Russian empire and subsequent assertion of China post-1949 proved decisive to British aspirations. Already by 1950, the British policy alternated between two aims:

> that of establishing a sphere of influence, especially in the Kashgar region and the Tarim Basin, tacitly conceding to Russia a sphere of influence in the Ili Valley and Jungaria, and that of cooperating with the Chinese

243 Lattimore (1950) *op.cit.* 235, 46.
244 *Ibid.* 51.
245 Wen-wu Tseng, *Chung Ku Kin Ying Hsi Yu Shih* (Shanghai, 1936) 599 as cited and quoted in English by Lattimore *Ibid.* 56.
246 *Ibid.* 103–151.

authorities and supporting the full claims of Chinese sovereignty thus indicating that the extension of Russian influence would be undesirable.[247]

Russia, China, and Territory

The Pamir Boundary Commission was established in 1895 to delimit the boundary between the Russian and British Empires.[248] Thomas H. Holdich, discussed earlier, was a key commentator and player in the demarcation of boundaries at that time.[249] The commission report resulted in the *Agreement between the Governments of Great Britain and Russia with regard to the sphere of influence of the two countries in the region of the Pamirs (1895).* The participation of Afghanistan and China in the commission and subsequent delimitation gives the boundary added legitimacy in the politics of the time.[250] As Holdich puts it, this achieved the following:

> [The treaty]... defined a buffer between ourselves and Russia. It is not an imposing buffer – the long attenuated arm of Afghanistan reaching out to touch China with the tips of its fingers. It is only eight miles wide at one part, and could be ridden across in a morning's ride.[251]

The interesting question that is partly raised by the agreement is how what may seem like a capitulation by a then weak State in international law (China) can be weighed against its growing strength now in territorial terms. As with many boundary questions, it raises questions of equity in the negotiations of the boundary treaties and the ability to be able to fully delineate the lines drawn on maps into coherent boundaries.

The story of the imperial rivalry for territory between the Chinese and Russian Empires[252] is depicted in a series of international legal documents. This includes the *Treaty of Nerchinsk* (1689), *Treaty of Bura* (1727), and the *Treaty of Kiakhta* (1727), which remained in force for nearly 100 years until contestation and subsequent renegotiation as Russia advanced its claims in the Pamir Plateau to the Northern bank of the Amur through acquisition of Maritime Provinces. There was also a subsequent spurt of treaties between 1858 and 1924 which set the frame for understanding Sino-Russian

247 *Ibid.* 200.
248 *Ibid.* 259.
249 See *Report of the Proceedings of the Pamir Boundary Commission* (Calcutta, India: Office of the Superintendent of Government Printing, 1897); also see Thomas H. Holdich, *The Indian Border Land, 1880–1900* (London: Methuen & Co., 1901).
250 Lattimore (1950) *op.cit.* 235, 260–261.
251 Holdich (1901) *op.cit.* 250, 284.
252 Also see Edmund Chubb, *China and Russia: The 'Great' Game* (New York: Columbia University Press, 1971).

relationships.[253] Among the treaties negotiated were *Treaty of Tientsin and Aigun* (1858), the *Treaty of Peking* (1860), *The Treaty of Livadia* (1879), *The Treaty of St. Petersburg* (1881), *The Russo-Chinese Anti-Japanese Alliance* (1896), *The Lia-tung Peninsula Concession* (1898), *The Russian Troop Withdrawal Agreement* (1902), *The Russo-Mongolian Agreement* (1912), *The Russo-Chinese Declaration* (1913), and *The Tripartite Kiaktha Conference* (1915).

The period between 1858 and 1924 was crucial in the determination of boundary lines in Asia on the back of this relationship. Firstly, many of the border tensions between the two regimes trace to this time. Secondly, the actual boundary as it emerged forms the contemporary fault line between 'west' and 'east'. Thirdly, the tensions of that period still impact Sino-Soviet relations and were material to the famous Sino-Soviet split in the 1960s. Fourthly, they explain the last major shift of power from China away to Russia which is now becoming reversed.[254] These reasons are important in understanding China's reorientation and redressal of territorial power dynamics to accompany its financial clout.[255]

Paine selected two quotes from previous Russian and Chinese leaders that are worth reproducing to capture some attitudes to boundaries that may still be relevant. Krushchev stated:

> As far as we were concerned, we weren't responsible for what our tsars had done, but the lands gained from those tsarist treaties were now Soviet territory. We weren't the only socialist country which had to administer and defend the territory inherited from a pre-Revolutionary regime. We were afraid that it we started remapping our frontiers according to historical considerations, the situation would get out of hand and lead to conflict. Besides, a true Communist and internationalist wouldn't assign any particular importance to the question of borders, especially borders between fellow socialist states.[256]

Mao Tse-Tung, in 1964, had a very different view:

> There are too many places occupied by the Soviet Union... The Russians took everything they could. Some people have declared that the Sinkiang area and the territories north of the Amur River must be included in the

253 SCM Paine, *Imperial Rivals: China, Russia and Their Disputed Frontier* (London: M. E. Sharpe, 1996) 2.

254 *Ibid.* 2.

255 For a work that examines Russo-Chinese boundaries, see John Robert Victor Prescott, *Map of Mainland Asia by Treaty* (Melbourne: Melbourne University Press, 1975).

256 Nikita Krushchez, *Kruschev Remembers: The Last Testament* (London: Little Brown, 1974) 284

> Soviet Union… The Soviet Union has an area of 22 million square kilometres and its population is only 220 million. It is about time to put an end to this allotment. …About a hundred years ago, the area to the east of [Lake] Baikal became Russian territory, and since then Vladivostok, Khabarovsk, Kamchatka, and others areas have been Soviet territory. We have not yet presented our account for this list.[257]

By the end of the twentieth century, the Sino-Soviet boundary was among the world's longest and had been completely demarcated, effectively ending territorial contestations. Against that Russia's current expansion into Ukraine and the threat of other potential incursions suggest that acquisition of territory further west and south may yet be an option. China's own Belt and Road Initiative and territorial advances may seem benign in comparison, but the issue of territorial demarcations may not seem as settled in perpetuity as it is currently presented. In terms of Chinese history, its boundaries have always varied tremendously over its long-documented history. The territory was greatest under the Yuan dynasty (Mongol) and the Ch'ing (Manchu) dynasty, neither of which were Han Chinese Empires.[258] However, Chinese history often fails to emphasize the territory in the Ming dynasty which followed the Yuan dynasty, thereby giving the impression of an aggrandized Han Chinese Empire, as reflected in the historical maps published by the Cartographic Publishing House.[259]

Japanese Forays into the Mainland and Oceans

To complete the picture, it is worth touching on a few facets of the reach of the Japanese into Asia. From the Meiji Restoration in 1868 onwards until defeat alongside Germany in World War II, Japan pursued expansionist empire-building activities that saw its ready acceptance as a Great Power in World Politics.[260] At its zenith, this enabled holding of territories well beyond the Japanese archipelago, including colonies, protectorates, mandates, and other territories. The lands, in the Western Pacific and East Asia, were gained through military victories that commenced with the defeat of the Qing in China in 1895 (First Sino-Japan War). This yielded Japan control

257 As captured in Dennis J. Doolin, *Territorial Claims in the Sino-Soviet Conflict: Documents and Analysis* (Stanford, CA: Hoover Institute Studies, Stanford University Press, 1965) 43–44.

258 See Morris Rossabi, *China and Inner Asia: From 1360 to the Present Day* (London: Thames & Hudson, 1975).

259 Sarah C. Paine *Imperial Rivals: China, Russia and Their Disputed Frontier* (London: M. E. Sharpe, 1996) 17.

260 Takatsu Kuwasaburo et al., *History of the Empire of Japan* [Frank Brinkley trans.] (Tokyo: Dai Nippon Tosho Kabushiki Kwaisha, 1893).

over Taiwan which it held as colony ceded by China under the *Treaty of Shimonoseki* (1895). Japan exercised control for five decades, which only ended with the Japanese surrender in World War II when Taiwan was placed under Chinese rule. Japan also gained effective control over the Korean peninsula which it had been intimidating since the latter half of the nineteenth century, including through coercion into signing the *Japan–Korea Treaty* (1876) which granted extraterritorial rights to Japanese citizens with preferential control over Korean ports. These actions were significant to the commencement of the First Sino-Japan War two decades later. Korea was occupied and declared a protectorate in 1905 via the *Japan–Korea Treaty* (1905), annexed in 1910 and remained within the Japanese Empire until its defeat in World War II. The Japanese seafaring tradition also facilitated capture of islands, including Sakhalin island, which had attracted Japanese settlers in the aftermath of the Meiji Restoration. While initially ceding control over to the island to Russia in exchange for the Kuril islands via the *Treaty of St. Petersburg* (1875), it regained the territory through military victory in the *Russo-Japanese War* of 1905. A colonial government was established which was renamed as a Japanese prefecture by 1907.

Japan also declared war on Germany following the outbreak of World War I, seizing its Pacific colonies – Northern Mariana, Caroline, and Marshall Islands. The *Treaty of Versailles* formally recognized Japanese title over these territories, including to Micronesia, which were held under a *League of Nations* Mandate as the *South Seas Mandate*, though some were lost in World War II to the United States and the rest formally revoked by United Nations Security Council Resolution 21(II) and awarded to the United States as trusteeship territories. Sino-Japanese relationships were always tense, and were at their nadir with the Japanese invasion of Manchuria and the subsequent massacre of Nanking in 1939. The invasion of Manchuria commenced in 1931 leading to declaration of the puppet State of Machukuo (1932) from where Japan sought to expand its industrial base. In keeping up with developments on the continent on other side of the Pacific Ocean, Manchukuo was fully equipped with the trappings of Statehood – a defined territory, a fixed population, an installed government, and an ability to trade with Japan. It formed the base for aggression against China and Mongolia during World War II until Japan's eventual defeat by the Soviet Union and the *Treaty of Surrender* which terminated Japanese imperialism and restored territories. Modern Japan, nonetheless, does have some claims to territory pending, including the Dodko/Takeshima island in the South China Sea.[261]

261 See K. Taijudo, 'The Dispute Between Japan and Korea Respecting Sovereignty over Takeshima' 12 *Japanese Annual of International Law* (1968) 1. Also see C. I. Chee, 'Legal Status of Dok Island in International Law' 42 *Korean Journal of International Law* (1997) 1; H. K. Lee, 'Korea's Territorial Rights to Todko in History and International Law' 20

Its relevance stems from codification of the Law of the Sea and its impact in creating an Exclusive Economic Zone (EEZ). Dodko/Takeshima (Liancourt Rocks) is referred to in the *San Francisco Treaty of 1951* signed between the Allies and Japan in the aftermath of World War II. Consisting two rocky islets and other outcrops classified as reefs, they lie 93 kilometres east of the Korean island of Ullung. Korea claims Dodko/Takeshima on the basis of the geographical contiguity of Ullung.[262] Located 157 kilometres northwest of Oki Islands and adjacent to the Hokkaido, Japan's claim is based on adjacency.[263] Historical arguments of the competing parties contradict each other:[264] Korea claims sovereignty since 512 AD[265] while the Japanese claim goes back to 1650[266] with official incorporation deemed to have occurred in 1905.[267] In Dodko/Takeshima even though the Korean claim may be valid, questions remain about whether the rocks were habitable. The matter is addressed by the *San Francisco Treaty* which sought to determine the disposition of the territories held by Japan.[268] This addressed sovereignty over Kurile, contested between the Soviet Union and Japan, and Senkaku, contested between China and Japan. However, on Dodko/Takeshima, there were considerable differences between the early and later drafts which still leave claims open.[269]

Korea Observer (1998) 1, and B. J. Lee, *A Study of the Legal Status of Dodko* (Oxford, OH: Miami University, 1957).

262 See Benjamin K. Sibbett, 'Tokdo or Takeshima? The Territorial Dispute Between Japan and the Republic of Korea' 21 *Fordham International Law Journal* (1997–1998) 1606, 1637.

263 Jonathan I. Charney, 'Central East Asian Maritime Boundaries and the Law of the Sea' 89 *American Journal of International Law* (1995) 724, 731.

264 For the Korean perspective on the disputed history see Y. Shin, 'A Historical Study of Korea's Title to Tokdo' 28 *Korean Observer* (1997) 333. Also see H. Lee, 'Dispute over Territorial Ownership of Tokdo in the Late Chosen Period' 28 *Korea Observer* (1997) 389 and B. J. Lee, "Title to Dodko' in International Law' 2 *Korean Journal of Comparative Law* (1974) 85.

265 The governmental position is captured in Ministry of Foreign Affairs, Republic of Korea, *An Outline of the Possession of Dodko* (Seoul: Ministry of Foreign Affairs, 1955).

266 Ministry of Foreign Affairs, Japan, *Outline of Takeshima Problem*, Press Release, Vol. III No. 76, October 28, 1954.

267 K. Hori, 'Japan's Incorporation of Takeshima into Its Territory in 1905' 28 *Korea Observer* (1997) 477.

268 For a discussion of the Treaty and its various drafts of it, see Seokwoo Lee, 'The 1951 San Francisco Peace Treaty with Japan and the Territorial Disputes in East Asia' 11 *Pacific Rim Law & Policy Journal* (2002) 63.

269 For more, see B. J. Lee (1974) *op.cit.* 826, 85. For an assessment of how the dispute could be addressed under the rules governing title to territory, see Joshua Castellino & Elvira Dominguez Redondo, 'The Title to Dokdo/Takeshima: Addressing Legacies of World War II Territorial Settlements' 22(4) *International Journal on Minority & Group Rights* (2015) 550–577.

Conclusion: Boundaries and the Future

This chapter presented insights into how matters concerning territorial acquisition and return have played out in the history of different parts of the world. It emphasizes how the world's boundaries have been impacted by expansionism in the previous century. Notwithstanding difficulties concerning the construction of the original boundaries and the lack of overlap between the ethno-linguistic communities and the political dimensions of the average post-colonial State, this chapter ends by enunciating six compelling reasons why territorial disputes will likely grow in intensity and volume over the next quarter of a century, at a time when greatest attention ought to be paid to other considerations, notably the existential fight against climate change.

First, significant numbers of international borders around the globe, especially in the context of maritime boundaries, have not been delimited and demarcated, leading to legal uncertainty.[270] Claimants are likely to increasingly seek remedies for these pushed by scarcity driven by climate change. Second, the average post-colonial State has, in many cases, been relatively unsuccessful in building pluralistic identity; as a consequence, border communities, especially those with kin on the opposite side of the border, have begun to express fervent claims which gain greater traction at a time of political polarization. Third, in the heightened sense of competition invoked by globalization, access to resources including in the Polar Regions, Arctic and Pacific, will likely become crucial, with it potentially becoming feasible for States with claims to advance these hitherto impractical claims due to melting glaciers and the potential emergence of new sea routes. Fourth, increased awareness of questions of identity have raised greater possibilities for political mobilzation around these, not least using social media. Fifth, there is a general ambience of instability caused by the transition of power between west and east,[271] with a number of values, including post-colonial citizenship, coming into question. Finally, because it may be possible, through increased disclosure and/or manipulation of documents and the possibility of collecting and evaluating other kinds of geo-scientific evidence, to advance claims that could not have had appropriate levels of evidentiary backing in previous eras.[272]

270 It is interesting that Russia and China appear to have delimited their boundaries between each other, while both have strong claims to their boundaries with others. See [Editors], *Approaches to Solving Territorial Conflicts* (2010) *op.cit.* 40. Also see [Editorial], 'The Sino-Russia Border: The Cockerel's Cropped Crest' *Economist* (24 July 2008) available at https://www.economist.com/asia/2008/07/24/the-cockerels-cropped-crest

271 See Joshua Castellino, *The End of the Liberal State and the First Terrorist* (London: Middlesex University Press, 2008).

272 See B. Donohue, N. Otte & B. Smith, 'An Ontological Approach to Territorial Disputes' in *Proceedings of the Conference on Semantic Technology in Intelligence, Defense and*

Two additional points need to be made to support the hypothesis that territorial disputes are likely to come into sharper focus. First, there has been an increasing proliferation of violence, with a clear phenomenon emerging of substate actors, with tacit or overt support of States, seeking reorientation of maps. These actions are often motivated by a desire on the part of kin communities to link better with their 'mother/father' State; and often receives logistical or moral support from the State keen to advance a claim and acquire more territory, possibly in the belief of increasing economic competitiveness.[273] Second, if the principle of *uti possidetis juris* is to be followed strictly, a territory in dispute would be awarded to the possessor until such time as the claimant could make a greater claim to it. In its more recent century-old application within public international law, *uti possidetis juris* was called upon to settle questions over possession and territory at a time of transition. It is perhaps time to entertain the idea that this transitional period has passed with the average post-colonial State entering its fifth decade of existence and with perpetual peace not on the horizon in most places. This is especially so since many States have now had a longer post-colonial life than the experience under colonisation. If in that time adequate measures have not been put in place towards accommodation, consolidation, and establishment of firm title, this ought to be debated in a court of law as a potential failure of effective control, especially since the incumbent ostensibly had full territorial jurisdiction and the claimant had none.

Security (Conference on Semantic Technology in Intelligence Defese & Security) (2014), CEUR (Conference Proceedings), Vol. 1304, 2–9.

273 Walter Kemp, Vesselin Popovski & Ramesh Thakur (eds.), *Blood and Borders: The Responsibility to Protect and the Problem of the Kin State* (Tokyo: United Nations University, 2011).

Conclusion

The Quest for Order and Justice?

Introduction

The most used substantive phrase in the UN Charter is the 'maintenance of international peace and security' and fittingly, it is the apex body of the structure, the UN Security Council, that is tasked with the duty of ensuring that it reacts to threats to peace and breaches of the peace. Much has been written about how the nature of the security questions facing the globe has changed since their articulation as a form of interstate conflict in the aftermath of World War II. The UN vision, premised on the global will to create a bulwark against threats to peace, is based on a system of collective security policed by the Security Council. This scenario envisages a global collective response to any threat or breach of peace committed by a single State or group of States against the territorial integrity of another. In the original vision, such an action would have warranted the matter being seized upon by the Security Council, who could then, via a decision with the explicit or implicit consent of the five veto-bearing members, authorize all means necessary to restore international peace and security. The idea that a standing army built from among the membership (Article 43) created immediate problems among competing States, and one element of that vision became inoperative right from the start. In nearly 80 years, the mechanism has faced significant challenges: permanent members' direct involvement in the conflict; permanent members' vested interests leading to the use of the veto to obstruct response; processes undertaken outside the framework of the collective security mechanism; the growth in intrastate conflict making collective global action more difficult; the sheer volume of threats to peace that abound in conjunction with limited willingness and capacities for intervention. The crisis over Gaza commencing from 2023 shows that rather than maintaining peace and security, the veto power has been used in a partisan manner by two members (the United States and the United Kingdom) acting against the weight of global consensus on an issue of a conflict already determined by the ICJ to be potentially of genocidal intent. This is notwithstanding the

DOI: 10.4324/9781003503279-6

fact that the original limited vision itself paid no heed to the extent to which the climate emergency may well be the most significant threat to peace and security, directly and indirectly.

While the development of a mechanism for collective security within the United Nations was an inevitable consequence of the atrocities that created the organization itself, the UN vision for a peaceful and prosperous world encompassed two other pillars: human rights and development. Through pronouncements in the General Assembly, the Security Council, and ECOSOC, a sophisticated machinery emerged in the post-colonial UN era that sought to guarantee the inherent dignity and worth of every individual, with the express backing of States. This latter point is important since global human rights standards have emerged through active State participation, with the documents framed, designed, agreed upon, signed, and ratified by States, despite the obvious intrusion such standards represent into the domestic jurisdiction of States as enshrined in Article 2(7) of the *United Nations Charter* (1945). The formalization of the human rights mandate through the creation of the *Commission on Human Rights* in 1946, reinforced under the denomination *Human Rights Council*, with its relocation as the General Assembly's subsidiary body in 2006, as well as the creation of the *Office of the High Commissioner for Human Rights* in 1993 to serve the human rights machinery, provides ample evidence of the seriousness of this element of the UN mandate.

The UN role has been equally accentuated in the quest for human development, albeit in a manner that reinforced anthropocentricity and was ignorant of wider planetary and biodiversity concerns. Driven by calls for global solidarity in ensuring equitable trade and development, emphasis was placed on growth as an imperative within States, with a focus on the erection of adequate infrastructure to enable societies, especially those in dire poverty, to fully emerge in global society. The presence of UNDP in-region and attempts to bring technological know-how to questions of entrenched poverty have been key features of UN work. The articulation of the *Millennium Development Goals* helped place emphasis on the importance of this agenda, while the *Sustainable Development Goals*, framed against a better acknowledgement of the threat of climate change, have sought to create a vision for global society in 2030 and beyond.

Yet the centrepiece of UN work, the one that touched the greatest number of lives across the globe and had the most significant impact on the history of the era, was probably its active sponsorship of the decolonization process. This was framed as a blueprint for a world where nations would emerge free from subjugation to constitute an international society of equal States, where the States would collaborate and cooperate with each other in a spirit of fraternity to tackle peace and security questions by building interdependent trading relationships that would assist their development, while conducting themselves in a manner that upheld the inherent dignity and worth of everyone within their jurisdictions. While many decolonization conversations were simply a process by which movements oriented towards 'national' liberation negotiated, coerced, and defeated their colonial masters, the official UN mechanism assisted under the guidance of the Fourth Committee of the General Assembly and the UN Trusteeship Council, whose role was to oversee the transfer of power in non-self-governing territories. While some discussions did arise about the dimensions of the self-determining unit, notably in the context of Portuguese objections to reporting and in the *Belgian Thesis* argument,[1] what followed was adherence to a strict rule of respecting colonial boundaries as sacrosanct, ostensibly driven by the belief that this would be most effective in maintaining order. Arguments for the aggrandizement of the existing colonial governing units, as represented by the Pan-Africanist and Pan-Arab movements, were defeated, attributed by historians to the vested interests of the power brokers of the time, and also, to a certain extent, to the expediency of completing the process as swiftly as possible. In some cases, the units did break down further, notably in the subdivision of colonial India into independent India and the two wings of Pakistan (West and East – later to become Bangladesh), which took protracted discussion but still could not prevent one of the most significant massacres of the previous century in the mass border crossings.[2] If anything, that experience probably reinforced belief in the absolute sanctity of the pre-existing boundaries, in the name of preventing bloodshed.

This book has highlighted how the decision to conserve pre-existing boundaries in the name of order formed the backdrop to Latin American decolonization (1810–1825); was repeated in the break-up of the Ottoman Empire, including by maintaining lines such as those drawn by the *Sykes–Picot Agreement*, but also in other decisions that fell under or were overseen by the League of Nations and the *Treaty of Versailles* (1919 ff); and was enshrined in UN decolonization (1945–1990). Strands of an attempt to create supervening identities were present on each occasion – in the real developments of a confederacy and the subsequent establishment of the Organization of American States in 1905, the Pan-Arab movement, and the much more developed idea of Pan-Africanism. It is worth emphasizing that even in the dissolution of the Soviet Union, an attempt was made to establish the *Commonwealth of Independent States* (CIS) to maintain the benefits of being part of a larger conglomerate faced with shared problems. While it is impossible to prove whether these ventures would have yielded peace, greater

1 See Fernand Van Langenhove, *The Question of Aborigines Before the United Nations: The Belgian Thesis* (Brussels: Royal Colonial Institute of Belgium, 1954) UN Doc A/AC.67/2 pp. 3–31.

2 Yasmin Khan, *The Great Partition: The Making of India and Pakistan* (New Haven, CT: Yale University Press, 2008).

development, or more robust human rights, it can be asserted that the promise of peace and security, development, and human rights under the current trajectory has been less than successful.

Decolonization in the Americas did not yield representative government, did not prevent territorial wars and disputes, and did not contribute to even-handed development across populations. The outstanding territorial claims of indigenous peoples against the State 200 years later suggest that land tenure remains to be decolonized. Rigid implementation of the *Sykes–Picot* line and the *Balfour Declaration* are among many colonial decisions that contribute to current tensions in the 'Middle East' rather than guaranteeing peace and security. The decolonization process that commenced after British and French rule usually sponsored proxies to maintain hegemonic access to lucrative natural resources of the region, rather than promote development or human rights. The inherited African boundaries have been ineffective in preventing war and separatist conflict, which, despite calls from the *Organisation of African Unity*, have detracted from the development agenda on the continent. The boundaries and incoming governments proved unable to stop the drain of African wealth towards Europe, and, like post-colonial governments the world over, fell prey to mass arms sales peddled by the former colonial masters, which heightened cross-border insecurity and hindered collaboration and cooperation in pursuit of other goals.

Instead of creating the blueprint for a peaceful, more representative world, the decolonization project privatized the assets and natural wealth of the persons from whom it was first extracted. This is not necessarily the fault of the former colonial powers, or the United Nations, nor even necessarily the post-colonial governments themselves, though all remain collectively culpable. In approaching the bicentennial of the end of one of the first decolonization drives (Latin America 1810–1825), the world may be at its most precarious moment, with the prospects of perpetual peace farther away than at any other point in the last two centuries.

That this may be the case despite past challenges, which include intensive global and local wars, Cold War insecurities over nuclear weapons, and overwhelming terrorism and counterterrorism threats is remarkable. Rather than establishing the grounds through which the international society of States can come together to implement the systemic change called for by the climate crisis, intense competition, reflected as a race to the bottom, is developing, where scarce resources are fought over through wars and other proxy means. This makes the final quarter of the UN centenary most fraught in terms of threats to peace and security, countenanced by inaction, inability, and unwillingness to make the necessary changes that are imperative. The complex direct dangers of the climate crisis to peace and security are well documented. The indirect impacts, including refugee flows and intense competition for finite resources, create more of a traditionally understood threat to international peace and security.

The end of the Cold War was accompanied by hope of the spread of democracy. However, 'democracy' has become a game of numbers within predetermined units, rather than one of values. It has not engendered the greater sense of security it was believed to produce. For the vast majority of post-colonial countries, drawn on the basis of the interests of departing colonial rulers, their national boundaries cut across kin communities, creating majority and minority groups based on proximity to power. Vaunted ideas of 'nation-building' – patronizingly sold from Europe as unifying forces to unite disparate communities under a common 'national unity' rubric have dimmed as virulent and exclusivist forms of 'nationalism' – linked to vested masculine readings of ethnicity, religion, or language have flourished. This has bred intense internal strife and fragmentation within States. Scapegoat politics have emerged as a key driver in nourishing anger through historically selective nationalist narratives that promote hate against non-conformers who are deemed 'anti-national'. As the crisis in Gaza shows, the danger of adverse, historically flawed, politically motivated attention to identity, especially towards minority and marginalized communities, can devastate societies, creating push factors towards the kind of conflict that the founding parents of the United Nations warned about.

The result is a sharp rise in the threat and persistence of ethnic conflict, ethnic cleansing, crimes against humanity, war crimes, and even genocide. The modalities of twenty-first-century life, not least the extent to which social media can be captured to amplify negative messaging and ratchet-up action, have resulted in atrocities that have spilt over international boundaries. The situation is not restricted to countries in the developing world. In wealthy countries, identity politics are used as a tool to strengthen scapegoat politics, tap into latent xenophobia, and transform political landscapes through polarization and fragmentation. The rise in the use of hate speech and attacks based on identity is a clear indicator of this trend. Two further factors are likely to augment the threat to international peace and security in the last quarter of the UN centenary. First, the intermixing of diverse populations within each State that was already the result of significant long-term global migrations caused by trade and flight over centuries has grown sharply and led to further cross-germination of identities. Second, identity-oriented politics, especially when manifested in exclusivist nationalisms, are likely to come into greater focus. This could set minorities – those of a different ethnicity, religion, or language – in one country, with kin across a national border, to mobilize across national frontiers as the threat to them in their current state grows.

When national boundaries are viewed through regional perspectives, their artificiality becomes accentuated, especially in post-colonial countries where borders were not drawn based on cohesion, homogeneity, or even shared historical experience of the communities. This is particularly true in East Asia, Southeast Asia, South Asia, Central Asia, the Gulf countries, the Levantine

States of the 'Middle East,' North Africa and the Maghreb, East Africa and the Great Lakes region, Southern Africa, Central Africa, West Africa, and Central America. In each of these regions, many of the national boundaries are less than a century old and were drawn without regard to any of the factors that ought to be salient in such a decision. Such factors are also present in the countries of North America, Western Europe, and Eastern and Central Europe, where boundaries are older and bear the scars of significant previous contestations. In these regions, intra-regional antagonisms feature less than collective antagonisms towards incoming communities from outside. In South America, the neglect and erasure over 200 years of indigenous rights and livelihoods are also becoming fiercely contested. The mostly island countries in the Pacific region are not immune to this threat either, as intrastate cross-fertilization has become inlaid against in-migration from Asia, creating identity-based tensions.

The actual threat to peace and security within any given State and its potential to cross national boundaries to become 'international' varies tremendously by country and region. Yet five commonalities emerge which significantly weaken the peace and security agenda:

(a) Assertion of flawed 'nationalist' identities often based on colonial existence enhances fragmentation.
(b) Failures to combat the dissemination of hate designed to privilege a vote bank by generating enmity against another generate preconditions for conflict.
(c) Neighbouring State rivalries augment threats against kin populations of those States that are often the direct consequence of colonial boundary demarcations.
(d) Biased historical narratives geared towards short-term political control promote deep legacies that weaken polities and compromise long-term prospects of inter-community peace.
(e) Failures to adopt international response-oriented measures to support peace and security undermine the legitimacy of international actors and the rule of law.

In the orchestrated campaign against the Rohingya in Myanmar over the last two decades, a theme that drove hate towards the community was the allegation that they were 'Muslim' and 'foreign'. It did not seem pertinent in the dissemination of this hate that being Buddhist and belonging to Myanmar was a mere construction that was barely a reference to an autochthonous history. Islam did spread to the region from the west through the Ottoman Empire and the trade that flourished within and along the Silk Road. But Buddhism also came from the near west, from India, and what can be determined as 'home' and 'foreign' is based on boundary lines drawn by the

British to better administer their crown jewel colony India, which originally included Myanmar.

While the aspiration to prevent the outbreak of World War III through the UN system has held firm for nearly 80 years, war has been omnipresent throughout. Testimony to this can be seen in the number of countries that have been under threat, or in breach of the peace. It is revealing that, in a series of analyses of attempts to act in support of the maintenance of peace and security from the period of 1945 to around 2006, instances of violations of minority rights have featured strongly, but attempts to resolve these have been slow to identify this animus driving the conflict. Minorities form a crucial litmus test to the failures of state-building and, as a consequence, act as a weathervane on the potency of identity-based fissures that, if coaxed, can become conflictual. After all, it is the drawing of the governance unit line that determines which community forms a majority. The imposition of the sovereign State in decolonization transferred power, explained as 'democratic legitimacy,' to this majority, and unless it was accompanied by an inclusive agenda, identity fissures became accentuated.

A simple analysis of UN deployments shows that 23 of the 61 documented peacekeeping operations in the UN period were in response to the violation of identity-oriented or minority rights, in diverse contexts such as the Middle East, Kashmir, (then) Republic of Congo, Syria and the Golan Heights, Lebanon, Afghanistan, Western Sahara, former Yugoslavia, Somalia, Rwanda, Burundi, Sudan, and Kosovo. As many as 10 of the 25 United Nations authorized military operations in that period, including in Bosnia and Herzegovina, Rwanda, Kosovo, Afghanistan, Iraq, Sudan, and the DRC, featured such factors prominently. UN authorized sanctions show the same trend with 8 instances (of 21) pertaining to similar contexts (Rhodesia, South Africa, Yugoslavia, Somalia, Rwanda, DRC, and Sudan). In none of these instances were racialized communities or minorities directly mentioned despite identity-oriented issues being the root cause of the conflict.

Since 2010 the following countries/areas have featured regularly in Security Council resolutions: Sudan, South Sudan, Central African Republic, Liberia, Somalia, Iraq, Cyprus, Mali, Western Sahara, Haiti, Burundi, Middle East, North Korea, Afghanistan, Bosnia and Herzegovina, Democratic Republic of Congo, Syria, Cote d'Ivoire, Libya, Guinea-Bissau, Sierra Leone, Yemen, Abyei (Ethiopia). While underlying tensions are often identity-based, in the following countries it could be argued that minority status is either a driver of conflict or is significant in the identity of the victims of the conflict: Sudan, South Sudan, Somalia, Iraq, Syria, Afghanistan, Bosnia and Herzegovina, Democratic Republic of Congo and Yemen. Yet none of the resolutions in the last 12 years draw attention to the specific need to protect marginalized communities, never mind the more specific use of the word 'minorities'.

In *Sudan,* conflict has brewed along lines of identity for over 40 years, with the emergence of South Sudan leaving crucial questions concerning boundaries and population transfers in each of the two States, making ethno-religious identity a new boundary line to the tension. While the peace and security situation in *Somalia* has been compromised for at least two decades, leading to failed statehood, the current hold of majority clans, the ongoing inter-clan conflict, and the specific marginalization of minority clans are significant features of the continued state of war. The failure for urgent humanitarian need to reach segments of the populations based on their minority clan status is significant to the human upheaval in the State. Identity issues are at the very forefront of *Iraq* since the illegal invasion led by the United States and the United Kingdom. The previously suppressed Shi'a majority has mobilized to claim governance, while Saddam Hussein's favoured ethno-religious Sunni community faced significant backlash, leading some to flee to *Syria* and remobilize as *Daesh*, generating mass atrocities in the region. Meanwhile, Yezidi, Kurdish, and other smaller suppressed nations within the borders of Iraq and Syria have faced diverse violations, from persistent systemic harassment, ethnic cleansing, crimes against humanity, war crimes, and genocide. A similar situation is live in *Afghanistan*, where another dubious invasion in the name of the protection of international peace and security forcibly maintained peace for a while but was unable to make the structural changes to generate long-term sustained stability. Instead the ousted Taliban regime returned invigorated, targeting minority communities alongside a widespread and sustained attempt to eliminate women from the public gaze as part of its ideology. The *Dayton Peace Accord* of 1995 may have brought the Yugoslav wars to an end, but it created a blueprint for ethnic segregation. While that yielded relative stability in five of the six former Yugoslav Republics, the sense of crisis remained in the former autonomous region of *Kosovo* and the former Republic of *Bosnia and Herzegovina*. The internationally mandated consociational agreement, another Western-developed remedy peddled voraciously as a post-conflict panacea, created an uneasy détente along ethnic lines. However, rather than fostering medium-term stability, it festered simmering tension which remains palpable. Similarly while the *DRC* features often in Security Council dispatches due to the internecine war in substantial parts of its territory, the persistent purge against the Batwa, using weaponry acquired for war against mostly unarmed communities, rarely features, despite documented crimes against humanity against the community in the name of conservation. The violation of the arms embargo, with apparent tacit support of Member States, has not warranted attention or action.

A key point to note in any assessment of global conflict through the lens of Security Council resolutions is that the veto-bearing powers of the five permanent members take conflicts where they have a direct interest off the table. Thus identity-oriented conflicts in Chechnya, Dagestan, Ingushetia, Transdniestr, Crimea, Eastern Ukraine, Xinjiang Autonomous Region, and the Tibet Autonomous Regime do not feature. The struggle to get a ceasefire in Gaza in 2023–2024 shows that Israel and the Occupied Territories should also feature on that list. In any case the 'Friends in High Places' syndrome indemnifies India along with Israel as obvious beneficiaries. In India, neither the revocation of the special status of Kashmir nor the significant peace and security hazards to Muslims in India, nor the direct threat of the creation of millions of stateless people by nationality stripping in Assam appears to feature in meaningful discussions about threats to international peace and security. The failed attempts to censure Israel throughout its history of building an apartheid State through the illegal augmentation of land to attract migrants safeguarded by the most sophisticated war machinery show how ally-oriented politics render the Security Council a bastion of vested interests rather than a body charged with the maintenance of international peace and security.

Much has been written about the anachronistic nature, appropriateness, and effectiveness of the State-oriented collective security arrangements at the United Nations. Despite its faults and lack of accountability, the mechanism remains the only legally mandated global regime to react to threats to peace and security. This brief section seeks to articulate key features that make it imperative for the UN machinery to prioritize understanding and action in the escalation of threats to minorities.

Despite articulations of narrow nationalism in States in every region of the world, the populations of these States have become increasingly *diverse* through historical and contemporary migration; influx of trade, investment, and labour; flight from persecution elsewhere; and intermarriages across ethno-religious and ethno-linguistic barriers. Changing values, including around gendered identities, make the notion of unitary nationalistic narratives outdated and dangerous in their ability to polarize and stigmatize segments of the population. The recent rise in flawed nationalistic narratives could be viewed as a direct consequence of the need to combat societal diversity through a thrust towards capturing political power. The consequence of such actions places significant State machinery, including the ability to make and revoke laws and use significant policing and military arsenals, against those deemed to fall outside the exclusivist narrative. The consequences of this have led and could continue to lead to significant tensions, which could further escalate into compromising local, national, regional, and international peace and security.

The scapegoating of populations through active and, on occasion, systematic hate dissemination is growing. Fuelled by ease of access and saturation of social media across the socio-economic spectra in society, such messages and fake news appear to galvanize action in a manner that could approach genocide, as documented in Rwanda. The unwillingness and inability to rein in social media corporations, alongside the breadth of personal data available online, has made the targeting of direct and subliminal actions possible to a level far beyond the reach of radio stations such as *Radio Télévision Libre des Mille Collines* (RTLM) – deemed key to the Rwandan genocide. The hostility of messaging on social media has created acceptance of aggressive speech in the public realm, making it possible for hate-oriented sentiments to be expressed even by Heads of States. This has polarized societies with a deeply fragmenting impact. Such divisive and anger-fuelled situations act as a powder keg for violence, with steps from fighting words to action well understood, including its ability to flare up into much larger societal incidents that can draw in many others in locales far removed from the site of the conflict.

Societal fragmentation has provided significant political opportunities, especially in democracies where it has been possible to establish political parties on racially motivated grounds. Sold as anti-political narratives at a time of austerity and economic stagnation, this tapped into mainstream vote banks, turning hitherto unacceptable values, regulated by strong constitutional provisions, into electable agendas. On seizing power, these political parties have sought to change the basic structure of societies, with institutions in favour of the rule of law and human rights becoming hollowed out and unable to contest actions that are blatantly against constitutional and international legal values. With the agendas of these political parties driven and supported by scapegoat politics, it is inevitable that as they form governments, the direct threat to peace and security will grow, resulting in greater investment in violent policing and militarization. Contestation through institutions is becoming nearly impossible, with strong repressive measures applied directly as civic spaces close, pushing societies towards conditions where the threat of the violation of peace and security grows exponentially unless communities accept the harassment and oppression that may rain down on them. The prevalence of hate within societies, often nourished through an education system, means that it is not merely State institutions that are to be feared in such instances. Rather, there appears to be significant growth in self-help paramilitaries and 'citizen-action' groups, emboldened by governmental messages, who claim to act in the name of 'popular values'. These paramilitaries and vigilantes rarely face sanction due to the tacit acceptance of their actions, often by police forces and criminal justice mechanisms that implicitly or explicitly share their biases. This has undermined the rule of law, challenging the monopoly of the State on tools of violence, germinating reactions with the potential to escalate threats to peace and security.

The polarization within State boundaries is often watched closely by kin communities across borders, where the majority–minority paradigm may well be reversed. In these situations, a government that may have been formed on similar grounds of scapegoating minorities could feel justified in acting, usually on the basis of pre-existing interstate rivalries and simmering tension. Before long, such actions could become classically interstate in the manner that led to the devastation that motivated the formation of the United Nations in 1945. The polarization within States is also mirrored at the international level, with complex allegiances that extend beyond borders as the global kaleidoscope of power shifts and new allegiances are formed. The interconnected nature of global societies has been recently demonstrated in grave terms with the spread of the COVID-19 pandemic. This interconnection also extends to the ability to divert funding and influence activities in other sovereign States. Thus, it is now possible for vested foreign interests to sustain and fuel conflict on the basis of their own national interests, which could prolong conflict and pose a significant threat to global peace and security.

The path to rethinking an apparatus to address the threats to peace and security articulated here seems beyond the remit and interest of many who are confronted with such issues. Besides this, obvious power dynamics make such a path nearly impossible to achieve, not least because of the significant implication of many of the protagonists in maintaining the system as it stands, using it when suited, and ignoring it on other occasions. It would seem that as an intergovernmental organization set up to ensure that such threats to peace and security are de-escalated, the United Nations ought to be in a prime position to act. Yet the United Nations itself is deeply influenced by the States, and despite progressive thinking from within the agencies that make up the thrust of the implementation of its agendas on peace, security, development, and human rights, it is State membership that has the controlling interest, with the more powerful footing the bill, who could progress or restrict the agenda. It is thus to these States, the civil servants, and the significant masses of populations who wish to live in a peaceful and prosperous world that can operate within its planetary boundaries that this conclusion is addressed.

The first step towards action would be to acknowledge the extent to which the current structural model of global society directly impedes the addressing of questions at the heart of human insecurity: climate-related and beyond. Whether explicitly or implicitly, the value of accepting this causal link can play a significant role in galvanizing prevention and redress mechanisms. Such an acknowledgement need not be dramatic since the agendas of every State and existing international organizations already posit values that are inherently inclusive, oriented towards peace and security, and pay attention to development needs.

Periodic odes devoted to the death of the sovereign State, often framed by progressive scholars, are usually defeated by the deep attraction that the exclusive powers of sovereignty bestow upon its holders, over territories, resources, and peoples. Drawing on Enlightenment Era ideas of emancipation, self-determination changed the global map, crystallizing new boundaries from lines drawn upon maps 'where no white man's foot had ever trod'. Hailed as emancipation, self-determination inspired decolonization reifying the sovereign State as the only recognizable form of legitimized 'national' political governance in international law. Determining the 'self' to be the former colonial unit had two impacts: it recognized these as the only legitimate holders of jurisdiction in their inherited territories and provided new sovereigns with exclusive beneficiary rights from the extractive economic system in place, enabling the escalation of resource exploitation ostensibly to generate wealth in aid of state-building. That the wealth generated did not accrue to communities facing loss and damage does not feature prominently in discussions.

The call for structural change struck a chord among populations in the midst of the climate emergency and COVID-19 pandemic. The palpable growth in inequality and decimation of public services feeds a simmering anger that has been stimulated by scapegoat politics within most sovereign states. These politics, often at the instigation of the super-wealthy who control media and messaging (and who are willing to provide the sought after health and education services at a premium price), aim to rile masses into a frenzy of distraction from the continued overexploitation of resources accompanied by an unwillingness to embark on the wholesale structural changes needed. Identity politics' incursion into mainstream consciousness has fragmented societies when societal unity focused on collective climate mitigation ought to be uppermost on policy agendas. Green Plans articulated with fanfare engage system-tinkering, avoiding the system-overhaul climate scientists and civil society demand. The nexus between governments and big businesses, especially extractive industries, is a key driver.[3]

Robert Lansing once stated that no one could determine what self-determination was until someone decided who the 'self' is.[4] Yet a changed approach to determining that 'self' that may be less of an artificial construct than has been foisted upon global imagination over the last two centuries can be framed against this backdrop.

Drawing on historical studies of the world's boundaries in tandem with communities' contestations, this book seeks to end with a practice-informed theoretical approach to viewing the world as 17 regions. The analysis is offered in a bid to offset the current reliance on a system that was designed by a few European men, schooled in their own values they believed to be supreme, who felt entitled to draw lines to protect their hegemony in competitions between themselves. That this system is deemed international and ostensibly supported with wide consensus is misleading when viewed through the privileging of the powerful male beneficiaries from other regions who then simply claim it to be so. As this book has sought to show, the legacy of contemporary governance derives from an absolute conviction in one system: that of the sovereign State – derived in one part of the world and imposed everywhere in the aftermath of an exploitative quest for wealth that treated the rest of the world as devoid of people. Rather than resulting

3 See *Big Oil versus the World* (London: BBC Production, 2022, 3 parts).

4 Whelan (1994) *op.cit.* 32, 99.

in a just transition when the pressure to change came, decolonization reified the boundaries drawn, maintaining colonial hegemonies through proxies on the argument that it was better for the maintenance of peace and security. Nearly two centuries later, it is irrefutable that the decision to maintain such boundaries did not result in peace. The conflicts that have raged since early in the nineteenth century have varied from the local to the global. The UN system established to maintain *inter*-national peace and security, i.e. peace and security between 'nations' used in this context as States has meant that numerous conflicts that have occurred within the realms of the problematic boundaries have been ignored as falling within the jurisdiction of the artificial entities that form its membership. In these conflicts incumbent governments have had uncontested power, due to their monopoly to legitimate weaponry, to act in a manner they determined fit, to maintain peace and security. Even where conflicts spread beyond national boundaries, the willingness to act in support of peace was reduced to individual calculations of sovereign States in the Security Council as to whether this warranted action. The full-fledged Russian invasion of Ukraine in 2022 on the grounds that it was seeking to protect its kin-based communities in that country shows how limited and flawed the entire system is, not least since it concerns a country whose historical acquisition of territory across the Eurasian landmass is rarely commented upon. The devastating failure to act as an Israeli army with genocidal intent physically destroys and inflicts starvation on a population over months of intense violence supported by Allies on the Security Council further underscores the absurdity of the mechanism.

The suggestion here is that contemporary governance crises – environmental, migration, and the need to generate growth through labour – are better realized through regionalism that downgrades the importance of the sovereign State. Rather than seek to dismantle the sovereign State, the suggestion is that Cooperation, Collaboration, and Construction (three very different C's than the Civilization, Christianity, and Commerce that drove colonial activity over the past two centuries) at two other levels may be imperative in addressing the governance agenda. Firstly, climate change, refugee flows, and sustainable development – in the sense of the generation of economic activity – may be realized far better at the regional level rather than at the level of the sovereign State. Benefitting from economies of scale and larger markets in a manner that is collaborative rather than competitive may not only yield more effective economic policy: it may also remove the hindrance and brake to economic growth that a persistent state of war, disruption, and tension creates. Secondly, sub-State entities including local governance may be better placed to address localized problems that pertain to specific geographical areas. Of course, these local governance units may, in some places, already correspond to an existing sovereign State, but in many instances the units may need to be much smaller to address specific problems. Historically there are a rich array of such governance contours from the Indian *panchayat* system to the system of emirates within a confederation, to the system of city-states that existed and have been able to successfully address governance issues. The overt focus on the sovereign State as the only site of responsible governance may have drowned out other more responsive mechanisms that need to be encouraged to flourish.

There are a range of factors that ought to be taken into account in understanding societies beyond 'nationality'. These include a shared geography, the existence of historical relationships – even if antagonistic – that shape entities; migratory flows of population leading to intermixing; common naturally occurring challenges; historical trade relations; regular interaction through intermediaries; shared language, religion, ethnicity, or culture and common values pertaining to indigeneity, among others. A combination of these, especially when consolidated into a larger whole, would make for more salient boundary lines, even if not delimited in the way that formal State boundaries currently are, rather than the ones drawn on the basis of the interests of those who first saw them as delimitations against each other, and then as a means to secure exclusive access to the exploitation of the territorial resources contained within. Viewing the world as 16 inhabited regions, along with the uninhabited Polar regions, would provide a better basis for answers to the pertinent questions of governance that ought to be highest on the agenda. At a macro-level, this approach may yield five regions in Africa; three in the Americas; five in the wider 'Asian' landmass of Eurasia; two on the rest of the Eurasian land mass; and the Pacific regional grouping. Mindful of not viewing the world as an uncharted territory where lines can be drawn on a map by an individual or a group of individuals motivated by serving their own interests, this book ends with a suggestion, contained in the appendix, for what these regions may be, with a call for greater attention and discussions, especially with the communities and countries contained within, as to whether these groupings may be accurate, and most importantly, as to whether they may represent a better prospect in addressing a long-standing but yet to be realized human ambition: the quest for perpetual peace.

Annex: Regional Groupings of Countries

Africa (54)

North Africa (6 +1)

Algeria, Egypt, Libya, Mauritania, Morocco, Tunisia, *Saharan Arab Democratic Republic*

West Africa (15)

Benin, Burkina Faso, Cabo Verde, Cote d'Ivoire, The Gambia, Ghana, Guinea, Guinea-Bissau, Liberia, Mali, Niger, Nigeria, Senegal, Sierra Leone, Togo

Central Africa (9)

Burundi, Cameroon, Central African Republic, Chad, Democratic Republic of Congo, Republic of Congo, Equatorial Guinea, Gabon, São Tomé & Príncipe

East Africa (14)

Comoros, Djibouti, Eritrea, Ethiopia, Kenya, Madagascar, Mauritius, Rwanda, Seychelles, Somalia, South Sudan, Sudan, Tanzania, Uganda

Southern Africa (10)

Angola, Botswana, Eswatini, Lesotho, Malawi, Mozambique, Namibia, South Africa, Zambia, Zimbabwe

NB: African States have been classified as per the African Union listing. The following are not listed because they are dependencies: St. Helena (UK), Mayotte & Reunion (France)

The Americas (35)

North America (3)

Canada, Mexico, United States of America.
Also: Saint Pierre & Michelon (France)

Caribbean & Central America (22)

Antigua & Barbuda, The Bahamas, Barbados, Belize, Costa Rica, Cuba, Dominica, Dominican Republic, El Salvador, Grenada, Guatemala, Guyana, Haiti, Honduras, Jamaica, Nicaragua, Panama, Saint Kitts & Nevis, Saint Lucia, Saint Vincent & the Grenadines, Suriname, Trinidad & Tobago.

Also Aruba, Curacao, Bonaire Sint Eastatius & Saba, Sint Maarten (all Netherlands) Anguilla, Bermuda, British Virgin Islands, Cayman Islands, Montserrat, Turks & Caicos Islands (all United Kingdom), Puerto Rico, US Virgin Islands, Guadeloupe, Martinique,Sant Barthelemy, Sant Martin (all France)

South America (10)

Argentina, Bolivia, Brazil, Chile, Colombia, Ecuador, Paraguay, Peru, Uruguay, Venezuela.

Also see: Bouvetoya (check spelling Carl, Norway), The Malvinas/Falklands, South Georgia & the South Sandwich Islands (UK), French Guiana (France)

Asia (48)

East Asia (5)

Democratic Peoples 'Republic of Korea, China, Japan, Mongolia, Republic of Korea.
Also see: "Republic of China" (Taiwan), Hong Kong Special Administrative Region, Macau Special Administrative Region (both China)

Southeast Asia (11)

Brunei Darussalam,Cambodia, Indonesia, Lao, Malaysia, Myanmar, Philippines, Singapore, Thailand,Timor Leste, Vietnam

South Asia (8)

Afghanistan, Bangladesh, Bhutan, India, Maldives, Nepal, Pakistan, Sri Lanka

Central Asia (6)

Azerbaijan, Kazakhstan, Kyrgyzstan, Tajikistan, Turkmenistan, Uzbekistan

Western Asia (including the Gulf) (17 +1)

Armenia, Bahrain, Cyprus, Georgia, Iran, Iraq, Israel, Jordan, Kuwait, Lebanon, Oman, Qatar, Saudi Arabia, *Palestine*, Syrian Arab Democratic, Turkey, United Arab Emirates, Yemen

Europe (42)

Central & Eastern Europe (17)

Albania, Bosnia & Herzegovina, Croatia, Belarus, Bulgaria, Czech Republic, Hungary, Poland, Moldova, Montenegro, North Macedonia, Romania, Russian Federation, Serbia,Slovenia, Slovakia, Ukraine

Western Europe (25 +1)

Andorra, Austria, Belgium, Denmark, Estonia, Finland, France, Germany, Greece, *Holy See*, Iceland, Italy, Ireland, Latvia, Liechtenstein, Lithuania, Luxembourg, Malta,Netherlands, Norway, Portugal San Marino, Spain, Sweden, Switzerland, United Kingdom of Great Britain & Northern Ireland.
Also see: Aaland Islands (Finland), Faroe Islands (Denmark), Gibraltar, Guernsey (incl. Sark), Jersey, Isle of Man, (UK) Svalbaard & Jan Mayen Islands (Norway), Monaco (France)

Australasia & The Pacific (16)

Australia & the Pacific (14+2)

Australia, New Zealand,*Cook Islands*, Federated States of Micronesia, Fiji, Kiribati, Marshall Islands, Nauru, *Niue*, Palau, Papua New Guinea, Samoa, Solomon Islands, Tonga, Tuvalu, Vanuatu.

Also see: Christmas Island, Cocos, Heard Island & McDonald Islands, Norfolk Island (Australia), French Polynesia, New Caledonia (Kanak), Wallis & Futuna (France), American Samoa, Guam, Northern Mariana Islands, United States Minor Outlying Islands – Baker, Howland, Jarvis, Johnston Atoll, Kingman Reef, Midway Atoll, Palmyra Atoll, Wake Island plus Navassa Island in the Caribbean Sea (USA), Pitcairn Islands (UK), Tokelau (New Zealand)

Bibliography

[Editorial] 'In the Matter of the Arbitration of the Boundary Dispute between the Republics of Costa Rica & Panama Provided by the Convention between Costa Rica and Panama of March 17th 1910' 8(4) *American Journal of International Law* (1914) 913–941.

[Editorial] 'The Sino-Russia Border: The Cockerel's Cropped Crest' *Economist* (July 24, 2008) available at https://www.economist.com/asia/2008/07/24/the-cockerels-cropped-crest

[Editors] 'Arbitration Convention between the United States and Ecuador' 4(4) *American Journal of International Law* (1910) 347–348.

[Editors] 'Report on a Proposed Pacific Charter of Human Rights, prepared under the auspices of LAWASIA, May 1989' 22 *Victoria University Wellington Law Review* (1992) 103.

[Editors] 'The Chaco Dispute' 28(4) *American Journal of International Law* (1934) 137–208.

[Editors] 'The First Pam-American Scientific Congress' 2(3) *American Political Science Review* (1908) 441–443.

[Editors] 'The Territorial Acquisitions of Russia during the Reign of Alexander II' 44(3) *Journal of the Statistical Society of London* (1881) 584–588.

[Editors] 'Letter: Emery Walker Ltd., London to Walter Wilson, sending a map for '*Turkey*' by Mark Sykes for approval and asking for spellings to be settled' Document 4/83 DDSY2/4 Foreign Affairs and travel (1888-1919) 6 May 1915 in *Papers of Mark Sykes* (Wakefield: Microform Academic Publishers).

[Editors] 'Notes by Mark Sykes' Document 4/96 of 1915 DDSY2/4 Foreign Affairs and travel (1888-1919) 6 May 1915 in *Papers of Mark Sykes* (Wakefield: Microform Academic Publishers).

[Editors] 'Outline Map of Turkey in Asia', form Document Nos. 69/4 to 78/4 taken from DDSY(2)/4/78, (3) Foreign Affairs and travel (1888-1919) in *Papers of Mark Sykes* (Wakefield: Microform Academic Publishers)

[Editors] 'Report on Pan-Arab Party in Syria' 5 September 1915 4/90 DDSY2/4 Foreign Affairs and Travel (1888-1919) in *Papers of Mark Sykes* (Wakefield: Microform Academic Publishers)

[Editors] *Correspondence between Sir Henry McMahon (His Majesty's High Commissioner at Cairo) and The Sherif Hussein of Mecca July 1915-March 1916* (London: HMSO Cmd 5957, 1939).

[Editors] *Correspondence between Sir Henry McMahon (His Majesty's High Commissioner at Cairo) and The Sherif Hussein of Mecca July 1915-March 1916* (London: HMSO Cmd 5957, 1939) 3.

[Editors] *Correspondence between Sir Henry McMahon (His Majesty's High Commissioner at Cairo) and The Sherif Hussein of Mecca July 1915-March 1916* (London: HMSO Cmd 5957, 1939) 4.

[Editors] *Documents Relating to the McMahon Letters* (London: Jewish Agency for Palestine, 1939).

[Editors] Mark Sykes Letter to Winston Churchill, 'Proposals for Prosecuting the War by Seizing Gallipoli and Constantinople, and attaching Germany via the Balkans, Austria and Bavaria' DDSY2/4 Foreign Affairs and Travel (1888-1919) 4/81 27 January 1915 in *Papers of Mark Sykes* (Wakefield: Microform Academic Publishers).

[Editors] Memorandum on Ports and Railways of Syria and Mesopotamia, by Major S F Newcombe, DDSY2/4 Foreign Affairs and Travel (1888-1919) 4/87 17 July 1915 in *Papers of Mark Sykes* (Wakefield: Microform Academic Publishers).

[Editors] *Report of the Proceedings of the Pamir Boundary Commission* (Calcutta, India: Office of the Superintendent of Government Printing, 1897).

[Editors] *The Baluch-Afghan Boundary Commission of 1896* (Calcutta, India: Baptist Mission Press, 1909).

[Editors] The Papers of Sir Mark Sykes, 1979-1919 with special reference to the Sykes-Picot Agreement and the *Middle East* from Hull University Archives ISBN-10: 1-85117-079-0; ISBN-13: 987-1-85117-079-1; Publishers' film no. R50041 [8 reels].

[Editors] Wingate Papers FO371/2486, 77713/34982, private letter from Wingate to Grey, Khartoum 15 May 1915.

[Editors] *Woodrow Wilson's Fourteen Points, January 8, 1918* (New York: Woodrow Wilson Foundation, 1943).

[Editors], *Approaches to Solving Territorial Conflicts: Sources, Situations, Scenarios and Suggestions* (Atlanta, GA: Carter Centre, May 2010) 40.

[Editors], *Common Crisis: North-South Cooperation for World Recovery, Report of the Brandt Commission* (London:Pan World Affairs, 1983).

[Editors] 'Evidence of Lieutenant-Colonel Sir Mark Sykes, BART MP, on the Arab Question' Meeting held at 10 Downing Street, Thursday December 16, 1915 at 11.30 am, 4/95 DDSY2/4 Foreign Affairs and Travel (1888-1919) in *Papers of Mark Sykes* (Wakefield: Microform Academic Publishers).

[Secretariat] *Juridical Regime of Historic Waters, Including Historic Bays*, A/CN.4/143, TILC, 1962, Vol. II.

[Various] *Essays on the Mabo Decision* (Sydney: Law Book Company, 1993).

[Editors] *Big Oil versus the World* (London: BBC Production, 2022, 3 parts).

[Editors] *The Sino-Indian Boundary: Texts of Treaties, Agreements and Certain Exchange of Notes Relating to the Sino-Indian Boundary* (New Delhi, India: Indian Society of International Law 1962).

Editors] Communication from Viceroy Lord Hardinge to London, 23 July 1914 I.O.R.:Pol.464 Pts 5 & 6 L/P & S/10/344 Political and Secret Memo B 206. No 90 of 1914 Government of India Foreign & Political Department.

Abdel Aal (AMSA), 'The Superpowers and Regional Security in the Middle East' in *Regional Security in the Third World: Case Studies from Southeast Asia and the Middle East* [M. Ayoob ed.] (London: Croom Helm, 1986) 196–213.

Adelson, Roger, *Mark Sykes: Portrait of an Amateur* (London: Jonathan Cape Thirty Bedford Square, 1975).

Ahmed, Dirdeiry M., *Boundaries and Secession in Africa and International Law: Challenging Uti Possidetis* (Cambridge: Cambridge University Press, 2015).

Ahrén, Matthias, "Indigenous Peoples' Culture, Customs and Traditions and Customary Law—The Saami People's Perspective' 21 *Arizona Journal of International and Comparative Law* (2004) 63.

Aitchison, C. U., *A Collection of Treaties, Engagements, and Sanads Relating to India and Neighbouring Countries* (Calcutta, India: Government of India Publications, 1929).

Alexandrowicz, Charles H., 'Paulus Vladimiri & the Development of the Doctrine of Coexistence of Christian and Non-Christian Countries (1963)' in *The Law of Nations in Global History* [David Armitage & Jennifer Pitts eds.] (Oxford: Oxford University Press, 2017) 59.

Alexandrowicz, Charles, H., *The European-African Confrontation* (Leiden: A. W. Sijthoff, 1973).

Alexandrowicz, Charles H., 'The Juridical Expression of the Sacred Trust of Civilization' 65 (1) *American Journal of International Law* (1971) 149–159.

Alexandrowicz, Charles H., 'The Role of Treaties in the European-African Confrontation in the Nineteenth Century' in *African International Legal History* [A. K. Mensah-Brown ed.] (New York: UNITAR, 1975) 27–68.

Allott, Anthony, 'Boundaries in Africa: A Legal and Historical Survey' in *African International Legal History* [A. K. Mensah-Brown ed.,] (New York: UNITAR, 1975 69.

Allsop, Harriet & van Wilgenburg, Wladimir, *The Kurds of Northern Syria: Governance, Diversity and Conflicts* (London: I. B. Taurus, 2019).

Alvarez, Alejandro, 'Latin American and International Law' 3 *American Journal of International Law* (1909) 286.

Anderson, Ben, *Imagined Communities: Reflections on the Origins and Spread of Nationalism* (London: Verso Books, 1983).

Anderson, G., 'Secession in International Law and Relations: What are We Talking About?' 35(3) *Loyola of Los Angeles International & Comparative Law Review* (2013) 343.

Andrews, J. A., 'The Concept of Statehood and the Acquisition of Territory in the Nineteenth Century' 94 *Law Quarterly Review* (1978) 408–427.

Anene, J. C., *International Boundaries of Nigeria* (London: Longman, 1970).

Antonious, George, *The Arab Awakening* (London: Simon Publications, 1938).

Ardley, Jane, *The Tibetan Independence Movement* (London: Routledge Curzon, 2002).

Atkin, M., 'Russian expansion in the Caucasus to 1813' in *Russian Colonial Expansion* [M. Rywkin ed.] (London: Mansell, 1988) 154–167.

Awisaju A. I. (ed.), *Partitioned Africans: Relations Across Africa's International Boundaries 1884-1984* (London: Palgrave Macmillan, 1985).

Aygoğan, Zeynep, 'Changing Perceptions along the Frontiers: The Moving Frontier with Rum in Late Medieval Anatolian Frontier Narratives' in *Living in the*

Ottoman Realm: Empire and Identity, 13th to 20th Centuries [Christine Isom-Verhaaren & Kent F. Schull eds.] (Bloomington, IN: Indiana University Press, 2016) 29–41.

Bagchi, Probodhachandra, *India and China: A Thousand Years of Cultural Relations* (Bombay, India: Hind Kitab, 1950).

Baker, Ray S. & Dobbs, William E. (eds.), *The Public Papers of Woodrow Wilson, Vol. V: War and Peace: Presidential Messages and Addresses 1917–1924* (New York: Harper and Brothers 1927) 231.

Baldwin, Simeon E., 'The International Congresses and Conferences of the Last Century as Forces Working towards the Solidarity of the World' 1(3) *American Journal of International Law* (1907) 808–829.

Barbour, K. M., 'A Geographical Analysis of Boundaries in Inter-Tropical Africa' in *Essays in African Populations* [K. M. Barbour & R. M. Prothero eds.] (London: Brown, 1961) 305.

Barfield, Thomas J., *The Perilous Frontier: Nomadic Empires and China, 221 BC to AD 1757* (Oxford: Blackwell, 1989).

Barkan, Elazar, *The Guilt of Nations: Restitution and Negotiating Historical Injustices* (Baltimore, MD: Johns Hopkins University Press, 2001).

Barr, James, *A Line in the Sand: Britain, France and the Struggle for the Mastery of the Middle East* (London: Simon & Schuster, 2011) 1.

Barsh, Russell L., 'Indigenous Peoples in the 1990s: From Object to Subject in International Law?' 7 *Harvard Human Rights Journal* (1994) 33–86.

Bendi, M., *Guinea-Bissau: Oil & Gas Industry* available at http://www.mbendi.co.za/indy/oilg/af/gb/p0005.htm.

Bengio, Ofra, *The Kurds of Iraq: Building a State within a State* (Westport, CT: Lynne Rienner, 2014).

Bengio, Ofra & Ben-Dor, Gabriel, *Minorities and the State in the Arab World* (London: Lynn Rienner, 1999).

Benton, Lauren & Straumann, Benjamin, 'Acquiring Empire by Law: From Roman Doctrine to Early Modern European Practice' 28(1) *Law & History Review* (2010) 1–38.

Biger, G., *The Boundaries of Modern Palestine 1840-1947* (London: Routledge, 2004).

Billé, Franck, Delaplace, Grégory & Humphrey, Caroline (eds.), *Knowledge & Practice at the Russian, Chinese & Mongolian Border* (Cambridge: Open Book Publishers, 2012).

Black, Jeremy, 'War and Cartography' in *Maps and the 20th Century: Drawing the Line* [Tom Harper ed.] (London: British Library 2016) 30–65, 38.

Blank, Paul, 'The Pacific: A Mediterranean in the Making?' 89(2) *Oceans Connect* (1999) 265–277.

Blay, S. Kwaw Nyameke, 'Self-Determination versus Territorial Integrity in Decolonization' 18(2) *New York University Journal of International Law & Politics* (1986) 441–472.

Blum, Y. Z., *Historic Title in International Law* (The Hague: M. Nijhoff, 1965).

Boggs, S. Whittmore, *International Boundaries: A Study of Boundary Functions and Problems* (New York: Columbia University Press, 1980).

Bower, Bruce, 'Rat DNA Points to Pacific Migrations' 166(2) *Science News* (2004) 30.

Bowman, Isaiah, 'A Note on the Political Map of Turkey' 1(2) *Foreign Affairs* (December 1922) 158–161.

Brading, David A., *Classical Republicanism & Creole Patriotism: Simon Bolivar (1783-1830) & the Spanish Revolution* (Cambridge: Cambridge University Press, 1983).

Briggs, Herbert W., [Editorial Comment] 'The Proposed European Political Community' 48(1) *American Journal of International Law* (1956) 110–122.

Brittain, Victoria, 'Colonialism and the Predatory State in the Congo' 236 *New Left Review* (1999) 133.

Broers, Laurence, 'Unrecognized Reality' in *Armenia and Azerbaijan: Anatomy of a Rivalry* (Edinburgh: Edinburgh University Press 2019.

Brooks, R. L., 'Getting Reparations for Slavery Right – A Response to Posner and Vermeule' 80 *Notre Dame Law Review* (2004–2005) 251.

Brophy, David, *Uyghur Nation: Reform and Revolution on the Russia-China Frontier* (Cambridge, MA: Harvard University Press, 2016).

Brownlie, Ian, *African Boundaries: A Legal and Diplomatic Encyclopedia* (London: C. Hurst, 1979).

Brownlie, Ian, *International Law and the Use of Force by States* (Oxford: Clarendon Press, 1963).

Brownlie, Ian, 'The Peaceful Settlement of International Disputes' 8(2) *Chinese Journal of International Law* (2009) 267.

Bryne, Alex, *The Monroe Doctrine and United States National Security in the Early Twentieth Century* (Cham: Palgrave Macmillan, 2020).

Buchanan, Allen, *Justice, Legitimacy, and Self-Determination: Moral Foundations for International Law* (Oxford: Oxford University Press, 2004).

Buckland, William W. & McNair, Arnold, *Roman Law and Common Law: A Comparison Outline,* 2nd ed. (Cambridge: Cambridge University Press, 1952) 70.

Buschmann, Rainer, 'Oceans of World History: Delineating Aquacentric Notions in the Global Past' 2(1) *History Compass* (2004) 1–10, 2.

Butt, Peter, Eagleson, Robert & Lane, Patricia, *Mabo, Wik & Native Title*, 3rd ed. (Canberra: Federation Press, 1998).

Callick, Rowan, 'Xi Jinping Launches New Era for China and the World' 52 *China Before a World in Crisis* (April 2021) available at https://revistaidees.cat/en/xi-jinping-launches-a-new-era-for-china-and-the-world/

Campbell, Ian C., *A History of the Pacific Islands* (Christchurch: University of Canterbury Press, 1989).

Cassidy, Julie, 'Observations on Mabo & Ors v. Queensland' 1 *Deakin Law Review* (1994) 37.

Castellino, Joshua, 'A Territorial Interpretation of Identity in International Law: The Case of the Western Sahara' 29(3) *Millennium Journal of International Studies* (1999) 523–559.

Castellino, Joshua, 'Liberté, Fraternité, Egalité: The Dubious Fruits of 'National' Self-determination in International Law' 1(1) *Turku Law Journal* (1999) 1–32.

Castellino, Joshua, 'National Identity & the International Law of Self-Determination: The Stratification of the Western Saharan 'Self'' in *Accommodating National Identity: New Approaches in International and Domestic Law* [Stephen Tierney ed.] (The Hague: Kluwer, 2000) 257, 270–281.

Castellino, Joshua, 'Territorial integrity and the Right to self-determination: an Examination of the Conceptual Tools' 33(2) *Brooklyn Journal of International Law* (2008) 503.

Castellino, Joshua, *The End of the Liberal State and the First Terrorist* (London: Middlesex University Press, 2008).

Castellino, Joshua & Allen, Stephen, 'The Doctrine of Uti Possidetis: Crystallization of Modern Post-Colonial Identity' 43 *German Yearbook of International Law* (2000) 205.

Castellino, Joshua & Allen, Stephen, *Title to Territory in International Law: A Temporal Analysis* (Dartmouth: Ashgate, 2003).

Castellino, Joshua & Cavanaugh, Kathleen A, 'Transformations in the Middle East: The Importance of the Minority Question' in *Multiculturalism and Minority Rights in the Arab World* [Will Kymlicka and Eva Pfostl eds.] (Oxford: Oxford University Press, 2014) 53–73.

Castellino, Joshua & Cavanaugh, Kathleen, *Minority Rights in the Middle East: A Comparative Legal Analysis* (Oxford: Oxford University Press, 2013).

Castellino, Joshua & Domínguez Redondo, Elvira, 'The Title to Dokdo/Takeshima: Addressing Legacies of World War II Territorial Settlements' 22(4) *International Journal on Minority & Group Rights* (2015) 550–577.

Castellino, Joshua & Keane, David P., *Minority Rights in the Pacific: A Comparative Legal Analysis* (Oxford: Oxford University Press, 2009).

Cavanaugh, Kathleen, 'Rewriting Law: The Case of Israel and the Occupied Territories' in *New Laws, New Wars? Applying the Laws of War in 21st Century Conflicts* [David Wippman & Matthew Evangelista eds.] (Leiden: Brill, 2005) 227.

Chacko C. J. et al., *The India-China Boundary Question: A Legal Study with a Brief Historical Introduction* (New Delhi, India: Indian Society of International Law, 1963).

Chang, The-Kuang, 'China's Claim of Sovereignty over Spratly and Paracel Islands: A Historical and Legal Perspective' 23 *Case Western Reserve Journal of International Law* (1991) 23.

Chari Chandra (ed.), *Superpower Rivalry and Conflict: The Long Shadow of the Cold War on the Twenty-first Century* (New York: Routledge, 2010).

Charney, Jonathan I., 'Central East Asian Maritime Boundaries and the Law of the Sea' 89 *American Journal of International Law* (1995) 724.

Charney, Jonathan I., 'Disputes Implicating the Institutional Credibility of the Court: Problems of Non-Appearance, Non-Participation, and Non-Performance' in *The International Court of Justice at Crossroads* [Lori Fisler Damrosch ed.] (New York: Transnational Publishers, 1987) 288.

Chee, C. I., 'Legal Status of Dok Island in International Law' 42 *Korean Journal of International Law* (1997) 1.

Chernow, Ron, *Titan: The Life of John D Rockefeller Sr* (New York: Knopf Doubleday Publishing Group, 2007).

Cheterian, Vicken, *War and Peace in the Caucasus: Russia's Troubled Frontier* (London: Hurst, 2008).

Chime, Samuel, 'The Organization of African Unity and African Boundaries' in *African Boundary Problems* [C. G. Widstrand ed.] (Uppsala: Scandinavian Africa Institute, 1969) 65–78.

Chubb, Edmund, *China and Russia: The "Great" Game* (New York: Columbia University Press, 1971).

Clark, Cameron, 'All Quiet on the Waterfront: Uncontacted Tribes in the Modern Era' 40(2) *Harvard International Review* (2019) 10–11.

Clarke, John & Martin, Camille (eds.), *Anarchy, Geography and Modernity: Selected Writings of Élisée Reclus* (Oakland, CA: PM Press, 2013 translation).

Clarke, R. Floyd, 'A Permanent Tribunal of International Arbitration: Its Necessity & Value' 1(2) *American Journal of International Law* (1907) 342–408.

Claude, Inis L., *Swords into Plowshares: The Problems and Progress of International Organization* (New York: Random House, 1984).

Clayton, Lawrence A., *Bartolomé de las Casas* (Cambridge: Cambridge University Press, 2012).

Clayton, Lawrence A., *Bartolome de las Cases and the Conquest of the Americas* (Chichester: John Wiley and Sons, 2011) 4.

Craven, Matthew C. R., 'The European Community Arbitration Commission on Yugoslavia' 66 *British Yearbook of International Law* (1995) 333.

Crawford, James, *Creation of States in International Law*, 2nd ed. (Cambridge: Cambridge University Press, 2007).

Crivenco, Andrei & von Löwis, Sabine, 'Shrinking Transnistria: Trends and Effects of Demographic Decline in De Facto State' 70(1) *Comparative Southeast European Studies* (2022) 47–79.

Crocombe, Ron, *The South Pacific: An Introduction* (Auckland: Longman Paul, 1987).

Crossley, Pamela Kyle, Siu, Helen F. & Sutton, Donald S. (eds.), *Empire at the Margins: Culture, Ethnicity and Frontier in Early Modern China* (Berkeley, CA: University of California Press, 2006).

Crowe, Sybil Eyre, *Berlin West-African Conference* (New York: Longmans, 1942).

Curzon, George Nathaniel, *Frontiers* (Oxford: Clarendon Press, 1907).

Danilovic, Vesna, *When the Stakes are High: Deterrence and Conflict among Major Powers* (Ann Arbor, MI: University of Michigan Press, 2002).

Dávila, Carlos G., *The Montevideo Conference: Antecedents & Accomplishments* (Washington, DC: Carnegie Endowment for International Peace, 1934).

Davis, Shelton H., 'Land Rights and Indigenous Peoples: The Role of the Inter-American Commission on Human Rights' (Cambridge, MA: Cultural Survival Report v 29, 1988).

Deutsche, Karl & Foltz, William, *Nation Building* (New York: Atherton Press, 1963).

Diamond, Jared and Bellwood, Peter, 'Farmers and their Languages: The First Expansions' 300 (2003) *Science* 597–603.

Distefano, G., 'The Conceptualization (Construction) of Territorial Title in the Light of the International Court of Justice Case Law' 19(4) *Leiden Journal of International Law* (2006) 1041–1075.

Dodwell, Horace H., *The Cambridge History of India*, Vol. VI (Cambridge: Cambridge University Press, 1943).

Domínguez Redondo, Elvira, *In Defense of politicization of human rights: The UN Special Procedures*, (Oxford: Oxford University Press, 2020).

Donohue, B., Otte, N. & Smith, B., 'An Ontological Approach to Territorial Disputes' in *Proceedings of the Conference on Semantic Technology in Intelligence, Defense and Security* (STIDS), CEUR, Vol. 1304, 2–9 (2014) available at https://philarchive.org/archive/OTTAOA

Doolin, Dennis J., *Territorial Claims in the Sino-Soviet Conflict: Documents and Analysis* (Stanford, CA: Hoover Institute Studies, Stanford University Press, 1965).

Doyle, Cathal, *Indigenous Peoples Title to Territory and Resources: The Transformative Role of Free Prior & Informed Consent* (New York & Oxon: Routledge, 2015) 11–70.

Drexler, Elizabeth F., *Aceh, Indonesia: Securing the Insecure State* (Philadelphia, PA: University of Pennsylvania Press, 2009).

Dugard, John, 'Namibia (South West Africa): The Court's Opinion, South Africa's Response, and Prospects for the Future' 11 *Columbia Journal of Transnational Law* (1972) 14.

Duggan, Stephen P., 'The Syrian Question' 11(4) *Journal of International Relations* (April 1921) 571–572.

Durand, Henry Marion, *First Afghan War and its Causes* (London: Longmans, Green and Co., 1879).

Dzurek, D. J., 'What Makes Some Boundary Issues Important?' in *IBRU Boundary and Security Bulletin* (1999–2000) 83–95 available at https://www.durham.ac.uk/media/durham-university/research-/research-centres/ibru-centre-for-borders-research/maps-and-databases/publications-database/boundary-amp-security-bulletins/bsb7-4_dzurek.pdf

Dzurek, D. J., 'What Makes Territory Important: Tangible and Intangible Dimensions' 64 *GeoJournal* (2005) 263–274.

Elton, Hugh, *The Frontiers of the Roman Empire* (Bloomington, IN: Indiana University Press, 1996).

Emory, Frederic, 'Russia in Asia' 15 *Annals of the American Academy of Political & Social Science* (May 1900) 114–120.

Erasmus-Khan, Daniel, 'Territory and Boundaries' in *Oxford Handbook of the History of International Law* [Bardo Fassbender & Anne Peters eds.] (Oxford: Oxford University Press, 2012) 231.

Evans, C., *The Right of Reparations in International Law for Victims of Armed Conflict* (Cambridge: Cambridge University Press, 2012).

Fage, John, *A History of Africa* (London: Routledge, 1995).

Fang, Hui, Feinman, Gary M. & Nicholas, Linda M., 'Imperial Expansion, Public Investment, and the Long Path of History: China's Initial Political Unification and Its Aftermath' 112(30) *Proceedings of the National Academy of Sciences of the United States of America* (2015) 9224–9229.

Farah, Caesar E., 'The Dilemma of Arab Nationalism' 8(3) *Die Welt des Islams* (1963) 140–164 at 140.

Farrington, Anthony, 'Trading Places: The East India Company and Asia' 52 *History Today* (2002) 40.

Farsakh, Leila H., *Rethinking Statehood in Palestine: Self-Determination and Decolonization Beyond Partition* (Oakland, CA: University of California Press, 2021).

Fassbender, Bardo & Peters, Anne (eds.), *Oxford Handbook of the History of International Law* (Oxford: Oxford University Press, 2012).

Fenwick, Charles G., 'The Third Meeting of Ministers of Foreign Affairs at Rio de Janeiro' 36(2) *American Journal of International Law* (1942) 169–203.

Filipec, Ondrej, *The Islamic State: From Terrorism to Totalitarian Insurgency* (London: Taylor & Francis, 2020).

Flint, John E., 'Chartered Companies and the Transition from Informal Sway to Colonial Rule in Africa' in *Bismarck, Europe, and Africa* [Stig Förster, Wolfgang J. Mommsen & Ronald Robinson eds.] (Oxford: Oxford University Press, 1988) 69.

Flint, John E., *Sir George Goldie and the Making of Nigeria* (Oxford: Oxford University Press, 1960).

Foot, Rosemary, Gaddis, John L. & Hurrell, Andrew (eds.), *Order & Justice in International Relations* (Oxford: Oxford University Press, 2003).

Forsyth, James, *A History of the Peoples of Siberia: Russia's North Asian Colony 1581-1990* (Cambridge: Cambridge University Press, 1992).

Franck, Thomas M., 'Clan and Super Clan: Loyalty, Identity and Community in Law and Practice' 90(3) *American Journal of International Law* (1996) 359.

Franck, Thomas M., 'The Emerging Right to Democratic Governance' 86(1) *American Journal of International Law* (1992) 46–91.

Franck, Thomas M., 'The Stealing of the Sahara' 70 *American Journal of International Law* (1978) 694.

Franckx, E., 'Dots and Lines in the South China Sea: Insights from the Lap of Map Evidence' 2 *Asian Journal of International Law* (2012) 89–118.

Fraser, Lovat, *Some Problems of the Persian Gulf - Proceedings of the Central Asian Society* (London: Central Asian Society, 1908) 4.

Frayne, Douglas, 'The Umma Lagash Border Conflict' available at http://cdli.ox.ac.uk/wiki/doku.php?id=umma_lagash_border_conflict [last consulted 10 August 2017].

Frettingham, Edmund & Hwang, Yih-Jye, *Maritime & Territorial Disputes in the South China Sea: Faces of Power and Law in the Age of China's Rise* (Oxford: Taylor & Francis, 2021).

Fry, James, D. & Loja, Melissa H., 'The Roots of Historic Title: Non-Western Pre-Colonial Normative Systems and Legal Resolution of Territorial Disputes' 27 *Leiden Journal of International Law* (2014) 727–754.

Fukuyama, Francis, *The End of History and the First Man* (New York: The Free Press, 1992).

Gall, Carlotta & de Waal, Thomas, *Chechnya: Calamity in the Caucasus* (New York: NYU Press, 1998).

Gammer, M., *Muslim Resistance to the Tsar: Shamil & the Conquest of Chechnia & Daghestan* (London: Routledge, 1944).

Gann L. H. & Duignan, Peter (eds.), *Colonialism in Africa 1870–1960* (Cambridge: Cambridge University Press, 1969).

Gann L. H. & Duignan, Peter, *The Rulers of British Africa 1870-1914* (Stanford, CA: Stanford University Press, 1978).

Gathii, James Thuo, 'Geographical Hegelianism in Territorial Disputes Involving Non-European Land Relations: An Analysis of the Case Concerning Kasiliki/Sedudu Islands (Botswana/Namibia)' 15(3) *Leiden Journal of International Law* (2002) 581–622.

Gathii, James Thuo, 'Promise of International Law: A Third World View' 114 *Proceedings of the ASIL Annual Meeting* (Cambridge University Press, 2020) 165.

Gavin, R. J. & Betley, J. A. (eds.), *The Scramble for Africa: Documents on the Berlin West African Conference and Related Subjects 1884/1885* (Ibadan: Ibadan University Press, 1973).

Geelani, Gowhar, *Kashmir: Rage and Reason* (New Delhi, India: Rupa Books, 2019).

Gelber, Harry G., *Nations out of Empires: European Nationalism and the Transformation of Asia* (London: Palgrave Macmillan, 2001).

Getachew, Adom, 'The limits of Sovereignty as Responsibility' 26(2) *Constellations: An International Journal of Critical and Democratic Theory* (2019) 225–240.

Getachew, Adom, *Worldmaking After Empire: The Rise and Fall of Self-Determination* (Princeton, NJ: Princeton University Press, 2019).

Ghosh, S., *Truth About McMahon Line* (Calcutta, India: Lalchand Roy & Co., 1962).

Gibbons, Ann, 'The Peopling of the Pacific' 291(5509) (2001) *Science* 1735–1737.

Gibbons, Herbert Adam, 'The Defects of the System of Mandates' 96 *Annals of the American Academy of Political and Social Science* (July 1921) 84–90 at 84.

Gifford, Prosser & Louis, William R., *France & Britain in Africa: Imperial Rivalry & Colonial Rule* (New Haven, CT: Yale University Press, 1971).

Gilbert, Geoff, 'Autonomy and Minority Groups: A Right in International Law?' 35 *Cornell International Law Journal* (2002) 307.

Giraud-Kinley, Catherine, 'The Effectiveness of International Law: Sustainable Development in the South Pacific Region' 12 *Georgetown International Environmental Law Review* (1999) 125–176.

Glatzer, Bernt, 'War and Boundaries in Afghanistan: Significance and Relativity of Local and Social Boundaries' 41(3) *Die Welt des Islams* (November 2001) 379–399.

Goldie, L. F. E., 'The Critical Date' 12 *International & Comparative Law Quarterly* (1963) 1251.

Gopal, Sarvepalli, *Jawaharlal Nehru: A Biography, Vol. III 1956-1964* (New Delhi, India: Oxford University Press, 1984).

Gozzi, Gustavo, *Rights & Civilizations: A History & Philosophy of International Law* (Filippo Valente trans.) (Cambridge: Cambridge University Press, 2010).

Gray, Christine, *International Law & the Use of Force* (Oxford: Oxford University Press, 2004) 24–50.

Grotius, Hugo, *De Mare Libero*, cap. III [Alexander VI.] (Leiden: Brill, 2009).

Grovogui, Siba N'Zatioula, *Sovereigns, Quasi-Sovereigns and Africans: Race and Self Determination in International Law* (Minneapolis, MN: University of Minnesota Press, 1996).

Gul Wazir, Babri, *Durand Line: A Discussion about the Legality of the Signing of the Durand Line Agreement between Afghanistan and British India on the 12th of November 1893* (Kabul: Shah Books, 2007) 28.

Gupta, Karunakar, 'The McMahon Line 1911-1945: The British Legacy' 47 *The China Quarterly* (1971) 521–545, 522.

Hargreaves, John D., 'The Making of the Boundaries: Focus on West Africa' in *Partitioned Africans* [A. I. Asiwaju ed.] (London: Hurst and Co. 1985) 19–27.

Hargreaves, John D., *West Africa Partitioned*, Vol. 1 (London: Macmillan, 1974).

Harper, Tom (ed.), *Maps and the 20th Century: Drawing the Line* (London: British Library 2016) 9.

Harris, David & Livingstone, Stephen (eds.), *The Inter-American System of Human Rights* (Oxford: Clarendon Press, 1998).

Hathaway Oona & Shapiro, Scott, *The Internationalists: How a Radical Plan to Outlaw War Remade the World* (London: Simon & Schuster, 2017).
Hauner, Milan, *What is Asia To Us Today: Russian Heartland Yesterday and Today* (London: Unwin Hayman, 1990).
Hay John (ed.), *Boundaries in China* (Oxford: Reaktion Books, 1994).
Hayward, Jack, *After the French Revolution: Six Critiques of Democracy and Nationalism* (London: Harvester Wheatsheaf, 1991) 1.
Heffernan, Michael, 'Maps and Peace' in *Maps and the 20th Century: Drawing the Line* [Tom Harper ed.] (London: British Library 2016) 66–93.
Heikal, Mohammed, 'Egypt's Foreign Policy' 56 *Foreign Affairs* (1978) 714–727.
Hensel, P. R., 'Territory: Theory and Evidence on Geography and Conflict' in *What Do We Know About War?* [J. A. Vasquez ed.] (Boulder, CO: Rowman & Littlefield, 2000) 57–84.
Herbst, Jeffrey, 'The Creation and Maintenance of National Boundaries in Africa' 43 *International Organization* (1989) 673–692.
Hertslet, Edward, *The Map of Africa by Treaty,* Vol. 2 (London: Harrison & Sons for HMSO, 1909).
Heywood, Colin, 'The Frontier in Ottoman History: Old Ideas and New Myths' in *Frontiers in Question: Eurasian Borderlands, 700-1700* [Daniel Power & Naomi Standen eds.] (New York: St. Martin's Press, 1999) 228-249.
Higgins, Rosalyn, 'Time and Law: International Perspectives on an Old Problem' 46 *International & Comparative Law Quarterly* (1997) 501.
Highet, Keith, 'The Peace Palace Heats Up: The World Court in Business Again?' 85(4) *American Journal of International Law* (1991) 646–654.
Hill, Norman, *Claims to Territory in International Law and Relations* (Oxford: Oxford University Press, 1944).
Hobsbawm, Eric, 'War and Peace in the 20th Century' 24(4) *London Review of Books* (February 2002).https://www.lrb.co.uk/the-paper/v24/n04/eric-hobsbawm /war-and-peace-in-the-20th-centur
Hobson, John Atkinson, *Imperialism: A Study* (London: J. Nisbet, 1902).
Hodges, Tony, *Western Sahara: The Roots of a Desert War* (Westport, CT: Lawrence Hill, 1983).
Holdich, Thomas H., *Political Frontiers and Boundary Making* (London: Macmillan, 1916).
Holdich, Thomas H., *The Indian Border Land, 1880-1900* (London: Methuen & Co., 1901).
Hori, K., 'Japan's Incorporation of Takeshima into Its Territory in 1905' 28 *Korea Observer* (1997) 477.
Hotta, Eri, *Pan-Asianism & Japan's War 1931–1945* (The Palgrave Macmillan Series in Transnational History) (New York: Palgrave Macmillan, 2007).
Howe, Kerry R., *Nature, Culture and History: The "Knowing" of Oceania* (Honolulu, HI: University of Hawai'i Press, 2000).
Hubbard, G. E., *From the Gulf to Ararat: Imperial Boundary Making in the Late Ottoman Empire* (London: I. B. Tauris, 2016).
Hughes, Charles E., 'Observations on the Monroe Doctrine' 17(4) *American Journal of International Law* (1923) 611–628.
Hughes, James, *Chechnya: From Nationalism to Jihad* (Philadelphia, PA: University of Pennsylvania Press, 2013).

Hung, Wu, 'Beyond the 'Great Boundary': Funerary Narrative in the Cangshan Tomb' in *Boundaries in China* [John Hay ed.] (London: Reaktion Books, 1994) 81–104.

Hussain, Shahla, *Kashmir in the Aftermath of Partition* (Cambridge: Cambridge University Press, 2021).

Iman, Jahanara, *Of Blood and Fire: The Untold Story of Bangladesh's War of Independence* (Dhaka: University Press, 2019).

Inlow, E. Burke, 'The McMahon Line' 63 *Journal of Geography* (September 1964) 261–272.

Isom-Verhaaren, Christine & Schull, Kent F. (eds.), *Living in the Ottoman Realm: Empire and Identity, 13th to 20th Centuries* (Bloomington, IN: Indiana University Press, 2016).

Jackson, Robert, 'Juridical Statehood in Sub-Saharan Africa' 46 *Journal ofInternational Affairs* (1992) 17.

Jackson, Robert, *Quasi-States: Sovereignty, International Relations and the Third World* (Cambridge: Cambridge University Press, 1990).

Jamison, Matthew C., *Weakness, Expansion and Disobedience: The Beginning of Russian Expansion into the Heart of Central Asia 1864-1854* (Oxford: Oxford University Press, 2007).

Jennings, Ivor, *The Approach to Self Governance* (Cambridge: Cambridge University Press, 1956).

Jennings, Paige, 'Chad: As Deserts Spread South, Pastoralists Face Scarcity & Drought' in *Key Trends Report 2019* (London: Minority Rights Group, 2019) available at https://minorityrights.org/app/uploads/2024/01/mrg-key-trends-report-2019-final-1.pdf

Jennings, Robert & Watts, Arthur (eds.), *Oppenheim's International Law, Peace*, 9th ed. (Oxford: Oxford University Press, 1992).

Jennings, Robert Yewdall, *The Acquisition of Territory in International Law* (Manchester: Manchester University Press, 1963).

Johnson, Hilde F., *South Sudan: The Untold Story from Independence to Civil War* (London: I. B. Taurus, 2016).

Jolowicz, H. F. & Nicolas, Barry, *Historical Introduction to the Study of Roman Law*, 3rd ed. (Cambridge: Cambridge University Press, 1972) 259–263.

Jones, Horace Leonard et al., *Geography* [Loeb Classical Library ed. and H. L. Jones trans.] (London: William Heinemann & Co., 1917).

Jongerden, Joost, *The Settlement Issue in Turkey and the Kurds* (Leiden: Brill, 2007).

Joseph, Abraham & Hamaguchi, Takako, *Timor Leste: The History and Development of Asia's Newest Nation* (Lanham, MD: Lexington Books, 2014).

Juricek, J. T., 'American Usage of the Word "Frontier" from Colonial Times to Frederick Jackson Turner' 110 *Proceedings of the American Philosophical Society* (1966) 10–34.

Kaikobad, Kayan H., 'Some Observations on the Doctrine of Continuity and Finality of Boundaries' 49 *British Yearbook of International Law* (1983) 126–127.

Kal Raustiala, *The Absolutely Indispensable Man: Ralph Bunche, the United Nations, and the Fight to End Empire* (New York: Oxford University Press, 2023).

Kamil, M. I., *The Camp David Accords: A Testimony* (London: KPI Publishers, 1986).

Kammen, Douglas, *Independent Timor-Leste: Between Coercion and Consent* (Cambridge: Cambridge University Press, 2019).

Kapil, Ravi L., 'On the Conflict Potential of Inherited Boundaries in Africa' 18 *World Politics* (1966) 656–673, 660.

Kaya, Zeynep, *Mapping Kurdistan: Territory, Self-Determination and Nationalism* (Cambridge: Cambridge University Press, 2020).

Kazemzadeh, Firuz, *Russia and Britain in Persia, 1814-1914: A Study in Imperialism* (New Haven, CT: Yale University Press, 1968).

Kazutada, Kataoka, *Shincho Shinkyo tochi kenkyu* (Tokyo: Yuzanakaku, 1991).

Keddie, Nikki, 'Is There a Middle East?' IV *International Journal of Middle Eastern Studies* (1973) 255–271.

Kedourie, Elie, *In the Anglo-Arab Labyrinth: The McMahon-Husayn Correspondence and its Interpretations 1914-1939* (Cambridge: Cambridge University Press, 1976).

Keller, Arthur S., Lissitzyn, Oliver J. & Mann, Frederick J., *Creation of Rights of Sovereignty through Symbolic Acts 1400–1800* (New York: Columbia University Press, 1938).

Kemp, Walter, Popovski, Vesselin, & Thakur, Ramesh (eds.), *Blood and Borders: The Responsibility to Protect and the Problem of the Kin State* (Tokyo: United Nations University, 2011).

Kinna, Ruth, *Kropotkin: Reviewing the Classical Anarchist Tradition* (Edinburgh: Edinburgh University Press, 2016).

Kirk, W., 'The Inner Asian Frontiers of India' 31 *Transactions & Papers* (December 1962) 131–168.

Klyuchevskii, Vladimir O., *Russya Istoriya: Polnii Kurs Lektsii v Trekh Knigakh*, 3 vols. (Moscow: Phoenix, 1993).

Korman, Sharon, *The Right of Conquest: The Acquisition of Territory by Force in International Law and Practice* (Oxford: Oxford University Press, 1996) 135–178.

Kozlowski, Artur, 'The Legal Construct of Historic Title to Territory in International Law – An Overview' 30 *Polish Yearbook of International Law* (2010) 61–100 at 62.

Kradin, Nikolay N., 'The Mongol Empire and the Unification of Eurasia' in *The Oxford World History of Empire* [Peter Fibiger Bang, C. A. Bayly & Walter Scheidel eds.] (Oxford: Oxford University Press, 2021) 507–532.

Krushchez, Nikita, *Kruschev Remembers: The Last Testament* (Boston, MA: Little, Brown, 1974).

Kunz, Josef L., 'Guatemala v Great Britain: in Re Belice' 40(2) *American Journal of International Law* (1946) 383–390.

Kurkov, Andrey, *Diary of an Invasion* (London: Mountain Leopard Press, 2022)

Kwiatkowska, Barbara, 'The International Court of Justice Doctrine of Equitable Principles Applicable to Maritime Delimitation and Its Impact on the International Law of the Sea' in *Forty Years International Court of Justice: Jurisdiction, Equity and Equality* [Ari Bloed & Peter van Dijk eds.] (Utrecht: Europa Institute, 1988) 158.

Kwiatkowska, Barbara, 'The Qatar v. Bahrain Maritime Delimitation and Territorial Questions Case' 33(3–4) *Ocean Development & International Law* (2002) 227–262.

Kymlicka, Will, *Politics in the Vernacular: Nationalism, Multiculturalism, and Citizenship* (Oxford: Oxford University Press, 2001).

Lalonde, S., *Determining Boundaries in a Conflicted World: The Role of Uti Possidetis* (Montreal: McGill-Queen's University Press, 2002).

Lamb, Alastair, *The McMahon Line*, 2 vols. (London: Routledge & Kegan Paul, 1966).

Lansing, H., 'Self-Determination in the Saturday' *Evening Post* (9 April 1921) 7.

Laquer, Walter & Rubin, B., *The Israel-Arab Reader: A Documentary History of the Middle East Conflict*, 4th ed. (New York: Facts on File, 1984).

Lattimore, Owen, *Pivot of Asia: Sinkiang and the Inner Asian Frontiers of China and Russia* (Boston, MA: Little, Brown, 1950).

Law of the Sea Institute, 'Oceans in the Nuclear Age' (University of California, Berkeley) available at http://www.law.berkeley.edu/centers/ilr/ona/pages/testing.htm

Leach, E. R., *Political Systems of Highland Burma* (Cambridge, MA: Harvard University Press, 1954).

Lee, B. J., *A Study of the Legal Status of Dodko* (Oxford, OH: Miami University, 1957).

Lee, B. J., "Title to Dodko' in International Law' 2 *Korean Journal of Comparative Law* (1974) 85.

Lee, C. J. (ed.), *Making a World After Empire: The Bandung Movement and its Political Afterlives* (Athens, OH: Ohio University Press, 2010).

Lee, H., 'Dispute over Territorial Ownership of Tokdo in the Late Chosen Period' 28 *Korea Observer* (1997) 389.

Lee, H. K., 'Korea's Territorial Rights to Todko in History and International Law' 20 *Korea Observer* (1998) 1.

Lee, Seokwoo, 'The 1951 San Francisco Peace Treaty with Japan and the Territorial Disputes in East Asia' 11 *Pacific Rim Law & Policy Journal* (2002) 63.

Legg, Michael, 'Indigenous Australians and International Law: Racial Discrimination, Genocide and Reparations' 20 *Berkeley Journal of International Law* (2002) 387.

Legum, Colin, *Pan Africanism: A Short Political Guide* (New York: Preager, 1965).

Lenin, Vladimir Ilyich, *The Right of Nations to Self-determination* (Moscow: Progress Publishers, 1914).

Leslie, Shane, *Mark Sykes: His Life and Letters* (London: Cassell and Company Ltd., 1923).

Lewis, Martin, 'Dividing the Ocean Sea' 89 *The Geographical Review* (1999) 188–214.

Lincoln, Bruce, *The Conquest of a Continent: Siberia and the Russians* (New York: Random House, 1994).

Lindley, Mark Frank, *The Acquisition and Government of Backward Territory in International Law* (London: Longman Green, 1926).

Lowe, Vaughan, 'The Role of Equity in International Law' 12 *Australian Yearbook of International Law* (1988–1989) 58–63.

Lugard, Frederick John Dealtry, *The Rise of Our East African Empire* (London: Blackwood & Sons, 1893).

Machiavelli, Niccolo, *Il Principe* (original 1532, G. Bull trans, London: Penguin Classics, 2003).

MacIver, Robert M., *The Modern State* (original London: Oxford University Press, 1926/ Redditch England: Read Books Ltd., 2006).

Maier, Georg, 'The Boundary Dispute Between Ecuador and Peru' 63(1) *American Journal of International Law* (1969) 28–46.

Malkin, I., 'Land Ownership, Territorial Possession, Hero Cults, and Scholarly Theory' in *Nomodeiktes: Greek Studies in Honor of Martin Oswald* [R. M. Rosen & J. Farrell eds.] (Ann Arbor, MI: University of Michigan Press, 1993) 225–234.

Mälksoo, Lauri, *Illegal Annexation and State Continuity* (Leiden: Brill, 2022) 70–139.

Manger, William, 'The Pan American Union at the Sixth International Conference of American States' 22(4) *American Journal of International Law* (1928) 764–775.

Marochkin, Sergey & Bezborodov, Yury (eds.), *The Shanghai Co-operation Organization: Exploring New Horizons* (London: Routedge, 2022).

Marques Antunes, Nuno Sérgio, 'The Eritrea-Yemen Arbitration: First Stage—The Law of Title to Territory Re-Averred' 48 *International & Comparative Law Quarterly* (1999) 362.

Marshall, Tim, *Prisoners of Geography: Ten Maps that Tell You Everything You Need to Know About Global Politics* (Chicago, IL: Elliot and Thompson Ltd., 2016).

Martin, Terry, *The Affirmative Action Empire: Nations and Nationalism in the Soviet Union 1923-1939* (Ithaca, NY: Cornell University Press, 2001).

Maynard, F. P. (ed.), *The Baluch-Afghan Boundary Commission of 1896* (Calcutta, India: Baptist Mission Press, 1909).

Mazrui Ali Al'Amin, *Towards a Pax Africana: A Study of Ideology and Ambition* (London: Weidenfield & Nicolson, 1967).

McHugh, A. M., 'Resolving International Boundary Disputes in Africa: A Case for the ICJ' 49 *Howard Law Journal* (2005–2006) 209.

McMahon, A. Henry, 'International Boundaries' 84 *Journal of the Royal Society of Arts* (15 November 1935) 9.

McMahon, A. Henry, 'The Southern Borderlands of Afghanistan' Paper Delivered at the *Royal Geographic Society* (22 February 1897) subsequently published as A. Henry McMahon, 'A. H. The southern borderlands of Afghanistan'. [London: Geographical Journal, no. 4 (April 1897)], 393-415.

McWhinney, Edward, *Conflict and Compromise: International Law and World Order in a Revolutionary Age* (Leiden: Sijthoff & Noordoff, 1981).

Mehra, Parshotam, *The McMahon Line and After: A Study of the Triangular Contest on India's North-eastern Frontier Between Britain, China and Tibet 1904-1947* (New Delhi, India: Macmillan, 1974).

Menon, P. K., 'International Boundaries – A Case Study of the Guyana – Surinam Boundary' 27 *International & Comparative Law Quarterly* (1978) 738–768.

Metchnikoff, Leon, *La civilisation et les grands fleuves historiques* (Paris: Hachette, 1889).

Meyers, Gary D. & Mugambwa, John, 'The Mabo Decision: Australian Aboriginal Land Rights in Transition' 23 *Environmental Law* (1993) 1203.

Moon, David, 'Peasant Migration and the Settlement of Russia's Frontiers 1550-1897' 40(4) *The Historical Journal* (1997) 859–893.

Moore, Gavney & Lemos, Maria Carmen, 'Indigenous Policy in Brazil: The Development of Decree 1775 & the Proposed Raposa/Serra do Sol Reserve, Roraima, Brazil' 21 *Human Rights Quarterly* (1999) 444.

Moore, John Bassett, 'Memorandum on Uti Possidetis: Costa Rica-Panama Arbitration 1911' in *The Collected Works of John Bassett Moore* (Oxford: Oxford University Press, 1944) 328. Available online as Moore, John Bassett, *Costa Rica-Panama arbitration: memorandum on uti possidetis* (Commonwealth Company, 1913) at https://repositorio.unal.edu.co/bitstream/handle/unal/9869/uti_possidetis.pdf?sequence=2&isAllowed=y

Morris, H. F. & Read, J. R. (eds.), *Indirect Rule and the Search for Justice: Essays in East African Legal History* (Oxford: Clarendon Press, 1972).

Muirhead, James, *Historical Introduction to the Private Law of Rome*, 3rd ed. [Henry Goudy & Alexander Grant eds.] (London: A&C Black, 1916) 89–212.

Muschik, Eva-Maria, *Building States: The United Nations, Development and Decolonization 1945-1965* (New York: Columbia University Press, 2022).

Mwa Bawele M., 'Afro-European Relations in the Western Congo Basin 1884-5' in *Bismarck, Europe, and Africa* [Stig Förster, Wolfgang J. Mommsen & Ronald Robinson eds.] (Oxford: Oxford University Press, 1988) 469–489.

Naldi, Gino J., 'The Case Concerning the Frontier Dispute (*Burkina Faso/Republic of Mali*): *Uti Possidetis* in an African Perspective' 36 *International & Comparative Law Quarterly* (1987) 893–903.

Nasaw, David, *Andrew Carnegie* (New York & London: Penguin Books, 2007).

Neuberger, Benjamin, *National Self-Determination in Postcolonial Africa* (Boulder, CO: Lynne Reinner, 1986).

Nguyen, Hong Thao, 'Vietnam's Position on the Sovereignty over the Paracel and the Spratlys: Its Maritime Claim' 5 *Journal of East Asia International law* (2012) 174–184.

Nobles, Gregory H., 'Breaking into the Backcountry: New Approaches to the Early American Frontier, 1750–1800' 46 *The William and Mary Quarterly* (1989) 641–670.

Noorani, A. G., India-China Boundary Problem 1846-1947 History and Diplomacy (New Delhi, India: Oxford University Press, 2011).

Nunn, Patrick, 'Recent Environmental Changes on Pacific Islands' 156(2) *The Geographical Journal* (1990) 125–140.

Odentun, Gbenga, 'Africa Before the International Court: The Generational Gap in International Adjudication and Arbitration' 44(4) *Indiana Journal of International Law* (October–December 2004) 701–748.

Oppenheimer, Stephen, 'The Express Train from Taiwan to Polynesia: On the Congruence of Proxy Lines of Evidence' 36(4) *World Archaeology* (2004) 591–600, 593.

Osakada, Yuko, 'An Argument for Relying on Article 27 of the ICCPR in the Ainu Fishery Lawsuit: Potential Basis for the Ainu's Group Right to Fish Salmon' 14(1) *Golden Gate University Environmental Law Journal* (2022) 53–68.

Paasi, Anssi, *Territories, Boundaries and Consciousness: The Changing Geographies of the Finnish Russian Border* (Chichester: John Wiley & Sons, 1996).

Paine, Sarah C., *Imperial Rivals: China, Russia and Their Disputed Frontier* (London: M. E. Sharpe, 1996).

Pakenham, Thomas, *The Scramble for Africa* (London: Little, Brown Book Group, 1991).

Palat, Ravi, 'Pacific Century: Myth or Reality?' 25(3) *Theory and Society* (1996) 303–347, 303.

Parish, M., *Mirages of International Justice: The Elusive Pursuit of Transnational Legal Order* (Cheltenham: Edward Elgar, 2011) 63.

Parker, Matthew, *Panama Fever: The Epic Story of One of the Greatest Human Achievements of All Time – The Building of the of the Panama Canal* (New York: Doubleday, 2007).

Pastor Bodmer, Beatrice, *The Armature of Conquest: Spanish Accounts of the Discovery of America 1492-1589* [Lydia Longstreth Hunt trans] (Stanford, CA: Stanford University Press, 1992).

Patnaik, Utsa & Patnaik, Prabhat, *A Theory of Imperialism* (New York: Columbia University Press, 2016).

Paulson, Colter, 'Compliance with Final Judgments of the International Court of Justice since 1987' 98 *American Journal of International Law* (2004) 434.

Pauwelyn, Joost, Maggetti, Martino, Büthe, Tim, & Berman, Ayelet (eds.), *Rethinking Participation in Global Governance: Voice and Influence After Stakeholder Reforms in Global Finance and Health* (Oxford: Oxford University Press, 2022).

Pavkovic, A. & Radan, P., *Creating New States: Theory and Practice of Secession* (Aldershot: Ashgate, 2007).

Peacock, Andrew C. S. (ed.), *The Frontiers of the Ottoman World* (Oxford: Oxford University Press, 2009).

Pellet, Allain, 'The Opinions of the Badinter Arbitration Committee: A Second Breath for the Self-Determination of Peoples' 3(1) *European Journal of International Law* (1992) 178–185.

Peters, Arno, *Die Neue Kartographie* (Klagenfurt: Universitäts Carinthia, 1983).

Pickles, John, *A History of Spaces: Cartographic Reason, Mapping and the Geo-Coded World* (London: Routledge, 2004).

Picon-Salas, Mariano, *A Cultural History of Spanish America from Conquest to Independence* (Berkeley, CA: University of California Press, 1962).

Plant, Glen, 'Case Report: Maritime Delimitation and Territorial Questions Between Qatar and Bahrain (Qatar v Bahrain)' 96 *American Journal of International Law* (2002) 198, 200–201.

Pokotilov, Dmitri D., *History of the Eastern Mongols in the Period of the Ming Dynasty 1368-1634* (St. Petersburg, 1893) – translated into English from Russian by R. Lowenthal (Chengdu: China Studies in History & Civilization, West China Union University Press, 1947).

Posner, Eric A., 'The Decline of the International Court of Justice' Issue 233 (JM Olin Program in Law & Economics Working Paper, School of Law, University of Chicago, Chicago, IL, 2004).

Posner, Eric A. & Vermeule, A., 'Reparations for Slavery and Other Historical Injustices' 103(3) *Columbia Law Review* (2003) 689.

Power, Daniel & Standen, Naomi (eds.), *Frontiers in Question: Eurasian Borderlands 711-1700* (Basingstoke: Palgrave Macmillan, 1999).

Pratt, John, *War and Politics in China* (London: Jonathan Cape, 1943).

Prescott, John Robert Victor, *Map of Mainland Asia by Treaty* (Melbourne: Melbourne University Press, 1975).

Rabl, Kurt, *Das Selbstbestimmungsrecht der Völker – Geschichtliche Grunlagen und Umriss der gegenwärtigen Bedeutung* (Köln: Böhlau, 1973) 5.

Radan, Peter, 'Post-Succession International Orders: A Critical Analysis of the Workings of the Badinter Commission' 24 *Melbourne University Law Review* (2000) 50.

Radan, Peter, 'Secession and Self-Determination: The Case of Slovenia and Croatia' 48 *Australian Journal of International Law* (1994) 183.

Radhakrishnan, S., *India & China* (Bombay, India: Hind Kitab Labs, 1947).

Rao, K. Krishna, *International Law Aspects of the Sino-Indian Boundary* (New Delhi, India: Indian Society of International Law, 1963).

Ratner, Stephen R., 'Drawing a Better Line: Uti Possidetis and the Borders of New States' 90 *American Journal of International Law* (1996) 590.

Reffell, Massala, *Echoes of Footsteps: Birth of a Negro Nation* (Bloomington, IN: Xlibris Corporation, 2012).

Regan, Bernard, *The Balfour Declaration: Empire, Mandate and Resistance in Palestine* (London: Verso Books, 2018).

Reid, W. C. Jameson, 'The Asiatic Problem and Its Relation to the United States' 18(2) *Political Science Quarterly* (1903) 181–196.

Ripert, G., 'Les regles du driot civil applicables auz rapports internationaux' 44 *Recueil des Court de l'Academie de Droit International* (1933–II) 575.

Rodrigues, Maria, G. M., 'Indigenous Rights in Democratic Brazil' 24 *Human Rights Quarterly* (2002) 487.

Rodríguez-Merino, Pablo A., *Violence, Discourse and Politics in China's Uyghur Region: The Terrorization of Xinjiang* (London: Taylor & Francis, 2022).

Root, Elihu, 'The Real Monroe Doctrine' 8(3) *American Journal of International Law* (1914) 427–442.

Rosenne, Shabtai, *The Law and Practice of the International Court*, Vol. II (Leyden: A. W. Sijthoff, 1965).

Rossabi, Morris, *China and Inner Asia: From 1360 to the Present Day* (London: Thames & Hudson, 1975).

Roy, Arundhati, Mishra, Pankaj & Bhatt, Hilal, *Kashmir: The Case for Freedom* (London: Verso Books, 2011).

Saad, R., 'Gulf Emirates Settle Debate' 526 *Al-Ahram Weekly Online* (March 22–28, 2001) .

Said, Edward, *Orientalism* (London: Penguin Books, 1978).

Sanghvi, Ramesh, *India's Northern Frontier and China* (Bombay, India: Contemporary Publishers, 1962).

Saraiva, Jose H., *Non Self Governing Territories and the United Nations Charter* (Lisboa: Agencia Geral do Ultramar, 1960)

Schofield, Richard, 'Foreword' in *From the Gulf to Ararat: Imperial Boundary Making in the Late Ottoman Empire* [G. E. Hubbard ed.] (London: I. B. Tauris, 2016) xv.

Schwarzenberger, Georg, 'Title to Territory: Response to a Challenge' 51 *American Journal of International Law* (1957) 313–314.

Schwarzenberger, Georg, *International Law*, 3rd ed. (London: Stevens & Sons, 1957) 289–309.

Schwarzenberger, Georg, *The Frontiers of International Law* (London: Steven & Sons, 1962).

Scott, Gary L. & Csajko, Karen D., 'Compulsory Jurisdiction and Defiance in the World Court: A Comparison of the PCIJ and ICJ' 16 *Denver Journal of International Law & Policy* (1987–1988) 377–392.

Segal, Gerard, *Rethinking the Pacific* (Oxford: Clarendon Press, 1990).

Shafir, Gershon, *A Half Century of Occupation: Israel, Palestine and the World's Most Intractable Conflict* (Oakland, CA: University of California Press, 2017).

Shaw, Malcolm N., 'People, Territorialism & Boundaries' 8 *European Journal of International Law* (1997) 478–508.

Shaw, Malcolm N., 'The Heritage of States: The Principle of Uti Possidetis Juris Today' 67 *British Yearbook of International Law* (1996) 97–101.

Shaw, Malcolm N., 'The Western Sahara Case' 44 *British Yearbook of International Law* (1978) 118.

Shaw, Malcolm N., *Title to Territory in Africa: International Legal Issues* (Oxford: Clarendon Press, 1986).

Shen, Jianming, 'China's Sovereignty over the South China Sea Islands: A Historical Perspective' 1 *Chinese Journal of International Law* (2002) 94.

Shen, Jianming, 'International Law Rules and Historical Evidences Supporting China's Title to the South China Sea Islands' 21 *Hastings International and Comparative Law Review* (1997) 1.

Sheshterinina, Anastasia, 'Mobilizing in Uncertainty: Collective Identities and War in Abkhazia' 22(1) *Ethnopolitics* (2023) 91–100.

Shin, Y., 'A Historical Study of Korea's Title to Tokdo' 28 *Korean Observer* (1997) 333.

Sibbett, Benjamin K., 'Tokdo or Takeshima? The Territorial Dispute Between Japan and the Republic of Korea' 21 *Fordham International Law Journal* (1997–1998) 1606–1637.

Simmons, B., 'Rules over Real Estate: Trade, Territorial Conflict and International Borders as Institution' 69(6) *Journal of Conflict Resolution* (2005) 823–848.

Simmons, B., 'See You in Court? The Appeal to Quasi-Judicial Legal Processes in the Settlement of Territorial Disputes' in *A Road Map to War: Territorial Dimensions of International Conflict* [P. Diehl ed.] (Nashville, TN: Vanderbilt University Press, 1998) 205–237.

Simpson, Gerry, 'Mabo, International Law, Terra Nullius and the Stories of Settlement: An Unresolved Jurisprudence' 19 *Melbourne University Law Review* (1993) 195.

Sloane, R. D., 'The Policies of State Succession: Harmonizing Self-Determination and Global Order in the Twenty-First Century' 30 *Fordham International Law Journal* (2007) 1288.

Soave, Tommaso, *The Everyday Makers of International Law: From Great Halls to Back* Rooms (Cambridge: Cambridge University Press, 2022).

Sokiri͡anskai͡a, Ekaterina Leonidovna, *Bonds of Blood? State-building and Clanship in Chechnya and Ingushetia* (London: Bloomsbury Academic, 2023).

Sorel, Jean-Marc & Wojcikiewicz Almeida, Paula (eds.), *Latin America and the International Court of Justice: Contributions to International Law* (London: Routledge, 2018).

Spate, Oscar Hermann Khristian, '"South Sea" to "Pacific Ocean": A Note on Nomenclature' 12(4) *Journal of Pacific History* (1977) 205–211.

Spitzer, R. M., 'African Holocaust: Should Europe Pay Reparations to Africa for Colonialism and Slavery' 35 *Vanderbilt Journal of Transnational Law* (2002) 1313.

Stalin, Joseph, *Marxism and the National Question* (Moscow: Foreign Languages Publishing House, 1947).

Stead, William T. (ed.), *The Last Will and Testament of Cecil J. Rhodes* (London: "Review of Reviews" Office, 1902).
Stohl, Rachel & Grillot, Suzette, *The International Arms Trade* (Cambridge: Polity Press, 2009).
Strausz-Hupé, Robert, *Geopolitics: The Struggle for Space and Power* (New York: G. P. Putnam's Sons, 1942).
Sud, Usha, *The United Nations and Non Self-Governing Territories* (Jalandhar, India: University Publishers, 1965).
Sumner, B. T., 'Note: Territorial Disputes at the International Court of Justice' 53 *Duke Law Journal* (2004) 1779–1812.
Sureda, Rigo, *The Evolution of the Right of Self-Determination* (Leiden: Martinus Nijhoff, 1973).
Sykes, Mark, *Dar-ul-Islam: A Record of a Journey Through Ten of the Asiatic Provinces of Turkey* (London: Bickers and Son, 1904).
Sykes, Mark, Letter to General C Calwell, 16 July 1915, FO/882/13.
Sykes, Mark, *The Caliphs' Last Heritage: A Shot History of the Turkish Empire* (London: Macmillan 1915).
Sykes, Mark, 'The Proposed Maintenance of a Turkish Empire in Asia without Spheres of Influence', 3 May 1915, Cab 27/1.
Sykes, Mark, 'The Question of a Railway Connecting Haifa with the Euphrates', 19 April 1915, Cab/27/1.
Sykes, Percy M., *A History of Persia* (London: Andesite Press, 1915) 324–325.
Sykes, Percy M., *Sir Mortimer Durand* (Lahore: Al-Biruni Press, 1977) 205.
Taagepera, R., 'An Overview of the Growth of the Russian Empire' in *Russian Colonial Expansion to 1917* [M. Rywkin ed.] (London: Mansell Publishing, 1988)1-7.
Taijudo, K., 'The Dispute Between Japan and Korea Respecting Sovereignty over Takeshima' 12 *Japanese Annual of International Law* (1968) 1.
Tate, G. P., *The Frontiers of Baluchistan: Travels on the Borders of Persia and Afghanistan* (London: Witherby & Co., 1909).
Terett, Steve, *The Dissolution of Yugoslavia and the Badinter Arbitration Commission* (Dartmouth: Ashgate, 2000).
Terrell, John Edward, Hunt, Terry L. & Gosden, Chris, 'The Dimensions of Social Life in the Pacific: Human Diversity and the Myth of the Primitive Isolate' 38(2) *Current Anthropology* (1997) 155–195.
Thatcher, John Boyd, *Christopher Columbus: His Life, his Work, his Remains, as Revealed by Original Printed and Manuscript Records, together with an Essay on Peter Martyr of Anghera and Bartolome de las Casas, the First Historians of America*, 3 vols. (New York and London: G. P. Putnam's Sons, I903–I904).
Thiong, Daniel Akech, *The Politics of Fear in South Sudan: Generating Chaos, Creating Conflict* (London: Zed Books, 2021).
Thirlway, Hugh, *The Law & Procedure of the ICJ: Fifty Years of Jurisprudence*, Vol. 1 (Oxford: Oxford University Press, 2013).
Thornberry, Patrick, 'The Democratic or Internal Aspect of Self-Determination' in *Modern Law of Self-Determination* [Christian Tomuschat ed.] (Leiden: Martinus Nijhoff, 1994).
Thruston, A. B., *African Incidents* (London: John Murray, 1900).

Tilly, Charles, 'Revolutions' in *Handbook of Political Science* [Fred I. Greenstein & Nelson W. Polsby eds.] (Reading, MA: Addison-Wesley, 1975) 521.

Torell, Jean-Pierre, *Saint Thomas Aquinas: The Person and his Work*, Vol. 1 (Washington DC: Catholic University of American Press, 2005).

Torpey, J., *Making Whole what Has Been Smashed: On Reparations Politics* (Boston, MA: Harvard University Press, 2006)

Touval, Saadia, 'Africa's Frontiers–Reactions to a Colonial Legacy' 42 *International Affairs* (1966) 641.

Touval, Saadia, *The Boundary Politics of Independent Africa* (Cambridge, MA: Harvard University Press, 1972).

Touval, Saadia, 'The Sources of *Status Quo* & Irrendentist Policies' in *African Boundary Problems* [C. G. Widstrand ed.] (Uppsala: Scandinavian Africa Institute, 1969) 101–118.

Agreement between the Republic of India & the Peoples' Republic of China on Trade and Intercourse Between Tibet Region of China and India (April 29, 1954) available https://www.mea.gov.in/bilateral-documents.htm?dtl/7807/Agreement+on+Trade+and+Intercourse+with+Tibet+Region.

Treadgold, Donald W., *The Great Siberian Migration: Government and Peasant in Resettlement from Emancipation to the First World War* (Princeton, NJ: Princeton University Press, 1957).

Trisotto, R., 'Seceding in the Twenty-First Century: A Paradigm for the Ages' 35(2) *Brooklyn Journal of International Law* (2010) 419.

Trout, F. E., 'Morocco's Boundary in the Guir-Zousfana River Basin' 3(1) *African Historical Studies* (1970) 37–56.

Tseng, Wen-wu, *Chung Ku Kin Ying Hsi Yu Shih* (Shanghai, 1936).

Turner F. J., *The Frontier in American History* (New York: Henry Holt, 1921) 3.

Tytler, Patrick Fraser, *Afghanistan: A Study of Political Developments in Central and Southern Asia* (Oxford: Oxford University Press, 1967).

Umozurike, Oji, *International Law and Colonialism in Africa* (Lagos: Nwamife Publishers, 1979).

Umozurike, Oji, *Self-Determination in International Law* (Hamden, CT: Archon Books, 1979).

Valentini, P. J. J., 'The Portuguese in the Track of Columbus' 21 *Journal of the American Geographical Society of New York* (1889) 167–196 at 167.

Vali, Abbas, *Kurds and the State in Iran: The Making of Kurdish Identity* (London: I. B. Taurus, 2014).

Van den Hout, T., 'Resolution of International Disputes: The Role of the Permanent Court of Arbitration – Reflections on the Centenary of the 1907 Convention for the Pacific Settlement of International Disputes' 21 *Leiden Journal of International Law* (2008) 643–661.

Van Langenhove, Fernand, *The Question of Aborigines Before the United Nations: The Belgian Thesis* (Brussels: Royal Colonial Institute of Belgium, 1954).

Vander Linden, H., 'Alexander VI and the Demarcation of the Maritime and Colonial Domains of Spain and Portugal, 1493-1494' 22(1) *The American Historical Review* (October 1916) 1–20.

Vattel Emmerich, *Le Droit des Gens*, Vol. 2 (reproduced, Paris: Adamant Media Corporation, 2001).

Vereté, Mayir, 'The Balfour Declaration and its Makers' 6(1) *Middle Eastern Studies* (1970) 48–76.

Verzijl, J. H. W., *International Law in Historical Perspective* (Heisenberg: Springer, 1970).

Vogel, Ezra F., *Deng Xiaoping and the Transformation of China* (Cambridge, MA: Harvard University Press, 2011).

Von Alten, 'The Powers in Asia' 181(589) *The North American Review* (December 1905) 834–844.

Waldron, Arthur, *The Great Wall of China: From History to Myth* (Cambridge: Cambridge University Press, 1990).

Walter, Christian, von Ungern-Sternberg, Anje & Abushov, Kavus (eds.), *Self-determination & Secession in International Law* (Oxford: Oxford University Press, 2014).

Wang Jiawei & Gyaincain, Nyima, *The Historical Status of China's Tibet* (Peking: China Intercontinental Press, 1997).

Ware, Robert Bruce & Kisriev, Enver, *Dagestan: Russian Hegemony and Islamic Resistance in the North Caucasus* (New York: Routledge, 2010).

Weller, Marc, 'The International Response to the Dissolution of the Socialist Federal Republic of Yugoslavia' 86 *American Journal of International Law* (1992) 569.

Wessling, H. L., *Divide and Rule: The Partition of Africa 1880-1914* (London: Praeger Westlake, 1996).

Westlake, John, *International Law*, Vol. 1 (Ann Arbor, MI: University of Michigan Press, 1910).

Whelan, Anthony, 'Wilsonian Self-Determination and the Versailles Settlement' 43 *International & Comparative Law Quarterly* (1994) 99–115.

Whittaker, Charles R., *The Frontiers of the Roman Empire: A Social and Economic Study* (Baltimore, MD: Johns Hopkins University Press, 1994).

Wieczynski, J. L., *The Russian Frontier: The Impact of the Borderlands upon the Course of Early Russian History* (Charlottesville, VA: University of Virginia Press, 1976)

Wiegand, K. E., *Enduring Territorial Disputes: Strategies of Bargaining, Coercive Diplomacy and Settlement* (Athens, GA: University of Georgia Press, 2011).

Williams, Basil, *Cecil Rhodes* (London: Constable, 1921).

Woronoff, Jon, *Organising African Unity* (Metuchen, NJ: Scarecrow Press, 1970).

Wright, Jane, 'Minority Groups, Autonomy, and Self-Determination' 19 *Oxford Journal of Legal Studies* (1999) 605.

Wright, Quincy, 'The Constitutionality of Treaties' 13(2) *American Journal of International Law* (1919) 242–266.

Wright, Quincy, 'The Goa Incident' 56 *American Journal of International Law* (1962) 617–632.

Xing, Li (ed.), *Mapping China's 'One Belt One Road' Initiative* (New York: Palgrave Macmillan, 2019).

Yates, Robin D. S., 'Body, Space, Time and Bureaucracy: Boundary Creation and Control Mechanisms in Early China' in *Boundaries in China* [J. Hay ed.] (Oxford: Reacktion Books, 1994) 1-55.

Yee, Sienho, 'The South China Sea Arbitration (Philippines v China): Potential Jurisdictional Obstacles and Objections' 13(4) *Chinese Journal of International Law* (2014) 663–739.

Zang, Xiaowei, *Handbook on Ethnic Minorities in China* (Cheltenham: Edward Elgar, 2016).
Zapato Barrero, Ricard (ed.), *Immigration and Self-Government of Minority Nations* (Brussels: Peter Lang, 2009).
Zinn, Howard, *A People's History of the United States 1492- Present* (London/New York: HarperCollins, 1980, new edition 2003).

Index

Made in the USA
Las Vegas, NV
19 September 2026

2e6873a5-ef21-4940-97ee-305da1a479b5R01